HARCOURT BRACE SPELLING

Thorsten Carlson

Richard Madden

HARCOURT BRACE SPELLING

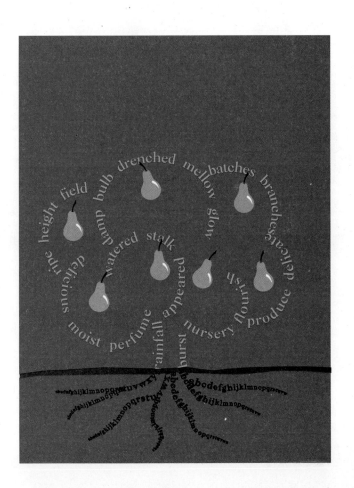

HARCOURT BRACE & COMPANY

Orlando Atlanta Austin Boston San Francisco Chicago Dallas New York Toronto London

http://www.hbschool.com

Acknowledgments

Letter forms from *HBJ Handwriting*. Copyright © 1987 by Harcourt Brace & Company. Definitions and the pronunciation key in the "Spelling Dictionary" are from the *HBJ School Dictionary*. Copyright © 1985, 1977 by Harcourt Brace & Company. Reprinted by permission of Harcourt Brace & Company.

PHOTO CREDITS

Key: T, Top; B, Bottom; L, Left; C, Center; R, Right.

Page 17, ALL, Anderson Studios/Derriak Anderson; 18, Vance Henry/Taurus Photos; 22, 26, 30, Anderson Studios/Derriak Anderson; 35, Gary Meszaros/Bruce Coleman; 37, Anderson Studios/Derriak Anderson; 38(BL), Steve Kasserman/Peter Arnold, Inc.; 38(T), Norman Owen/Bruce Coleman; 51, Anderson Studios/Derriak Anderson; 57, M. Timothy O'Keefe/Bruce Coleman; 58, Bruce Coleman; 60, Julie Bartlett/Bruce Coleman; 61, Anderson Studios/Derriak Anderson; 62, Dr. David Schwimmer/Bruce Coleman; 64, Cecile Brunswick; 65, 67, Anderson Studios/Derriak Anderson; 70, Owen Franken/Stock Boston; 84, Anderson Studios/Derriak Anderson; 87, Mickey Gibson/Animals, Animals; 88, 95, Anderson Studios/Derriak Anderson; 96, L.L.T. Rhodes/Taurus Photos; 104, 110, 116, ALL, Anderson Studios/Derriak Anderson; 120(T), J. Messerschmidt/Bruce Coleman; 120(B), J.L. Atlan/Sygma; 125, 137, Anderson Studios/Derriak Anderson; 138(T), RCA/NBC; 138(B), 142, Anderson Studios/Derriak Anderson; 146, Cecile Brunswick; 150, Anderson Studios/Derriak Anderson; 155, William F. Harrah/Automobile Museum, Reno, Nevada; 164, ALL, 165, Anderson Studios/Derriak Anderson; 169, Jack Couffer/Bruce Coleman; 170, Blaine Harrington/Stock Market; 173, S.J. Krasemann/Peter Arnold; 180, Richard Kolar/Earth Resources; 185, Focus on Sports; 186(L), Anderson Studios/Derriak Anderson; 186(R), Peter Menzel/Stock Boston; 190, J. Hoffman Studios; 193, Lawrence Smith/Photo Researchers; 194, Leonard Lee Rue/DPI; 197, H. Armstrong Roberts; 198(L), Mike Price/Bruce Coleman; 198(R), John Lei/Omni Photo Communications; 200, Honeywell Residential Controls Center; 201, Anderson Studios/Derriak Anderson; 202, J. Alex Langley/DPI.

Lodge
Textbook
PE
1145.2
.H37
1999
Gr. 6
SE

Contents

Study Steps to Learn a Word

 **SAY** the word. Recall when you have heard the word used. Think about what it means.

 **LOOK** at the word. Find any prefixes, suffixes, or other word parts you know. Think about other words that are related in meaning and spelling. Try to picture the word in your mind.

 **SPELL** the word to yourself. Think about the way each sound is spelled. Notice any unusual spelling.

 **WRITE** the word while looking at it. Check the way you have formed your letters. If you have not written the word clearly or correctly, write it again.

 **CHECK** your learning. Cover the word and write it. If you did not spell the word correctly, practice these steps until the word becomes your own.

Skills Check

Name _____ Date _____

A. Write the letter of the misspelled word.

1. _____ **a.** range **b.** tishue **c.** social
2. _____ **a.** twist **b.** thret **c.** daily
3. _____ **a.** screan **b.** twine **c.** coal
4. _____ **a.** coast **b.** squeze **c.** tense
5. _____ **a.** sence **b.** ticket **c.** pickle
6. _____ **a.** diaries **b.** solid **c.** acke
7. _____ **a.** porch **b.** slant **c.** thrif
8. _____ **a.** lied **b.** scowl **c.** dout

**number right
A.** _____ (8)

B. Write the correct spelling for each pronunciation.

9. /kwik/ _____ 10. /rēth/ _____

11. /chōz/ _____ 12. /di·rek′shən/ _____

13. /nā′shən/ _____ 14. /prōōv/ _____

15. /ois′tər/ _____ 16. /vej′(ə·)tə·bəl/ _____

**number right
B.** _____ (8)

C. The words in each column end with the sounds at the top of the column. Write the correct spelling of the whole word.

/ər/		/ən/	
17. coll _____		20. cart _____	
18. clev _____		21. apr _____	
19. may _____		22. cert _____	

/əl/

23. whist _____

24. hospit _____

25. tunn _____

**number right
C.** _____ (9)

2

Harcourt Brace School Publishers

D. Write the plural of each word.

26. bunch _____   **27.** tax _____

28. tray _____   **29.** battery _____

30. loaf _____   **31.** hinge _____

E. Add <u>ed</u> to each word on the left. Add <u>ing</u> to each word on the right. Write the words.

	ed		**ing**

32. drop _____   **35.** deny _____

33. study _____   **36.** depend _____

34. promise _____   **37.** lie _____

F. Add one of these prefixes to each word. Write the new word.

dis-   re-   un-

38. usual _____   **39.** pleasant _____

40. agree _____   **41.** write _____

42. build _____   **43.** approve _____

G. Add one of these suffixes to each word. Write the new word.

-less   -ion   -ful   -ness

44. educate _____   **45.** breath _____

46. tardy _____   **47.** force _____

H. Write a three-syllable word that fits each sentence.

48. Indent the first line of each _____ you write.

49. Enclose your letter in this _____ .

50. These sweaters come in small, _____ , and large.

---

number right
D. _____(6)

number right
E. _____(6)

number right
F. _____(6)

number right
G. _____(4)

number right
H. _____(3)

total right
_____(50)

3

1 Short Vowel Sounds

UNIT WORDS

1. chess ⑯
2. snack ⑬
3. glimpse ①
4. dock ⑦
5. crumpled ⑱
6. album ③
7. drenched ⑳
8. plastic ②
9. bristle ⑫
10. rapid ⑲
11. bronze ④
12. nozzle ⑭
13. publish ⑯
14. pulse ⑩
15. solve ⑪
16. absence ⑥
17. depth ⑮
18. against ⑧
19. system ⑤
20. oven ⑨

glimpse /i/ system

The Unit Words

All the words in this unit have short vowel sounds. These are the symbols for those sounds: /a/, /e/, /i/, /o/, /u/. Letters that come between two slanted lines show sounds.

Short vowel sounds are usually spelled with one vowel letter.

- The sound /a/ is spelled with **a.**   snack
- The sound /e/ is spelled with **e.**   chess
- The sound /i/ is spelled with **i.**   glimpse
- The sound /o/ is spelled with **o.**   dock
- The sound /u/ is spelled with **u.**   crumpled

Sometimes short vowel sounds are spelled with other letters.

- The sound /e/ is spelled with **ai** in *against*.
- The sound /i/ is spelled with **y** in *system*.
- The sound /u/ is spelled with **o** in *oven*.

Spelling Practice

A. Follow the directions using the Unit words.

1. Write the three words in which /e/ is spelled with *e*.

_____   _____   _____

2. Write the word in which /e/ is not spelled with *e*. _____

3. Write the five words in which /a/ is spelled with *a*. Circle the two words that also have /i/ spelled *i*.

_____   _____   _____

_____   _____

4. Write the three other words in which /i/ is spelled *i*.

_____   _____   _____

5. Write the word in which /i/ is not spelled with *i*. _____

6. Write the four words in which /o/ is spelled *o*.

_____   _____   _____

_____

7. Write the word in which *o* does not spell /o/. _____

B. Write the correct spelling for each of these pronunciations. Circle the word in which *u* does not spell /u/.

8. /puls/ _____   **9.** /al'bəm/ _____

10. /pub'lish/ _____   **11.** /krum'pəld/ _____

C. Complete each sentence using one of the Unit words. The short vowel sound in / / will help you.

12. My cat likes to chase balls of /u/ _____ paper.

13. Luis baked an eggplant dish in the /u/ _____ .

14. The small statue is made of /o/ _____ .

15. The lake has an average /e/ _____ of 100 meters.

16. I had to explain the reason for my /a/ _____ from school.

17. The earth is part of the solar /i/ _____ .

18. Are you for or /e/ _____ building a new stadium?

Spelling and Language · Plurals

UNIT WORDS

chess
snack
glimpse
dock
crumpled
album
drenched
plastic
bristle
rapid
bronze
nozzle
publish
pulse
solve
absence
depth
against
system
oven

A noun is plural when it names more than one person or thing. You add *s* to most nouns to form the plural.

system   systems<u>s</u>   nozzle   nozzle<u>s</u>

Complete each sentence by writing the plural form of a Unit word.

1. We like apples for after-school _____ .

2. My uncle has many new record _____ of country music.

3. The three _____ in the harbor are made of wood.

4. The _____ on the brush are plastic.

5. The attendance officer recorded Cindy's two _____ .

6. The restaurant has four _____ for baking pizza.

Writing on Your Own

Draw a picture of what you might see if you were to ride through an automatic car wash. Then write a paragraph for your classmates describing the picture. Use these and other Unit words: *nozzle, bristle,* and *glimpse.* Use as many plurals as you can.

 THESAURUS For help finding descriptive words, turn to page 205.

Using the Dictionary to Spell and Write

Each word given in a dictionary is called an **entry word.** Entry words are listed in alphabetical order. This will help you find a word quickly if you need to check its spelling or meaning.

Find each of these words in the **Spelling Dictionary.** Then write the entry word that comes right after each word.

1. doubtful _____   2. sweet _____

3. glacier _____   4. public _____

5. division _____   6. northwest _____

7. deposit _____   8. pivot _____

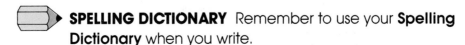 **SPELLING DICTIONARY** Remember to use your **Spelling Dictionary** when you write.

Harcourt Brace School Publishers

Spelling on Your Own

pl/a/st/i/c

Copy and complete this chart using the Unit words. Write each word under the symbol for the first short sound you hear in the word.

/a/	/e/	/i/	/o/	/u/

MASTERY WORDS

Complete each sentence using a Mastery word for each missing word. The short vowel sound for each word is given.

1. Bill grew a flower from a /u/ _____ .

2. The flower was a /i/ _____ first-place

   /i/ _____ at the fair.

3. Bill will /e/ _____ his prize money for more bulbs.

Finish these sentences with Mastery words.

4. I planted a tulip _____ in the garden.

5. The ground felt _____ after yesterday's rain.

6. I like to work _____ growing things.

7. I _____ most Saturdays working in the garden.

winner
among
damp
spend
bulb
solid

BONUS WORDS

1. Write one Bonus word that has each of these short vowel sounds: /a/, /e/.

2. Write two Bonus words that have each of these short vowel sounds: /i/, /u/.

3. Write three Bonus words with the short vowel sound /o/. Circle the word that has two pronunciations.

4. Rewrite this sentence. Replace the underlined words with Bonus words. Then add more sentences to write a mystery story.

   Harry's quick changes in behavior puzzle me.

bewilder
mystify
adopt
abrupt
conduct
remedy
atlas
modify

2 Long Vowel Sounds

UNIT WORDS

1. coach
2. shoulder
3. complain
4. ailment
5. detailed
6. breathe
7. squeak
8. disease
9. borrow
10. blown
11. failure
12. cease
13. release
14. growth
15. stow
16. grain
17. claim
18. brain
19. foam
20. aisle

The Unit Words

In this unit you will study words with three long vowel sounds: /ā/, /ē/, and /ō/. In the Unit words each of these long vowel sounds is spelled with two vowel letters. The name of the first letter in the spelling sounds the same as the vowel sound it helps to spell. When you say *a*, the sound you make is /ā/.

The Unit words show these spellings for the long vowel sounds.

- The sound /ā/ is spelled with **ai** as in *grain.*
- The sound /ē/ is spelled with **ea** as in *squeak.*
- The sound /ō/ is spelled with **oa** as in *foam.*
- The sound /ō/ is spelled with **ow** as in *stow.*
- The sound /ō/ is spelled with **ou** as in *shoulder.*

☐ The word *aisle* does not follow the usual pattern. In *aisle* the letters *ai* don't spell /ā/, but another long vowel sound: /ī/.

REMEMBER THIS

The word *breathe* is a verb. Memorize the sentence "Breathe easy" to help you remember that breathe has a long *e* sound and ends with *e*.

Harcourt Brace School Publishers

Spelling Practice

A. Follow the directions using the Unit words.

1. Write the two words in which /ō/ is spelled *oa*.

_____   _____

2. Write the four words in which /ō/ is spelled *ow*.

_____   _____

_____   _____

3. Write another word with the sound /ō/. Underline the letters for /ō/.

_____

4. Write three words with /ā/ that rhyme. Underline the letters for /ā/.

_____   _____   _____

5. Write four more words with the sound /ā/. Underline the letters for /ā/.

_____   _____

_____   _____

6. Write the word that sounds like *I'll*. _____

7. Write the five words in which /ē/ is spelled *ea*.

_____   _____   _____

_____   _____

B. Write a Unit word that rhymes with each of these words.

8. sorrow _____   9. both _____

10. speak _____   11. frame _____

C. Finish the story with Unit words. The vowel sound will help you.

The whistle had just /ō/ __12__ . We were behind 50–49 as we ran back onto the basketball court with two minutes left in the game. I looked over to the bench. The /ō/ __13__ raised her left hand for the last play. As Mei passed me the ball, I felt a sharp pain in my /ō/ __14__ . I could hardly /ē/ __15__ as I ran down the court. I couldn't be a /ā/ __16__ now! I raised my arms to /ē/ __17__ the ball and watched it curve toward the basket.

12. _____   13. _____   14. _____

15. _____   16. _____   17. _____

Harcourt Brace School Publishers

Spelling and Language · Verb Endings

UNIT WORDS

coach
shoulder
complain
ailment
detailed
breathe
squeak
disease
borrow
blown
failure
cease
release
growth
stow
grain
claim
brain
foam
aisle

You add *ed* to most verbs to talk about what already happened: *squeaked*. You add *ing* to make a word you can use with a form of *be*: were *squeaking*.

Complete the paragraph by writing the verb in ( ) with *ed* or *ing*. Remember that when you add *ed* or *ing* to a verb that ends with *e*, you must drop the final *e*.

The neighbors were (complain) __1__ about my brother again. Soap suds were (foam) __2__ out of the washing machine. Jay (claim) __3__ it wasn't his fault. The machine was (release) __4__ too much soap. He (borrow) __5__ a wrench to fix it. Now it is completely useless. We all (breathe) __6__ a sigh of relief when Jay finally went back to school.

1. _____   2. _____   3. _____

4. _____   5. _____   6. _____

Writing on Your Own

Pretend you are Jay's sister or brother. Write a story for the family scrapbook about another time Jay got in trouble. Use as many of the Unit words as you can. Add *ed* and *ing* to some verbs.

 WRITER'S GUIDE For help editing and proofreading your story, use the marks on page 268.

Using the Dictionary to Spell and Write

Suppose you want to make sure you used a word correctly in your writing. You can find the word quickly in the dictionary by using guide words. **Guide words** are the two words at the top of each dictionary page. The word on the left is the first entry word on the page, and the word on the right is the last word. The rest of the words on the page are in alphabetical order between the guide words.

Write the three Unit words that would appear on a dictionary page with each pair of guide words. Write the words in alphabetical order.

1. ship   straw   2. blue   brush   3. catch   coin

_____   _____   _____

_____   _____   _____

_____   _____   _____

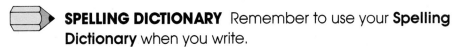 **SPELLING DICTIONARY** Remember to use your **Spelling Dictionary** when you write.

Harcourt Brace School Publishers

Spelling on Your Own

UNIT WORDS

Write the Unit word that would follow each word below in alphabetical order.

1. aid	**2.** aim	**3.** blame	**4.** bone	**5.** brag
6. breakfast	**7.** cart	**8.** city	**9.** clown	**10.** compete
11. deliver	**12.** diet	**13.** fade	**14.** fly	**15.** grab
16. ground	**17.** read	**18.** short	**19.** speech	**20.** sting

MASTERY WORDS

Follow the directions using the Mastery words.

1. Write the two words in which /ē/ is spelled _ea._

_____   _____

2. Write the two words in which /ō/ is spelled _ow._

_____   _____

heat
pain
throw
goal
steam
glow

Finish each sentence with a Mastery word. The long vowel sound is given to help you.

3. Tom scored the first /ō/ _____ in the soccer game.

4. But the /ō/ _____ of success quickly faded.

5. A sharp /ā/ _____ shot through Tom's leg.

6. Tom had managed to /ō/ _____ out his knee.

7. The coach sent Tom to the /ē/ _____ bath.

BONUS WORDS

Write a Bonus word to complete each sentence. The vowel for each word is given.

1. When will you be _/ā/_ to baby-sit?
2. We want to go _/ō/_ tonight.
3. Jamie is in a _/ō/_ mood today.
4. The chef will _/ō/_ the fish in milk.
5. How did the Austins survive the _/ē/_ ?
6. Angie's strongest _/ā/_ are honesty and courage.
7. At last the masked man _/ē/_ his identity.
8. I can't _/ā/_ this jogging pace much longer.

available
mellow
bowling
revealed
sustain
poach
ordeal
traits

11

More Long Vowel Spellings

UNIT WORDS

1. height
2. weigh
3. reindeer
4. receive
5. hygiene
6. field
7. brief
8. freight
9. veil
10. ceiling
11. achieve
12. neighbor
13. believe
14. seize
15. vein
16. chief
17. sleigh
18. niece
19. grief
20. friendship

believe /ē/
receive /s/ + /ē/
weigh /ā/

NAME: *Jay Town*
HEIGHT: 4'8"
WEIGHT: 85 lbs.

The Unit Words

The two vowel letters *e* and *i* combine in different ways to spell long vowel sounds. Which letter comes first? Here are some ways to remember.

- Most of the time, the spelling of /ē/ is *i* before *e*, as in *field* and *niece*.

- If the word has a long *a* sound /ā/, *e* comes before *i*, as in *neighbor* and *veil*.

- If the word has a long *e* sound /ē/ after the sound /s/, the spelling is also *ei*, as in *receive* and *seize*.

☐ The words *height* and *weight* look the same in print, but they do not sound the same. *Height* has a long *i* sound: /ī/. *Weight* and *weigh* have a long *a* sound: /ā/. The letters *eigh* can spell both vowel sounds, although long *i* is not usually spelled this way.

☐ One word in this unit has a short vowel sound spelled with *i* and *e*. In *friendship*, /e/ is spelled *ie*.

Spelling Practice

A. Follow the directions using the Unit words.

1. Write the word that sounds like *sees*. _____

2. Now write two more words that have /ē/ spelled *ei*.

_____   _____

3. Write the word in which *ei* stands for /ī/. _____

4. Write the word that sounds like *way*. _____

5. Now write three more words that have /ā/ spelled with *eigh*.

_____   _____   _____

6. Write the three words that have /ā/ spelled with *ei*.

_____   _____   _____

7. Write the three words that rhyme with *leaf*.

_____   _____   _____

8. Now write five more words that have /ē/ spelled *ie*.

_____   _____   _____

_____   _____

9. Write the word in which *ie* stands for /e/. _____

B. Write the Unit word that rhymes with each of these words.

10. fleece _____   **11.** right _____

C. Finish this story with Unit words.

Last Saturday I baby-sat for my three-year-old __12__, Sarah, and our next-door __13__, Kenny, who is two and a half. What a job that was! First I took them out to the big __14__ behind our house to play. They both ran around so much I couldn't keep up with them. I couldn't __15__ how fast those two could run! Then we went inside for lunch. Sarah decided to throw her peanut butter sandwich up at the __16__ to see if it would stick. Kenny thought it would be fun to drink his milk from his shoe. I guess good __17__ doesn't mean much to Kenny. Finally their mothers came. I spent the afternoon cleaning up.

12. _____   **13.** _____   **14.** _____

15. _____   **16.** _____   **17.** _____

Spelling and Language · Adding -er

UNIT WORDS

height
weigh
reindeer
receive
hygiene
field
brief
freight
veil
ceiling
achieve
neighbor
believe
seize
vein
chief
sleigh
niece
grief
friendship

You can add the suffix -er to some words to make nouns that name persons or things that do something. For example, when you add -er to the word *farm*, you get *farmer*, "a person who farms." Remember to drop the final *e* in a word before you add -er.

Add -er to the words in boldface. Write the words that complete the sentences.

field   **1.** The center _____ dropped the baseball.

believe   **2.** Sandra is a strong _____ in regular exercise.

Writing on Your Own

Imagine that you are a famous writer working on a joke book of directions for solving unusual problems. Write funny directions for weighing a reindeer. Use as many of the Unit words as you can.

 WRITER'S GUIDE   For a sample how-to paragraph, turn to page 270.

Using the Dictionary to Spell and Write

A **dictionary entry** has a lot of information to help you when you write. It gives the meaning of a word. It also shows the syllable breaks, the pronunciation, the part of speech, inflected forms, and sometimes examples of the word used in context. Study this entry for *receive* with the parts of the entry labeled. Then answer the questions.

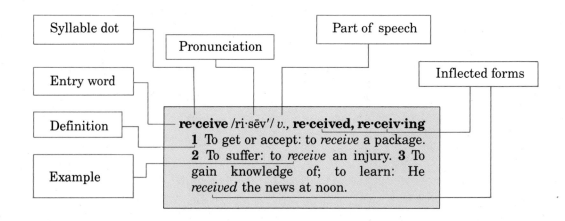

Syllable dot · Pronunciation · Part of speech · Entry word · Inflected forms · Definition · Example

re·ceive /ri·sēv'/ *v.*, **re·ceived, re·ceiv·ing**
1 To get or accept: to *receive* a package.
2 To suffer: to *receive* an injury. **3** To gain knowledge of; to learn: He *received* the news at noon.

1. What part of speech is the entry word? _____

2. Write the *ing* form of the entry word. _____

3. How many syllables are there in the entry word? _____

Spelling on Your Own

UNIT WORDS

Write each Unit word correctly using the letters *ei* or the letters *ie*.

1. v __ l
2. fr __ ndship
3. br __ f
4. gr __ f
5. fr __ ght
6. h __ ght
7. w __ gh
8. v __ n
9. n __ ce
10. s __ ze
11. sl __ gh
12. n __ ghbor
13. ach __ ve
14. f __ ld
15. r __ ndeer
16. ch __ f
17. hyg __ ne
18. rec __ ve
19. c __ ling
20. bel __ ve

MASTERY WORDS

| piece |
| neither |
| grape |
| ripe |
| agree |
| waist |

Write the Mastery words in which you hear each of these sounds. Underline the letter or letters that spell the sounds.

1. /ā/ (two words) _____ _____

2. /ē/ (three words) _____ _____

   _____

3. /ī/ _____

Finish each sentence with a Mastery word.

4. A _____ can be either green or purple.

5. Ari tossed _____ olives into the salad.

6. Did the belt fit around your _____ ?

7. Ben wrote the note on a _____ of yellow paper.

8. Do you _____ that cats make the best pets?

BONUS WORDS

| shriek |
| receipt |
| deceive |
| siege |
| beige |
| yield |
| shield |
| conceited |

1. Write four Bonus words with /ē/ spelled *ie*.
2. Write three Bonus words with /ē/ spelled *ei*. Underline the letter that comes before *ei* in each word.
3. Write the Bonus word with /ā/.
4. Add *ed* and *ing* to these verbs: *shriek, deceive, yield, shield*.
5. Write the Bonus word that has the same base word as *deception*. Write a sentence using that word.

4 Plurals

UNIT WORDS

1. radishes
2. tomatoes
3. potatoes
4. batches
5. starches
6. dominoes
7. heroes
8. wristwatches
9. cargoes
10. masses
11. radios
12. stereos
13. mice
14. geese
15. oxen
16. tornadoes
17. volcanoes
18. echoes
19. lenses
20. autos

The Unit Words

All of the words in this unit are plural. Usually we form the plural by adding *s* or *es* to a word, but there are exceptions. For most of the Unit words, the plural is formed in one of the following ways:

● For words ending in *s, ss, x, sh, ch, tch,* and *zz,* the plural is formed by adding *es: mass   masses.*

● Words that end with a consonant and *o* also form the plural with *es: hero   heroes.*

● Words that end with a vowel and *o* add only *s* to form the plural: *radio   radios.*

☐ *Autos* is an exception to the rules for plurals; add just *s* to form the plural.

☐ *Mice, geese,* and *oxen* are called irregular plurals because they are not formed by adding *s* or *es.*

REMEMBER THIS

The *ch* in *echo* is pronounced the same as the *ch* in *chorus:* /ek'ō/ /kôr'əs/. To help you remember the correct spelling for *echo,* think of this: *The sound of the chorus echoes through the school.*

Harcourt Brace School Publishers

Spelling Practice

A. Write the plural form of each of these words.

1. batch _____ **2.** starch _____

3. mass _____ **4.** radish _____

B. Write the plural form of each of these words.

5. mouse _____ **6.** goose _____

7. ox _____

C. Write the plural form of each of these words. Circle the word with the plural ending that is different from the rest.

8. potato _____ **9.** domino _____

10. tomato _____ **11.** cargo _____

12. hero _____ **13.** tornado _____

14. volcano _____ **15.** auto _____

D. Follow the directions using the Unit words.

16. Write the word that is a compound word. _____

17. Write the word that has the sound /k/ spelled *ch*. _____

18. Two Unit words end in a vowel and *o* in the singular form. Write the plural form of each. Underline the plural endings.

_____ _____

19. Write the plural form of *lens*. _____

E. Complete these questions with Unit words.
Did you know that . . .

20. the winds in _____ can reach speeds of 300 miles per hour?

21. the first _____ were powered by steam engines?

22. _____ are fruit because they have seeds?

23. sweet _____ grow underground?

24. _____ fly in a V-shaped formation?

25. bats are guided in flight by _____ from sounds they make?

Spelling and Language·Subject and Verb Agreement

The subject and verb in a sentence must agree in number. If the subject is plural, the verb must also be plural.

Singular   This *tomato is* not ripe.
Plural   The other *tomatoes are* ripe.

Complete each sentence with the singular or plural form of a Unit word.

1. A fresh _____ of rolls is on the table.

2. There are also radishes and sliced _____ .

3. Baked _____ go well with the roast beef.

Writing on Your Own

Imagine that you have just discovered that music makes certain vegetables grow faster. Write a short article for *Farming Magazine*. Describe your experiments and try to persuade farmers to use music in their fields. Use as many of the Unit words as you can.

 WRITER'S GUIDE   For help in persuasive writing, turn to the sample opinion paragraph on page 271.

Using the Dictionary to Spell and Write

Some words have more than one spelling for the plural form. When a word has more than one correct spelling, the one used most often appears first in a dictionary entry. Look at the dictionary entry for *volcano.* It shows two spellings for the plural form. The more common one, *volcanoes,* is given first.

> **vol·ca·no** /vol·kā′nō/ *n., pl.* **vol·ca·noes 1** An opening in the earth's surface through which lava, steam, ashes, etc., are released, forming a cone-shaped hill or mountain. **2** The hill or mountain itself. *Alternate plural:* **volcanos.**

Look up these words in the **Spelling Dictionary.** Write the plural form or forms for these words. If there are two forms, circle the more common one.

1. tornado _____

2. hero _____

3. cargo _____

4. stereo _____

5. domino _____

Spelling on Your Own

Write the Unit words in alphabetical order. Add the plural form of each of these words: *juice, niece, yoyo, use, inch, kiss, flash, zoo.* You will have at least one word for each letter of the alphabet except *q* and *x.*

MASTERY WORDS

addresses
branches
losses
sheep
peaches
women

Follow the directions using the Mastery words.

1. Two words end with *ch* in the singular form. Write the singular and the plural form of each one.

   _____   _____

   _____   _____

2. Two words end with *ss* in the singular form. Write the singular and the plural form of each one.

   _____   _____

   _____   _____

Write the plural form of each of these nouns.

3. sheep _____   **4.** woman _____

Use a Mastery word to complete each item.

5. one _____ from the flock

6. two _____ for the fruit salad

7. three _____ from an elm tree

8. four _____ applying for the job

BONUS WORDS

lassos
broncos
rodeos
mosquitoes
burros
pueblos
gumbos
patios

Items that are related in some way fit into the same category. For example, apples, oranges, and bananas all fit the category of types of fruit. Write the Bonus word that is part of the same category as each pair of words given below.

1. ponies, donkeys (two words) **2.** wasps, flies
3. apartments, homes **4.** ropes, cords
5. contests, roundups **6.** terraces, yards **7.** soups, stews

Choose four words; use them to write a paragraph about the Old West.

5 The Sounds /kw/, /ks/, /gz/

UNIT WORDS

1. quake
2. suffix
3. exact
4. equator
5. mixture
6. taxi
7. examine
8. example
9. squad
10. squirm
11. quiz
12. prefix
13. quality
14. exist
15. request
16. axle
17. expert
18. quarrel
19. exert
20. exhaust

That was quite a quake.

The Unit Words

The English alphabet has just 26 letters, although there are about 40 sounds in our language. Many vowel sounds are represented by combinations of letters.

Most consonant letters stand for one consonant sound. However, there are some consonant letters that stand for more than one sound. Among those consonants are *c*, *q*, and *x*. The letter *c* represents either /k/ or /s/.

- The letter *q* always combines with the vowel letter **u** and usually spells the sounds /kw/, as in *quake*.

- The letter *x* usually represents the different sounds /ks/, as in *suffix*, and /gz/, as in *exact*.

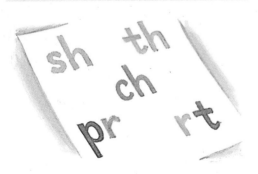

REMEMBER THIS

Two consonant letters that stand for one sound (*sh*, *ch*, and *th*) are called a **consonant digraph**. A **consonant cluster** is two or more consonant letters together in which you hear each consonant sound: *pr* in *prefix* and *rt* in *exert* are examples.

Spelling Practice

A. Follow the directions using the Unit words.

1. Write the four words that begin with the sounds /kw/.

_____   _____   _____   _____

2. Write the two words that begin with the sounds /skw/.

_____   _____

3. Write two more words that contain the sounds /kw/.

_____   _____

4. Write the two words that end with the sounds /ks/. Then underline the word that begins with a consonant cluster.

/tak'sē/
/ak'səl/

_____   _____

5. Write four more words that contain the sounds /ks/.

_____   _____   _____   _____

6. Write the six words that contain the sounds /gz/.

_____   _____   _____

_____   _____   _____

7. Does a vowel or a consonant sound follow /gz/ in these words? _____

B. Follow the directions using Unit words that have consonant clusters.

8. Write the words that end with each of these consonant clusters.

ct _____

rm _____

st (3 words) _____   _____   _____

9. Write the word that ends a consonant cluster and begins with the

sounds /skw/. _____

C. Finish these sentences. Write the six Unit words that have the sounds /gz/. You will write each word once.

10. The mechanic will carefully _____ the

_____ pipes of Dad's car.

11. If you _____ effort at school, you will set a good _____ .

12. An _____ copy of this rare vase does not _____ .

Spelling and Language · Synonyms

UNIT WORDS

quake
suffix
exact
equator
mixture
taxi
examine
example
squad
squirm
quiz
prefix
quality
exist
request
axle
expert
quarrel
exert
exhaust

Synonyms are words that have the same or nearly the same meaning. *Example* and *model* are synonyms in these sentences: Please give us an *example* to follow. We need a *model.* Use synonyms to vary your writing and to make your meaning clear.

Write a Unit word that is a synonym for each underlined word.

1. Mr. Henley will give us a short <u>test</u> on Friday. _____

2. The <u>precise</u> starting time will be noon. _____

3. I will <u>investigate</u> the possibility of taking the test later. _____

4. Mr. Henley may <u>ask</u> that I take it now. _____

Writing on Your Own

Pretend you are an education expert. Write a paragraph for a booklet for students your age. Explain the benefits of relaxing before tests. Describe some of the problems nervousness causes and reasons for remaining calm. Use as many of the Unit words as you can.

 THESAURUS For help finding vivid synonyms, turn to page 205.

Proofreading

This notice for the A-V club meeting has six spelling errors.

1. Read the notice and circle the spelling errors.

Notice to the A-V Squad

Mr. John Cleveland of the High Quality Video Company will speak to the sqwad next Thursday. The ixact time will be announced later.

Mr. Cleveland is an ekspert on audio-visual equipment. He will show us an exsample of a video disc and a video camera. We riquest that all squad members be on time.

---

2. Write the six misspelled words correctly.

_____   _____   _____

_____   _____   _____

Spelling on Your Own

UNIT WORDS

Make a word chain using the Unit words. Write one word. Use a letter in that word to write another word. Then keep going, writing words across and down in a chain.

MASTERY WORDS

Follow the directions using the Mastery words.

quiet
quickly
tax
excellent
square
except

1. Write the three words that have the sounds /kw/ heard in *quiz*.

_____   _____   _____

2. Write the three words that have the sounds /ks/ heard in *box*.

_____   _____   _____

Write *accept* or *except* for each meaning.

3. "but" _____   4. "take or receive" _____

Now finish each sentence with *accept* or *except*.

5. Everyone _____ Joan went bowling.

6. We _____ your invitation to go bowling.

Finish each sentence with a Mastery word.

7. This vacation went slowly instead of _____ .

8. Cut the patch in a _____ instead of a triangle.

9. Please be _____ , not noisy.

BONUS WORDS

banquet
acquaint
exile
extinct
exit
aquarium
qualify
existence

Add *ed* to each of these words.

1. exile   2. acquaint   3. exist   4. qualify

Write the Bonus word that answers each question.

5. What word describes a lavish feast?
6. What word describes a place where fish are kept?
7. What word applies to the dinosaur?
8. What word most frequently appears over doors in public buildings?
9. What word has the same base word as *qualification*?
10. What word has *exist* as its base word?

Review

Follow these steps when you are unsure of how to spell a word.
- **Say** the word. Recall when you have heard the word used. Think about what it means.
- **Look** at the word. Find any prefixes, suffixes, or other word parts you know. Think about other words that are related in meaning and spelling. Try to picture the word in your mind.
- **Spell** the word to yourself. Think about the way each sound is spelled. Notice any unusual spelling.
- **Write** the word while looking at it. Check the way you have formed your letters. If you have not written the word clearly or correctly, write it again.
- **Check** your learning. Cover the word and write it. If you did not spell the word correctly, practice these steps until the word becomes your own.

UNIT 1

oven
solve
rapid
depth
against
plastic
publish
absence
system
snack

UNIT 1 Follow the directions using words from Unit 1.
Write the words that have the same vowel sounds as the words below.

1. bronze _____

2. other (2 words) _____ _____

3. bristle (4 words) _____ _____

_____ _____

4. chess (2 words) _____ _____

5. pass (4 words) _____ _____

_____ _____

6. stump (2 words) _____ _____

UNIT 2

breathe
shoulder
growth
grain
borrow
aisle
coach
complain
release
brain

UNIT 2 Write words from Unit 2 that have these long vowel sounds.

7. /ē/ (2 words) _____ _____

8. /ī/ _____

9. /ā/ (3 words) _____ _____

_____

10. /ō/ (4 words) _____ _____

_____ _____

Follow the directions using words from Unit 3.
Add *ei* or *ie* to complete each word below.

11. rec__ve _____

12. v__n _____

13. h__ght _____

14. bel__ve _____

15. n__ghbor _____

16. f__ld _____

17. w__gh _____

18. n__ce _____

Write the correct spelling for each underlined word.

19. The <u>ceeling</u> was at least eight feet high. _____

20. She set out to <u>acheeve</u> her goal. _____

21. Use words with the sound /ē/ to complete the poem. The beginning
   sound for each word is given to help you.
   Judge how generously you give
      by how worthily you /r/ _____
   Judge how truthfully you speak
      by how honestly you /b/ _____
   Judge how bravely you fail
      by how grandly you /ə/ _____

UNIT 3
receive
neighbor
believe
height
vein
weigh
field
ceiling
achieve
niece

Follow the directions using words from Unit 4.
Write the plural form of each of these words.

22. hero _____

23. mouse _____

24. tomato _____

25. radish _____

26. batch _____

27. cargo _____

28. lens _____

29. auto _____

30. Use the plural form of each of these words in a sentence.

   radio _____

   stereo _____

UNIT 4
radios
heroes
radishes
mice
tomatoes
batches
cargoes
stereos
lenses
autos

WORDS IN TIME

The word *tomato* came from the Nahuatl language of Mexico and Central
America. This familiar garden plant is actually a South American fruit. The early
Spanish explorers took the plant, along with the word *tomatl,* back with them to
Europe. In Spain, they called the plant *tomate.* Before long the word began to
appear in English as *tomato.*

equator
expert
exact
example
quarrel
suffix
mixture
quiz
prefix
request

UNIT 5 Follow the directions using words from Unit 5.

31. Write four words that would appear on a dictionary page with the guide words *equal* and *export*.

_____ _____ _____

_____

Write the words that have these sounds.

32. /kw/ (four words) _____ _____

_____ _____

33. /ks/ (four words) _____ _____

_____ _____

34. /gz/ (two words) _____ _____

Write the word that fits each definition.

35. a word part that goes at the end of a word _____

36. a word part that goes at the beginning of a word _____

37. a combination of things all together _____

Complete the story.

One day, Marta overheard two students studying for a __38__ on South America. Suddenly the students began to __39__ . One student said Ecuador was near the South Pole. The other said it was next to Brazil. Finally Marta said, "You could go to the library and __40__ a map of South America to find the __41__ location, but that shouldn't be necessary. I'm no __42__ in geography, but isn't *Ecuador* the Spanish word for __43__ ?"

38. _____   **39.** _____

40. _____   **41.** _____

42. _____   **43.** _____

WORDS IN TIME

No one is sure how the word *quiz* originated. It seems to have just popped into British English sometime in the eighteenth century. Originally it meant "an odd person." The verb form, "to quiz," meant "to play a joke on someone." Then, in the late nineteenth century, the word appeared in American English wirh a different meaning: "to seek out an answer." Some dictionaries say the American word *quiz* is probably a form of *inquisitive*.

Spelling and Reading
A Research Report

Read the following research report on the South American rain forest. Notice how the information is organized.

The Amazing Amazon Rain Forest

The Amazon rain forest in South America is one of the most surprising places on earth. It stretches 3,000 miles along the equator, and through its heart flows the mighty Amazon River. It is the largest and wettest tropical forest in the world. In fact, about 100 inches of rain fall in this rain forest each year.

The hot, wet climate of the rain forest encourages rapid growth. Trees shoot up to great heights, forming a leafy ceiling that shuts out the sunlight. As a result, few plants grow along the forest floor. In some places, where people have cut down the trees, you may find large farms, or plantations. From these plantations, rich cargoes of tropical fruits are shipped all over the world.

The rain forest is far from quiet. High in the trees, monkeys quarrel and complain. More than 1,500 types of brightly feathered birds cackle and call. Fantastic insects, some as large as baseballs, buzz and click and whir.

How many life forms live in the Amazon rain forest? No one knows. Until more of this great green world is explored, we can only guess what secrets lie hidden in its depths.

Write the answers to the questions.

1. In this report, where does the writer say the Amazon rain forest is located?
2. What does the hot, wet climate of the rain forest encourage?
3. Why can plants grow where people have cut down trees?
4. Does the writer feel that the monkeys make a pleasant or an unpleasant sound? Why do you think as you do?

Underline the review words in your answers. Check to see that you spelled the words correctly.

Harcourt Brace School Publishers

Spelling and Writing
A Research Report

Think and Discuss

A research report is a form of writing that gives facts about a single topic. A good research report is well organized and presents facts in an interesting way.

Writers usually begin a report with an introduction that states the topic. In this first paragraph, they also give one or two striking details to hook the reader's interest. The body of a report is organized around several main ideas. Each of the main ideas is developed in a separate paragraph.

When writing a research report, most writers start by gathering information about the subject, taking notes, and then making an outline. In the outline, each Roman numeral stands for the main idea of a paragraph. Each capital letter stands for a detail that supports the main idea. Here, for example, is how an outline for the research report on page 27 might begin:

Title: *The Amazing Amazon Rain Forest*

  I.   Introduction
    A.   Size and location
      1.   3,000 miles long
      2.   Located on the equator and Amazon River
    B.   Climate
      1.   Wettest, hottest place on earth
      2.   100 inches of rain per year

Look over the introduction of the report on page 27. What striking details does the writer give in the first paragraph? How do these details work to catch the reader's interest? Now reread the rest of the report. What main ideas are covered in the second, third, and fourth paragraphs?

Apply

Now write a **research report** on a topic that interests you. Use the library to find out more about your topic. You will share your report with your classmates. Follow the writing guidelines on the next page.

Words to Help You Write

solve
rapid
depth
against
system
release
receive
believe
achieve
expert
example
exact

Prewriting

Think of a topic about which you would like to write a report.

- Go to the library and research your topic. Take notes.
- Make an outline by arranging your notes into main ideas and supporting details.
- Choose some striking details to use in your introduction.

 THESAURUS For help finding words to make your details more striking, turn to page 205.

Composing

Use your outline to write a first draft of your report.

- Write your title.
- Write an introduction in which you state your topic and give a few details that will catch the reader's interest.
- Write a paragraph about each main idea in your outline.
- Look over your outline. Have you left out any details?

Revising

Read your report and show it to a classmate. Then follow these guidelines to improve your work. Use the editing and proofreading marks on this page to indicate corrections.

 WRITER'S GUIDE For help revising your report, use the checklist on page 267.

Editing

- Make sure your report is well organized and interesting.
- Make sure your introduction states the topic and you have included striking details to catch the reader's interest.
- Make sure that you have written a paragraph for each main idea in your outline.
- Make sure you have written detail sentences to support each of your main ideas.
- Check that your title fits your report.

Proofreading

- Check your spelling, capitalization, and punctuation.

Copy your report onto clean paper. Write carefully and neatly.

Publishing

Share your report with your class. Ask what facts about your topic interested them the most. Then have students suggest other main ideas you might use to expand your report.

Editing and Proofreading Marks	
	capitalize
⊙	make a period
∧	add something
	add a comma
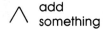	add quotation marks
ℯ	take something away
◯	spell correctly
⊬	indent the paragraph
/	make a lowercase letter
	transpose

7 The Sound /j/

UNIT WORDS

1. *genuine*
2. *junk*
3. *gigantic*
4. *fringe*
5. *wage*
6. *lodge*
7. *jumble*
8. *image*
9. *pledge*
10. *language*
11. *adjust*
12. *hedge*
13. *germs*
14. *genes*
15. *garbage*
16. *junior*
17. *budge*
18. *ridge*
19. *objection*
20. *pigeon*

The Unit Words

Genuine and *junk* both begin with the sound /j/. The sound is spelled with *g* in *genuine* and with *j* in *junk*. At the beginning of words and syllables, /j/ is usually spelled with *g* or *j*. The vowel letter that follows /j/ can often help you decide whether to use *g* or *j*.

- /j/ is usually spelled **g** before *e* or *i*

- /j/ is usually spelled **j** before *a, o,* or *u*

☐ *Objection* is an exception you will need to remember.

The Unit words also show two ways to spell /j/ at the end of words.

- **ge**, as in *fringe*

- **dge** after short vowel sounds, as in *lodge*

☐ Notice that *pigeon* is an exception. In *pigeon, ge* spells /j/ in the middle of a word.

30

Spelling Practice

A. Follow the directions using the Unit words.

1. Write the five words that have /j/ spelled *j*.

_____ _____ _____

_____ _____

2. Write the word that sounds like *jeans*. _____

3. Write three more words that begin with /j/ spelled with *g*. Circle the word that has a second *g* that does not stand for /j/.

_____ _____ _____

4. Write the six words that have /j/ spelled *ge*.

_____ _____ _____

_____ _____ _____

B. Write the Unit words in which /j/ follows these short vowel sounds.

5. /e/ (two words) _____ _____

6. /o/ _____ 7. /u/ _____

8. Write the other word that ends with *dge*. _____

C. Write the Unit word that rhymes with each of these words.

9. hinge _____ 10. tumble _____

11. worms _____ 12. page _____

13. dodge _____ 14. scrimmage _____

D. Complete each sentence using a Unit word.

15. A raccoon has overturned the _____ can.

16. The belt buckle is made of _____ silver.

17. Please _____ the clock to show the right time.

18. Spanish is the first _____ I learned to speak.

19. The judge overruled the lawyer's _____ .

20. My sister will change schools after her _____ year.

21. A _____ landed on the windowsill.

Spelling and Language · Nouns and Verbs

UNIT WORDS

genuine
junk
gigantic
fringe
wage
lodge
jumble
image
pledge
language
adjust
hedge
germs
genes
garbage
junior
budge
ridge
objection
pigeon

Some of the Unit words can be either nouns or verbs. A **noun** names a person, place, or thing. A **verb** shows action or being.

Noun The mountain *lodge* is made of natural stone.
Verb A stone *lodged* in the wheel of my bike.

Complete each pair of sentences using Unit words. The word will be a noun in the first sentence and a verb in the second sentence. Add *ed* to the verb if necessary. Remember to drop final *e* before adding *ed*.

1. We have all made a _____ to help with the project.

2. Janet has _____ two hours of her time each week.

3. The _____ on the porch awning is coming off.

4. Aunt Margaret _____ the scarf for me.

Writing on Your Own

Imagine that you think a neighborhood clean-up program in your area has been unsuccessful. Write a letter to the editor to express your opinion. Use as many Unit words as you can. Use some words as both nouns and as verbs.

 WRITER'S GUIDE   For a sample opinion paragraph, turn to page 271.

Using the Dictionary to Spell and Write

Knowing how to pronounce a word can help you remember how to spell a word. A pronunciation follows each entry word in the dictionary. The **pronunciation** is the word written in sound symbols. The **pronunciation key** lists the sound symbols and gives a sample word for each sound. You will find a complete pronunciation key at the beginning of the **Spelling Dictionary** and a key on every right-hand page.

| act, āte, câre, ärt; | egg, ēven; | if, īce; | on, ōver, ôr; | bŏok, fōod; | up, tûrn; |

ə = a in *ago*, e in *listen*, i in *giraffe*, o in *pilot*, u in *circus*;   yōo = u in *music*;   oil;   out;   chair;   sing;   shop;   thank;   that;   zh in *treasure*.

Use the key to read each pronunciation below. Then write the correct spelling of a Unit word.

1. /jen′yōo·in/ _____
2. /wāj/ _____

3. /pij′ən/ _____
4. /jēnz/ _____

Harcourt Brace School Publishers

Spelling on Your Own

Replace the sound symbol /j/ in each word with the correct spelling; write the Unit word.

1. /j/erms
2. lo/j/
3. ob/j/ection
4. /j/unk
5. ple/j/
6. /j/umble
7. wa/j/
8. ad/j/ust
9. langua/j/
10. /j/unior
11. /j/enes
12. he/j/
13. ima/j/
14. frin/j/
15. pi/j/on
16. /j/igantic
17. /j/enuine
18. ri/j/
19. garba/j/
20. bu/j/

MASTERY WORDS

Write the three Mastery words that would appear on a page with each pair of guide words. Write the words in alphabetical order.

1. chair   engineer

2. jet   orchard

orange
engine
dodge
charge
judge
join

Follow the directions using the Mastery words.

3. Write the two words in which /j/ is spelled *dge*.

4. Write the two words that begin with /j/ spelled *j*. Underline the vowel letter that follows *j*.

BONUS WORDS

1. In four of the Bonus words, the sound /j/ is spelled with *g*. Write the four words.

2. Write the three Bonus words that have the sound /j/ spelled *j*.

3. Use three of the Bonus words that are nouns in sentences. Make each word plural.

4. Use the last two Bonus words in sentences. Use the words as verbs.

5. Write a brief story about a "juvenile genius." Use as many Bonus words as you can.

surgery
prejudice
juvenile
vegetarian
projector
genius
apologize
wedge

8 The Sounds /sh/ and /zh/

UNIT WORDS

1. precision
2. destination
3. decision
4. usual
5. measure
6. explosion
7. version
8. friction
9. situation
10. initial
11. gracious
12. treasure
13. pleasure
14. vision
15. division
16. glacier
17. pronunciation
18. correction
19. condition
20. equation

The Unit Words

We use the sound /sh/ by itself to tell someone to be quiet. In words, /sh/ is usually spelled with the letters *sh*, as in *hush*. But look at the word *motion*. In *motion*, the letters *ti* spell the sound /sh/. Words that end with /shən/ are usually spelled with *tion*.

In the Unit words, the sound /sh/ is spelled these two ways:

- with **ti** as in *initial* and *friction*

- with **ci** as in *gracious*

The sound /zh/ is heard in *usual*. Before the letter *u*, /zh/ is spelled with *s*. Words that end with /zhən/ are usually spelled with *sion*.

In the Unit words, the sound /zh/ is spelled these two ways:

- with **s** as in *measure*

- with **si** as in *decision*

☐ The word *equation* is an exception to these rules. In this word /zh/ is spelled with *ti*.

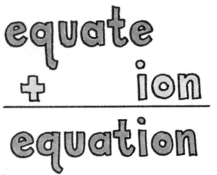

34

Spelling Practice

A. Follow the directions using the Unit words.

1. Write the six words that end with /shən/.

_____   _____   _____

_____   _____   _____

2. Write three more words with the sound /sh/.

_____   _____   _____

3. Write the word that ends with *tion* pronounced /zhən/.

_____

4. Write six more words that end with /zhən/.

_____   _____   _____

_____   _____   _____

5. Write four words with /zh/ spelled *s*. Underline the vowel letter that follows *s* in each word.

_____   _____

_____   _____

6. Write the word that has five syllables. _____

B. Words that end with *-ion* are nouns. Write the Unit words that are the noun forms of these base words. In each case, notice how the spelling changes.

7. explode _____ **8.** decide _____

9. divide _____ **10.** situate _____

11. equate _____ **12.** precise _____

13. correct _____ **14.** pronounce _____

C. Write the Unit word that best completes each sentence.

15. The pirates left the _____ buried on the island.

16. The _____ retreated in the Ice Age.

17. French was difficult because of the _____ .

18. The _____ caused by rubbing the two sticks together made a lot of heat.

Spelling and Language · Word Families

precision
destination
decision
usual
measure
explosion
version
friction
situation
initial
gracious
treasure
pleasure
vision
division
glacier
pronunciation
correction
condition
equation

A **word family** is a group of words with the same base word. The words *pleasure, pleasant,* and *displeasing* all belong to the same word family. They all have the base word *please.*

The underlined word in each sentence belongs to the same family as one of the Unit words. Write the Unit word that has the same base word.

1. Hillary has an explosive temperament. _____

2. How do you pronounce your name? _____

3. The ink is invisible in this light. _____

4. It is his destiny to be successful. _____

5. The skaters glided gracefully around the rink. _____

 Writing on Your Own

Imagine that you are a newspaper reporter. A huge glacier is moving rapidly toward Noname, a small fishing village on the Canadian coast. Write a news item about this event. Use as many Unit words as you can.

WRITER'S GUIDE   For a sample news story, see page 278.

Using the Dictionary to Spell and Write

A dictionary entry gives you a lot of information that will help you when you write. When you look up a word in the dictionary, you will sometimes find other words given at the end of the main entry. These additional words are called run-on entry words. A **run-on entry word** is a word formed by adding a suffix to the entry word. The part of speech is given after the run-on entry word.

Entry Word

gra·cious /grā′shəs/ *adj.* **1** Kind and polite. **2** Elegant; refined: *gracious* living. **—gra′cious·ly** *adv.*

Run-on Entry Word

Look up these entry words in the **Spelling Dictionary.** Write the run-on entry word given for each one and its part of speech.

1. usual _____   **2.** division _____

3. examine _____   **4.** exact _____

SPELLING DICTIONARY   Remember to use your **Spelling Dictionary** when you write.

36

Harcourt Brace School Publishers

Spelling on Your Own

Use all the Unit words in sentences. Include as many of the words as you can in each sentence. See how few sentences you can write. Here is an example: "Your *version* of the *situation* was told with *precision*."

MASTERY WORDS

confusion
action
social
delicious
motion
attention

Follow the directions using the Mastery words.

1. Write the three words in which /sh/ is spelled *ti*.

_____   _____

2. Write the two words in which /sh/ is spelled *ci*.

_____   _____

Write the Mastery words that have these base words.

3. move _____   4. confuse _____

5. attend _____   6. act _____

Finish each sentence with a Mastery word.

7. It is important to pay _____ to traffic lights.

8. There was some _____ about when the program would start.

9. A glass of cold milk tastes _____ .

10. The big _____ event in the spring is the school picnic.

BONUS WORDS

stationary
affectionate
supervision
transfusion
beneficial
precious
leisure
exposure

1. Write the headings NOUNS and ADJECTIVES. Then list each Bonus word under the appropriate heading. You will need to list one word twice.

2. Write the word that means "useful or helpful." Then write three more words that belong to the same word family. Use a dictionary if you need help.

3. Write the Bonus word that is a homophone for *stationery*. Then use each homophone in a sentence.

4. Write a sentence that includes two Bonus words with the suffix *-ion*.

9 The Sounds /ou/ and /oi/

UNIT WORDS

1. poise
2. porpoise
3. devour
4. disloyal
5. vow
6. flounder
7. surround
8. chowder
9. grouchy
10. soybean
11. employer
12. cower
13. rejoice
14. stout
15. poisonous
16. appoint
17. bound
18. fowl
19. coil
20. tortoise

The Unit Words

The words in this unit show two spellings for each of the vowel sounds /ou/ and /oi/.

The vowel sound /ou/ is spelled these two ways:

- with **ou** as in *devour*

- with **ow** as in *vow*

The vowel sound /oi/ is spelled these two ways:

- with **oi** as in *poise*

- with **oy** as in *disloyal*

☐ The Unit words *porpoise* and *tortoise* are not like the other words on the list. In these two words, the letters *oi* are in the unstressed syllable and have the sound /ə/.

Harcourt Brace School Publishers

Spelling Practice

A. Follow the directions using the Unit words.

1. Write the three words in which /oi/ is spelled *oy.*

_____ _____ _____

2. Write five more words with the vowel sound /oi/.

_____ _____ _____

_____ _____

3. Write the two words in which *oi* stands for /ə/.

_____ _____

B. Follow the directions using Unit words with the sound /ou/.

4. Write the word that is a homophone for *foul.* _____

5. Write three more words spelled with *ow.*

_____ _____ _____

6. Write two words that rhyme with *sound.*

_____ _____

7. Write four more words that have /ou/ spelled *ou.*

_____ _____ _____

_____ _____

C. Complete these "word math" problems. Write the word.

8. grief — /ēf/ + /ou/ + /chē/ = _____

9. chief — /ēf/ + /ou/ + /dər/ = _____

D. Complete Ann's diary entry with Unit words. Add *ed* to all the verbs.

Our first day on Uncle Will's boat was perfect. We spent the morning fishing for __10__ near shore. In the afternoon, Uncle Will took the boat out to sea. We spotted a __11__ in the water ahead of us. All of a sudden, a whole school of them __12__ the boat. They played and swam near us for hours. Later, Uncle Will made a huge pot of seafood __13__. We were so hungry we __14__ it all. Then Uncle Will __15__ Jan and me to the cleanup crew.

10. _____   11. _____   12. _____

13. _____   14. _____   15. _____

Spelling and Language · Antonyms

poise
porpoise
devour
disloyal
vow
flounder
surround
chowder
grouchy
soybean
employer
cower
rejoice
stout
poisonous
appoint
bound
fowl
coil
tortoise

Antonyms are words that mean the opposite of each other. *Old* and *new* are antonyms. Write a Unit word that is an antonym for the underlined word in each sentence.

1. Tom is always <u>cheerful</u> when he is hungry. _____

2. We noticed the speaker's <u>awkwardness</u>. _____

3. Was Avery <u>faithful</u> to the club's code? _____

4. The paint contains <u>nontoxic</u> chemicals. _____

5. Did the team <u>dismiss</u> the captain yet? _____

Writing on Your Own

Pretend you have just enjoyed dinner at a restaurant. Write a business letter to the manager praising the meal. Use antonyms for *disloyal, grouchy,* and *poisonous.* Use five other Unit words in your letter.

 WRITER'S GUIDE For help with the parts of a business letter, turn to page 273.

Using the Dictionary to Spell and Write

Knowing how to pronounce a word can help you remember how to spell a word. A dictionary **pronunciation** shows you how to say a word. It gives the sounds that make up the spoken word. The pronunciation for a word with more than one syllable also includes an **accent mark** ('). The accent mark shows which syllable is the accented syllable, the one said with greater force. The accent in *flounder* is on the first syllable.

/floun′dər/

Write the spelling for each of these pronunciations. Then underline the letters that spell the accented syllable.

1. /pôr′pəs/ _____   2. /kou′ər/ _____

3. /im·ploi′ər/ _____   4. /chou′dər/ _____

5. /di·vour′/ _____   6. /ri·jois′/ _____

7. /sə·round′/ _____   8. /ə·point′/ _____

act, āte, câre, ärt;   egg, ēven;   if, īce;   on, ōver, ôr;   bŏŏk, fŏŏd;   up, tûrn;
ə = a in *ago,* e in *listen,* i in *giraffe,* o in *pilot,* u in *circus;*   yŏŏ = u in *music;*   oil;   out;
chair;   sing;   shop;   thank;   that;   zh in *treasure.*

 SPELLING DICTIONARY Remember to use your **Spelling Dictionary** when you write.

Spelling on Your Own

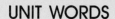

UNIT WORDS

Write the Unit word that is a synonym for each word below. Then write a sentence using either the Unit word or the synonym.

1. stew	**2.** balance	**3.** tied	**4.** turtle	**5.** boss
6. name	**7.** consume	**8.** promise	**9.** twist	**10.** tremble
11. encircle	**12.** chubby	**13.** unfaithful	**14.** sulky	**15.** toxic
16. dolphin	**17.** celebrate	**18.** bird	**19.** flatfish	**20.** plant

MASTERY WORDS

choice
moist
annoy
drown
royal
mountain

Follow the directions using the Mastery words.

1. Write four words with /oi/. Underline the letters that spell /oi/.

_____ _____

_____ _____

2. Write two words with /ou/. Underline the letters that spell /ou/.

_____ _____

3. A *Rhyme Styme* is a riddle with two rhyming words for the answer. Use a Mastery word and another word to finish this Rhyme Styme.

What do you call a hill that spurts water?

_____ _____

BONUS WORDS

allowance
boundary
corduroy
outrageous
browse
hoist
boycott
announcement

Write the Bonus words that have these meanings. Then use each word in a sentence.

1. fabric with ridges
2. refuse to buy
3. look around
4. lift up

Write the Bonus words that have these base words.

5. outrage   **6.** announce   **7.** bound   **8.** allow

Play a word association game with the Bonus words.

9. Write each word. Then write the first word that you think of when you read the word.

10. Now use both words in a sentence.

10 The Sounds /yo͞o/ and /yo͝o/

UNIT WORDS

1. musician
2. mural
3. museum
4. review
5. secure
6. curious
7. fuse
8. perfume
9. menu
10. universe
11. view
12. cure
13. pure
14. excuse
15. refuse
16. furious
17. community
18. amuse
19. abuse
20. preview

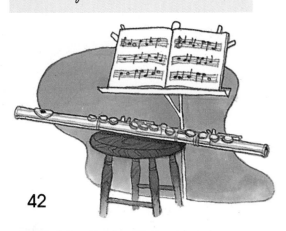

The Unit Words

The words *musician* and *mural* begin with the same two letters, *mu*. But they do not begin with the same two sounds: /myo͞o zish′ən/, /myo͝or′əl/. The vowel sound /yo͞o/ in *musician* and the vowel sound /yo͝o/ in *mural* are both spelled with *u*.

The Unit words show other ways to spell both /yo͞o/ and /yo͝o/.

- /yo͞o/ in *fuse* is spelled **u**-consonant-**e**

- /yo͝o/ in *cure* is spelled **u**-consonant-**e**

There is also a third way to spell /yo͞o/—with the letters *iew*, as in *view*.

REMEMBER THIS

Each of the words *refuse, abuse, excuse* has two pronunciations. When the word is a verb, the *s* is pronounced /z/. When the word is a noun, the *s* is pronounced /s/.

Spelling Practice

A. Complete the exercises using the Unit words.

1. Write the three words in which /yo͞o/ is spelled with *iew*.

_____   _____   _____

2. Write the three words in which /yo͝or/ is spelled with *ure*.

_____   _____   _____

3. Write the two words that rhyme and have /yo͝o/ spelled with *u*.

_____   _____

4. Write five words in which /yo͞oz/ is spelled with *use*.

_____   _____   _____

_____   _____

5. Write another word with /yo͞o/ spelled *u*-consonant-*e*. _____

6. Write three words that begin with *mu*. Circle the word with the sound /yo͝o/.

_____   _____   _____

7. Write a word that begins with *u* and a word that ends with *u*.

_____   _____

B. Complete each sentence with a Unit word.

8. There will be a square dance at the _____ hall.

9. One _____ will call the dances.

10. He always gives a _____ of the steps before each dance.

11. There is no _____ not to join in.

12. Aren't you _____ to see what it is like?

C. Write the correct spelling for each pronunciation in the limerick.
   "I've discovered a medicine /pyo͝or/ **(13)**
   For the cold! A prize I'll /si·kyo͝or'/." **(14)**
   But, alas it was /kyo͝or'ē·əs/, **(15)**
   And it made Jill /fyo͝or'ē·əs/, **(16)**
   That her own cold it just couldn't /kyo͝or/. **(17)**

13. _____   14. _____   15. _____

16. _____   17. _____

Spelling and Language · Nouns and Verbs

As a noun, *use* is pronounced /yo͞os/. When it is a verb, *use* is pronounced with a /z/: /yo͞oz/. *Excuse* and *abuse* change pronunciation the same way.

excuse   n. /ik·skyo͞os'/   v. /ik·skyo͞oz'/
abuse   n. /ə·byo͞os'/   v. /ə·byo͞oz'/

Complete each pair of sentences with *abuse* or *excuse*. Then write *n.* or *v.* to show the part of speech.

1. Let's not ____ the privilege. _____

2. This book can't take any more ____ . _____

3. What was his ____ for being late? _____

4. Can you ____ me for the afternoon? _____

Writing on Your Own

Imagine you are traveling through two U.S. states. Write a comparison paragraph for a friend. Tell how the two states are alike and different. Use some Unit words both as nouns and as verbs.

 WRITER'S GUIDE   For a sample comparison paragraph, turn to page 272.

Using the Dictionary to Spell and Write

Words that have the same spelling but are different in meaning and origin are listed as separate entries in the dictionary. A number follows each entry word to help you locate the meaning.

Read the two entries for *refuse*. Then answer the questions.

> **re·fuse**[1] /ri·fyo͞oz'/ *v.* **re·fused, re·fus·ing** To say that one will not give, take, allow, or agree to something; to decline: to *refuse* to help; to *refuse* candy.
> **ref·use**[2] /ref'yo͞os/ *n.* Trash: Throw out the *refuse*.

act, āte, câre, ärt;   egg, ēven;   if, īce;   on, ōver, ôr;   bo͝ok, fo͞od;   up, tûrn;
ə = a in *ago*, e in *listen*, i in *giraffe*, o in *pilot*, u in *circus*;   yo͞o = u in *music*;   oil;   out;
chair;   sing;   shop;   thank;   that;   zh in *treasure*.

1. Write the pronunciation for the verb *refuse*. _____

2. Write the pronunciation for the first syllable of each word.

   n. _____   v. _____

Spelling on Your Own

UNIT WORDS

Write the Unit words in alphabetical order. Then write the plural form of each word that begins with *m*. Add *ed* to each word that ends with *use*. Remember to drop the final *e* before you add *ed*.

MASTERY WORDS

huge
cube
music
humid
future
misuse

Follow the directions using the Mastery words.

1. Write the three words in which /yo͞o/ is spelled with *u*.

_____

2. Write the three words in which /yo͞o/ is spelled with *u*-consonant-*e*.

_____

Write the Mastery word that belongs with each group of words.

3. past   present   _____

4. mistreat   _____   abuse

5. square   rectangle   _____

6. _____   sticky   muggy

7. big   _____   large

Use each pair of Mastery words in a sentence.

8. huge cube   _____

9. future music   _____

BONUS WORDS

contribute
immature
commuter
persecute
peculiar
manicure
immune
humorous

Add noun-forming suffixes to the Bonus words to form new words.

1. persecute + -or   **2.** contribute + -or   **3.** manicure + -ist
4. immature + -ity   **5.** immune + -ity   **6.** peculiar + -ity

Write the Bonus word that is a synonym for each of these words.

7. odd   **8.** donate   **9.** amusing

Write a paragraph entitled "The Student Commuter." Use as many Bonus words as you can.

11 Compound Words

UNIT WORDS

1. airmail
2. already
3. background
4. billboard
5. brainstorm
6. earthquake
7. eavesdrop
8. northwest
9. offshore
10. outlaw
11. proofread
12. rainfall
13. roommate
14. somebody
15. streamlined
16. throughout
17. touchdown
18. turnpike
19. whatever
20. workshop

The Unit Words

A **compound word** is made up of two or more words. The words are usually written together as one word.

air + mail = airmail
brain + storm = brainstorm

Often you can tell the meaning of a compound word from the words that make it up. For example, airmail is mail that is sent by air. But the meaning of a compound word is not always the combined meaning of its parts. A brainstorm is not violent weather happening inside the brain. A brainstorm is a sudden bright idea.

Look for the two smaller words that make up each compound word. Usually the spellings of the separate words remain the same when they are combined. Sometimes, however, a letter is dropped. This happens with *already:* all + ready = already.

Spelling Practice

A. Complete the exercises using the Unit words.

1. Write the four words that have the sounds /ôr/ heard in *corn*.

   _____   _____

   _____   _____

2. Write the three words that have the sounds /ûr/ heard in *nurse*.

   _____   _____   _____

3. Write the three words that have the sound /o͞o/ heard in *soon*.

   _____   _____   _____

4. Write the compound word that has one fewer letter than the two words that form it.

   _____

B. Change one word in each of these compounds to make a Unit word.

5. however _____   6. workbench _____

7. airline _____   8. rainbow _____

9. backstroke _____   10. somewhere _____

C. Read each sentence below. Write the Unit word that can take the place of the underlined words.

11. Its <u>smooth, flowing</u> design makes this car more economical.

12. I pressed my ear to the door to <u>listen in secretly</u> on the conversation.

13. The sheriff captured the <u>criminal</u>.

14. Sid scored a <u>play worth six points</u> in the big game.

15. We took the <u>highway that charges a toll</u> to Boston.

16. My <u>friend who lives with me</u> loves to cook.

17. The <u>amount of rain that fell</u> added up to more than a foot.

18. The ship anchored ten miles <u>in the sea beyond the shore</u>.

19. <u>Mail sent by air</u> arrives overnight.

11. _____   12. _____   13. _____

14. _____   15. _____   16. _____

17. _____   18. _____   19. _____

Spelling and Language · *All Ready* and *Already*

UNIT WORDS

airmail
already
background
billboard
brainstorm
earthquake
eavesdrop
northwest
offshore
outlaw
proofread
rainfall
roommate
somebody
streamlined
throughout
touchdown
turnpike
whatever
workshop

The two words *all ready* and the compound word *already* are often confused. The two words *all ready* mean "completely ready." The compound word *already* is an adverb meaning "before this time" or "by this time." Look at these examples.

I am *all ready* to go to the store.
Mother *already* left for the store.

Complete these sentences using *all ready* or *already*.

1. Melissa is _____ for her piano lesson.

2. Ted has _____ had his piano lesson.

3. The governor has _____ signed the new legislation.

4. The city is _____ for the parade.

Writing on Your Own

Pretend you have just traveled both major highways and scenic back roads. Write a business letter to the State Highway Commissioner comparing what was good and bad about these two kinds of roadways. Use some of these Unit words in your letter: *background, billboard, northwest, somebody, throughout, turnpike.*

 WRITER'S GUIDE   For help with the parts of a business letter, turn to page 273.

Using the Dictionary to Spell and Write

The dictionary gives the pronunciation after each entry word. The pronunciation shows you how to say the word. This can help you remember how to spell the word. Different spellings for the same sound are given in the full pronunciation key at the beginning of the **Spelling Dictionary**.

Write the correct spelling for each pronunciation.

1. Ed has /ôl·red′ē/ rehearsed his part. _____

2. I think /sum′bod′ē/ has my ticket. _____

3. Suki saw something in the /bak′ground′/. _____

4. Mr. Crow is painting an ad on the /bil′bôrd′/. _____

Spelling on Your Own

UNIT WORDS

Write each Unit word and a short definition of the word. Decide if the meaning of the compound word is the combined meaning of the two words that make up the compound. If it is not, use the compound word in a sentence that shows its meaning. Use the **Spelling Dictionary** if you need help.

MASTERY WORDS

basketball
upstairs
forever
outdoors
everyday
nobody

Follow this "word math" to write Mastery words.

1-basket	2-out	3-up	4-body
5-ever	6-ball	7-for	8-no
9-stairs	10-doors	11-every	12-day

1. 7 + 5 _____ **2.** 8 + 4 _____

3. 3 + 9 _____ **4.** 2 + 10 _____

5. 1 + 6 _____ **6.** 11 + 12 _____

Complete this story with Mastery words. Use each word only once.

My secret dream is to become a __7__ star. Each morning, I rush __8__ to practice my game. There is __9__ around but me. Then suddenly I remember it's almost time for school, and I race __10__ to my room to get ready.

7. _____ **8.** _____

9. _____ **10.** _____

BONUS WORDS

overdue
woodcut
hallway
stockholder
wholesale
patchwork
windshield
limelight

Each of these compound words contains part of a Bonus word. Copy each word and write the Bonus word that shares one of its parts.

1. spotlight **2.** windbreaker

3. groundwork **4.** halfway

5. wholehearted **6.** stockbroker

7. overhead **8.** woodpecker

Write the Bonus word associated with each word.

9. quilt **10.** theater **11.** automobile

12 Review

Follow these steps when you are unsure of how to spell a word.
- **Say** the word. Recall when you have heard the word used. Think about what it means.
- **Look** at the word. Find any prefixes, suffixes, or other word parts you know. Think about other words that are related in meaning and spelling. Try to picture the word in your mind.
- **Spell** the word to yourself. Think about the way each sound is spelled. Notice any unusual spelling.
- **Write** the word while looking at it. Check the way you have formed your letters. If you have not written the word clearly or correctly, write it again.
- **Check** your learning. Cover the word and write it. If you did not spell the word correctly, practice these steps until the word becomes your own.

UNIT 7 Follow the directions using words from Unit 7.

1. Write the three words that begin with /j/ spelled *g*.

    _____   _____   _____

2. Write the word in which /j/ before *e* is spelled *j*. _____

3. Write the four words that end with /j/. Circle the letters in each word that spell the sound.

    _____   _____

    _____   _____

UNIT 7

objection
pledge
language
germs
gigantic
genuine
wage
adjust
garbage
junk

Write the word that is a synonym for each word below.

4. huge _____   5. promise _____

6. real _____   7. change _____

8. trash (two words) _____

Complete each sentence.

9. The old car was nothing but a piece of _____

10. Hu Yan undertook the _____ task of rebuilding it.

11. It took him four days to _____ the carburetor.

12. Hu Yan said the car was a _____ antique.

Harcourt Brace School Publishers

13. Write the six words that have /zh/ as in *incision*. Circle the letters that spell the sound in the words.

_____   _____   _____

_____   _____   _____

14. Write the four words that have /sh/ as in *direction*. Circle the letters that spell the sound in the words.

_____   _____

_____   _____

UNIT 9 Follow the directions using words from Unit 9.

15. Write the six words that have /oi/ as in *boy*. Circle the two words in which /oi/ is spelled *oy*.

_____   _____   _____

_____   _____   _____

16. Write the four words that have /ou/ as in *cow*. Circle the letters that spell the sound in the words.

_____   _____

_____   _____

Complete each sentence.

17. The president will _____ a new secretary.

18. It would be _____ not to support our school team.

19. The bite of the common garden snake is not _____ .

20. I saw the hungry rabbit _____ a row of lettuce plants.

UNIT 8
usual
division
gracious
measure
correction
decision
situation
vision
condition
equation

UNIT 9
chowder
surround
appoint
poisonous
employer
devour
vow
rejoice
coil
disloyal

WORDS IN TIME

Chowder is an American word that goes back a long way. This thick soup is actually named for the pot it was made in. The French word for pot was *chaudiere*. This word came from the even older Latin word *caldaria*. In ancient Rome, the *cauldarium* was the room for hot baths. Our word *cauldron*, a large kettle, comes from the same root.

musician
excuse
view
pure
curious
museum
review
menu
amuse
community

UNIT 10 **Follow the directions using words from Unit 10.**

21. Write the two one-syllable words.

_____   _____

22. Write the word that fits both of these sentences.

Olga had a good _____ for being late.

The history teacher will _____ the class early.

23. Write the word that rhymes with *furious*. _____

24. Write the six words that have /yo͞o/ spelled *u* or *u*-consonant-*e*.

_____   _____   _____

_____   _____   _____

Finish these sentences.

25. The _____ played the violin for us.

26. She asked the class to _____ the test questions.

UNIT 11 **Follow the directions using words from Unit 11.**
Change one word in each compound below to spell a word from Unit 11.

UNIT 11

already
throughout
airmail
northwest
somebody
background
offshore
proofread
rainfall
roommate

27. northeast _____   28. someone _____

29. airplane _____   30. dugout _____

31. underground_____   32. waterfall _____

Write the word that fits each definition.

33. before or by this time _____

34. all through _____

35. to read and make corrections _____

36. a person sharing living quarters with another _____

Write the word that means the opposite of the underlined word or words in each sentence.

37. There is <u>no one</u> at the door. _____

38. I will meet you on the <u>southeast</u> corner. _____

39. Alden had <u>not yet</u> arrived. _____

40. Waves broke <u>on the beach</u>. _____

Spelling and Reading
A Character Description

Read this character description. Notice the overall impression of the character that the writer's details give you.

Maggie is a devoted musician. When she plays, she is the picture of concentration. There is something graceful and natural about the way she holds the cello. Her thick, black hair falls in coils around her shoulders as she bends over the instrument. Her long, slender fingers adjust rapidly to the various positions demanded by the music.

Music is not a hobby to Maggie. She made a solemn decision to become a musician when she was nine years old, and she has kept to that vow. Her teacher says, "Maggie gets a pure sound from the cello that only somebody very gifted could achieve. She has genuine talent. That's why music is a second language to her."

Yet Maggie is not singleminded about music. She will readily devour a good book. She has sometimes spent an entire day in an art museum. She will scream herself hoarse at a good soccer game. Maggie belongs to the musical community, but she thinks a broad background is essential to being a good musician. "Life is like a great feast," Maggie explains. "In my life, music is the main course. But I enjoy having a little chowder and dessert on the menu too."

Write the answers to the questions.

1. What is the first trait the writer mentions about Maggie in this character description?

2. What does the writer say about the way Maggie holds the cello?

3. What activities in her life is Maggie talking about when she says, "I enjoy having a little chowder and dessert on the menu too"?

4. Was the most important year of Maggie's life the year that she was nine years old? Why or why not?

Underline the review words in your answers. Check to see that you spelled the words correctly.

Spelling and Writing
A Character Description

Harcourt Brace School Publishers

Words to Help You Write

gigantic
usual
gracious
vision
condition
surround
disloyal
musician
excuse
view
pure
curious
amuse
community
already
throughout
background

Think and Discuss

In a character description, the writer tries to give an exact and vivid picture of what a person is like. Writers can do this by describing a person's appearance, interests, feelings, and activities. They can also tell key facts about the person's life. Look back at the character description on page 53. What does the writer tell about Maggie in the first paragraph? What do we find out in the second paragraph? What is revealed in the third?

A paragraph in a character description often starts with a topic sentence. Then come detail sentences that support the topic sentence. Look at the character description on page 53. What is the topic sentence of the first paragraph? How do the detail sentences support the topic sentence? Notice the vivid and specific details the writer presents in the paragraph. Why does the writer describe Maggie's fingers so carefully?

In a good character description, the writer gives details that reveal the person's key traits. This helps build a general impression of the person. The character description on page 53, for example, gives the impression that Maggie is serious, hard-working, and intense. How do the details in the second paragraph give this impression? How do the details in the third paragraph help build this impression?

Apply

Write a **character description** for your teacher of someone who is not in your school. Use details to give a general impression of the person. Follow the writing guidelines on the next page.

54

Prewriting

Decide on a person to write about. It could be a friend or relative, a character in a movie, or someone you imagine.

- Make a chart with four columns. Label the columns *Appearance, Personality, Achievements, Goals.*
- List words and phrases in each column that help describe that side of the person's character.

 THESAURUS For help finding more describing words, turn to page 205.

Composing

Use your chart to write the first draft of your character description.

- Choose three traits of your character. Write a paragraph describing each one.
- Write a topic sentence for each paragraph that tells what character trait the paragraph will discuss.
- Write detail sentences that help build a consistent impression of your character.
- Look over your prewriting chart. Do you want to add any details?

Revising

Read your description and show it to a classmate. Follow these guidelines to improve your work. Use the editing and proofreading marks on this page to show corrections.

 WRITER'S GUIDE For help revising your work, use the checklist on page 267.

Editing

- Make sure your description of the character is vivid and exact.
- Make sure each paragraph in your description describes a different trait of the character.
- Make sure all your details help to build the same overall impression of the character.

Proofreading

- Check your spelling, capitalization, and punctuation.

Copy your description onto clean paper. Write carefully and neatly.

Publishing

Show your character description to your teacher. Ask him or her to tell you what overall impression your description creates.

	Editing and Proofreading Marks
≡	capitalize
⊙	make a period
∧	add something
⋀̧	add a comma
⸌⸍	add quotation marks
⟋	take something away
◯	spell correctly
⊓	indent the paragraph
/	make a lowercase letter
∼ tr	transpose

13 Words with *ed* and *ing*

UNIT WORDS

1. picnicking
2. frolicking
3. coasting
4. wondered
5. filtered
6. appeared
7. steering
8. referred
9. panicked
10. mimicking
11. squirting
12. finished
13. offered
14. watered
15. occurred
16. printing
17. touching
18. delivered
19. preferred
20. transferred

The Unit Words

All of the Unit words are action verbs. Some express an action that can be seen or heard, such as *frolicking*. Others express an action of the mind, such as *wondered*.

Here are some helpful spelling rules for adding *ed* and *ing* to action verbs.

1. If a word ends with *ic*, add *k* before you add the ending.

    picnic   picnicked   picnicking

2. If a word ends with *er* or *ur*:

  a. double the *r* before you add the ending if the accent is on the last syllable.

        re fer'   referred

  b. just add the ending if the accent is on the first syllable.

        of'fer   offered

Although the accent can be on either syllable of *transfer*, always double the *r* before adding the ending.

3. If a word ends with two consonants or two vowels and a consonant, just add the endings.

    appear   appeared   coast   coasting

Spelling Practice

A. Add the letters *ed* or *ing* to these words to spell Unit words.

1. panic _____ **2.** frolic _____

3. picnic _____ **4.** mimic _____

B. Follow the directions using the Unit words.

5. Write the four words in which you
double the final consonant before   _____ _____
adding the letters *ed* or *ing*.
                                       _____ _____

6. Write the two words that end with two vowels and one consonant
before the letters *ed* or *ing* are added.

_____ _____

C. Complete this "word math."

7. printed − ed + ing = _____

8. coasted − ed + ing = _____

9. finishing − ing + ed = _____

10. squirted − ed + ing = _____

11. touched − ed + ing = _____

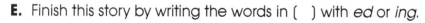

D. Add the letters *ed* to these words to spell Unit words.

12. wonder _____ **13.** deliver _____

14. filter _____ **15.** offer _____

16. water _____

E. Finish this story by writing the words in ( ) with *ed* or *ing*.

What a sticky day it was yesterday! I (offer) __17__ to take
Brad's paper route so he could go on a family picnic. At 5:30 I
(finish) __18__ . I (deliver) __19__ the last paper and headed for
home. Someone had already (water) __20__ our lawn, I noticed.
Just then Dad (appear) __21__ around the corner of the house,
(squirt) __22__ me with the hose! At our house, you never know
what will happen next.

17. _____ **18.** _____ **19.** _____

20. _____ **21.** _____ **22.** _____

Spelling and Language · Using Verbs with *ed* and *ing*

UNIT WORDS

picnicking
frolicking
coasting
wondered
filtered
appeared
steering
referred
panicked
mimicking
squirting
finished
offered
watered
occurred
printing
touching
delivered
preferred
transferred

You add *ed* to a verb to tell about something that already happened. You add *ing* to make a verb that can be used after forms of *be: am, is, are, was,* and *were.*

Add *ed* or *ing* to each underlined word. Write the verb that correctly completes each sentence.

1. Irene <u>panic</u> during the earthquake. _____

2. We are <u>print</u> a weekly newspaper. _____

3. The dogs were <u>frolic</u> in the deep snow. _____

4. Steve <u>finish</u> the book before dinner. _____

5. I <u>transfer</u> to another class. _____

Writing on Your Own

Draw a picture of several children playing at the ocean. Show some of them enjoying the waves and others building sand castles. Then write a paragraph describing the picture for a classmate. Use at least five of the Unit words in your descriptive paragraph. Add *ed* or *ing* to some verbs.

Proofreading

Henry found six misspelled words when he proofread this science report. He also found four mistakes in punctuation or capitalization.

1. Circle each misspelled word. Draw three lines under the letters that should be capitals. Add the missing punctuation.

> Have you ever wondered how animals protect themselves from danger Some insects protect themselves by mimiking nature. There is a butterfly that hides by appeering to be a dry brown leaf. This butterfly is sometimes refered to as the "dead leaf" butterfly. snowshoe rabbits can frolick in the snow without pannicking their white color in winter prevents them from being seen. The opossum's disguise is simply to pretend to be dead.

2. Write the six misspelled words correctly.

_____   _____   _____

_____   _____   _____

3. Write the sentences that need capitals or end punctuation on another piece of paper.

 WRITER'S GUIDE See the editing and proofreading marks on page 268.

Harcourt Brace School Publishers

Spelling on Your Own

ed ing

Add *ing* to the first ten words below. Add *ed* to the next ten. Then use three verbs with *ing* and three verbs with *ed* in sentences.

1. prefer	**2.** deliver	**3.** water	**4.** print	**5.** touch
6. frolic	**7.** squirt	**8.** wonder	**9.** picnic	**10.** filter
11. finish	**12.** offer	**13.** coast	**14.** mimic	**15.** appear
16. steer	**17.** transfer	**18.** refer	**19.** panic	**20.** occur

MASTERY WORDS

reached
counting
returned
chopped
begged
stepped

Add the letters *ed* or *ing* to each word to spell a Mastery word.

1. beg _____   **2.** step _____

3. count _____   **4.** reach _____

5. chop _____   **6.** return _____

Finish these sentences with Mastery words.

7. Father _____ down the old elm tree last week.

8. The top branches _____ above the roof.

Do this "word math."

9. begging − ing = _____ + ed = _____

10. stepping − ing = _____ + ed = _____

BONUS WORDS

depositing
shellacked
altered
succeeded
forgetting
forbidding
upsetting
recommended

Add *ed* or *ing* to each word to spell a Bonus word.

1. shellac   **2.** deposit   **3.** alter   **4.** upset

Write the Bonus word that has the same base word.

5. forgetful   **6.** forbidden   **7.** recommendation   **8.** successful

Follow the directions using the Bonus words.

9. Write five sentences that tell your opinions about things. Use one Bonus word in each sentence.

10. Write a sentence about something you recommended to someone. Use at least two Bonus Words.

14 The Sound /ô/

UNIT WORDS

1. hawk
2. dawn
3. walnut
4. stalk
5. fault
6. pause
7. caution
8. bossy
9. broth
10. install
11. laundry
12. sausage
13. daughter
14. lawn
15. awful
16. applaud
17. haunt
18. faucet
19. frost
20. broad

The Unit Words

There are several ways to spell the vowel sound /ô/ you hear in *hawk*. The Unit words show four ways.

- with **a** before *l* as in *walnut*
- with **au** as in *laundry*
- with **aw** as in *lawn*
- with **o** as in *frost*

☐ The word *broad* does not follow the regular spelling patterns. In *broad*, /ô/ is spelled *oa*.

REMEMBER THIS

Look carefully at the word *daughter*. The letters for /ô/—*au*—are followed by two "silent" consonant letters, *gh*.

daughter

Spelling Practice

A. Follow the directions using the Unit words.

1. Write the three words in which /ô/ is spelled *o*.

_____ _____ _____

2. Write the word that begins with the sound /ô/. _____

3. Now write three more words that have /ô/ spelled the same as in the word you wrote for **2**.

_____ _____ _____

4. Write the three words that have /ô/ spelled with *a* as in *walk*. Circle the word that has a "silent" *l*.

_____ _____ _____

5. Write the word in which /ô/ is spelled *oa* and rhymes with *applaud*.

_____

6. Write the word in which /ô/ is spelled *au* followed by two "silent" letters.

_____

7. Write in alphabetical order the other eight words with /ô/ spelled *au*.

_____ → _____ → _____

→ _____ → _____ → _____

→ _____ → _____

B. Finish each sentence using a Unit word.

8. Ernie ate a _____ of celery.

9. When the temperature is very cold, _____ forms on windows.

10. We began to _____ before the performance was over.

11. A large _____ soared overhead.

12. A yellow traffic sign means " _____ ."

13. Turn off the _____ while you brush your teeth.

14. My sister just had a baby _____ .

15. Please sort the _____ before you do the wash.

16. Workers will _____ the new dryer tomorrow.

Spelling and Language · Multiple Meanings of Words

UNIT WORDS

hawk
dawn
walnut
stalk
fault
pause
caution
bossy
broth
install
laundry
sausage
daughter
lawn
awful
applaud
haunt
faucet
frost
broad

Most words have more than one meaning. The word *stalk* as a noun means "the stem of a plant." As a verb, *stalk* means "to track animals or other prey": Four rangers *stalked* the injured deer.

Write the Unit words that have these meanings.

1. frozen dew _____   **2.** a large bird _____

Use the same two Unit words you wrote to complete these sentences. Add the endings *s, ed,* or *ing* if needed.

3. My cousin _____ peanuts at the football games.

4. I _____ the carrot cake with cream cheese icing.

Writing on Your Own

Write a story to amuse a young child. First make up a title with a few of the Unit words. Then make up events that will allow you to use many Unit words. Choose at least one word that has more than one meaning. Use that word at least twice to show the different meanings.

Using the Dictionary to Spell and Write

An **idiom** is an expression that has a specialized meaning. Often an idiom has a different meaning than the separate words do. Knowing the meaning of an idiom can help you use it correctly.

Read the dictionary entry for *fault.* At the end of the entry, three idioms that include *fault* are explained.

> **fault** /fôlt/ *n.* **1** Defect; failing: His only *fault* is that he is careless. **2** A mistake. **3** Responsibility for failure; blame: It was not her *fault* that she was late. **4** A break in the earth's crust that causes rock layers to shift. **–at fault** In the wrong. **–to a fault** To an almost excessively favorable degree. **–find fault with** To complain about or criticize.

Finish each sentence using one of the idioms for *fault.*

1. The driver of the red car was _____ in the accident.

2. We could not _____ Jessie's work.

3. Sal is neat _____ and never leaves things around.

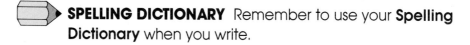

SPELLING DICTIONARY Remember to use your **Spelling Dictionary** when you write.

Harcourt Brace School Publishers

Spelling on Your Own

UNIT WORDS

Write the pairs of words that appear below. Under each pair, write all the Unit words that come alphabetically between those two words. Write the words in alphabetical order.

appear–cease　　**data–hazy**　　**ink–waterfall**

MASTERY WORDS

saucer
cause
moss
straw
strong
taught

Finish the exercises using the Mastery words.

1. Write the three words that have the sound /ô/ spelled *au*. Circle the word that has "silent" *gh*.

_____   _____   _____

2. Write the two words that have /ô/ spelled *o*.

_____   _____

3. Write the word that ends with /ô/. _____

4. Write the other word that begins with the same three letters as the

word you wrote for **3.** _____

5. My Uncle Hector _____ me about gardening.

6. He told me too much water can _____ plants to rot.

7. However, damp soil is just right for _____ .

8. A layer of dry _____ will keep roots warm in winter.

BONUS WORDS

auditorium
automation
authority
squall
auction
lawyer
scrawny
authentic

Write the Bonus word that is a synonym for each of these words. Use your **Thesaurus** for help.

1. attorney　　　**2.** genuine　　　**3.** skinny　　　**4.** storm

Complete the exercises using the Bonus words.

5. Write the words that begin with /ô/ in alphabetical order.

6. Write three sentences, using one of these word pairs in each sentence.

authentic	auction
lawyer	authority
scrawny	squall

15 The Sounds /ûr/

UNIT WORDS

1. emergency
2. hurl
3. journey
4. nursery
5. courtesy
6. courage
7. furnish
8. observe
9. deserve
10. flourish
11. journal
12. surface
13. terminal
14. sturdy
15. search
16. pearl
17. concern
18. perch
19. flurries
20. murmur

The Unit Words

Each Unit word has the vowel sound /û/ before the letter r—/ûr/.

The sounds /ûr/ are spelled four ways in the Unit words.

- with **ur** as in *sturdy*

- with **our** as in *journey*

- with **ear** as in *search*

- with **er** as in *terminal*

REMEMBER THIS

In the word *murmur* /mûr'mər/, the first *ur* stands for /ûr/ and the second *ur* stands for /ər/.

In the word *pearl*, the /ûr/ sound is spelled with *ear*. In ancient times, most of the valued natural pearls were in the shape of pears. You can still see the *pear* in the word *pearl*.

Harcourt Brace School Publishers

Spelling Practice

A. Follow the directions using the Unit words.

1. Write the four words that have just one syllable each. Underline the letters that spell /ûr/ in each word.

_____   _____

_____   _____

2. There are two pairs of words that start with the same letters. Write both pairs. Then underline the letters that spell /ûr/.

_____   _____

_____   _____

3. Add letters to *serve*. Write two different words.

_____   _____

4. Write the two-syllable word that has the same spelling for each syllable but two different vowel sounds. _____

5. Write the word that has the base word *nurse*. _____

6. Write the three words that start with consonant clusters.

_____   _____   _____

7. Write the four words that end with consonant digraphs.

_____   _____

_____   _____

B. Add the letters that spell /ûr/ to write Unit words.

8. j__nal _____   9. s__ch _____

10. em__gency _____   11. s__face _____

C. Finish the paragraph with Unit words.

　　Sue stared out the window of the airline __12__. What had started as snow __13__ was now a real blizzard. All around her she heard the impatient __14__ of passengers eager to start their __15__. Sue could __16__ the growing __17__ in people's faces. The snow would probably cause all planes to be grounded.

12. _____   13. _____   14. _____

15. _____   16. _____   17. _____

Spelling and Language · Nouns and Verbs

UNIT WORDS

emergency
hurl
journey
nursery
courtesy
courage
furnish
observe
deserve
flourish
journal
surface
terminal
sturdy
search
pearl
concern
perch
flurries
murmur

Some Unit words can be either nouns or verbs. A **noun** names a person, place, or thing. A **verb** shows action or being.

Noun   Our *search* is over.   **Verb**   We *searched* for her.

Complete each pair of sentences with Unit words. Write *n* or *v* after the word to show its part of speech. You may need to add *ed* or *ing* to verbs.

1. I heard a ____ from the room.   _____ __

2. You can ____ your answer to me.   _____ __

3. Do not ____ yourself with his problems.   _____ __

4. Eating on time is never a ____ for Val.   _____ __

Writing on Your Own

Pretend you are a diver searching for pearls. You keep a journal about your work. Choose five Unit words that can be used as both nouns and verbs. Then write two journal entries. In one, use some Unit words as nouns. In the other, use the same words as verbs.

 WRITER'S GUIDE   For a sample journal entry, see page 275.

Using the Dictionary to Spell and Write

Dictionary entries give information that helps you check if you used a word correctly in your writing. Read the definitions for *surface* given in the dictionary entry below. Two meanings are nouns, and one is a verb.

Parts of Speech

sur·face /sûr′fis/ *n., v.* **sur·faced, sur·fac·ing**
1 *n.* The face of any solid body, or the top of a liquid. **2** *v.* To rise to the surface, as a submarine. **3** *n.* The way a person or situation appears to be: He is always cheerful on the *surface*.

Write the number of the definition that fits each sentence. Then write *n* or *v* to show if *surface* is used as a noun or a verb.

1. To understand Pepe, look beneath the surface.   _____

2. The submarines surfaced near the island.   _____

3. Oil covered the surface of the water.   _____

Harcourt Brace School Publishers

Spelling on Your Own

UNIT WORDS

Copy and complete this chart, listing each Unit word under the correct spelling for /ûr/.

ur	ear	er	our

MASTERY WORDS

Write the Mastery words that have the sound /ûr/ spelled with these letters.

1. er _____ _____

2. ur _____ _____

3. ear _____ _____

Some words can be used either as nouns or as verbs. Complete each pair of sentences below using Mastery words. The word will be a noun in the first sentence and a verb in the second.

4. Denise is practicing her tennis _____ .

5. We can _____ juice at the club meeting.

6. The sudden _____ of rain came from that small cloud.

7. The balloon will _____ if it hits a sharp object.

8. She parked the car six inches from the _____ .

9. He could not _____ the frisky horse.

Mastery words: earn, burst, curb, serve, learn, person

BONUS WORDS

1. Write the Bonus words in four groups according to the letters that spell /ûr/ in each word.

2. Write the three words that have two syllables each.

3. Write the Bonus word that begins with a prefix meaning "not." Then use the word in a sentence.

4. Write the Bonus word that means the opposite of *rural.* Use each word in a sentence that shows its meaning.

5. Write the Bonus word that means the opposite of *forward.*

Bonus words: occurrence, courteous, reverse, rehearsal, submerge, imperfect, urban, thermostat

16 The Sounds /ôr/

UNIT WORDS

1. court
2. sports
3. cord
4. encore
5. mourn
6. coarse
7. ore
8. normal
9. chores
10. source
11. restore
12. ignore
13. portion
14. hoarse
15. scorch
16. storm
17. adore
18. fortress
19. afford
20. chord

CITY TENNIS COURTS

SPORTS PROGRAM
Every Saturday

The Unit Words

Each Unit word has the vowel sound /ô/ before the letter r—/ôr/. The sounds /ôr/ can be spelled in different ways. The words *court* and *sports* both have the sounds /ôr/, but the spellings for /ôr/ are different.

The sounds /ôr/ are spelled four ways in the Unit words.

- with **or** as in *sports*
- with **our** as in *court*
- with **ore** as in *ignore*
- with **oar** as in *coarse*

REMEMBER THIS

The words *cord* and *chord* are homophones. They sound exactly alike, but they have different spellings and different meanings. To help you remember the correct spelling of *chord*, think of this: A *chord* is a combination of musical tones often sung by a *chorus*. Both *chord* and *chorus* are words that come from Greek. In words from Greek, the sound /k/ is often spelled *ch*.

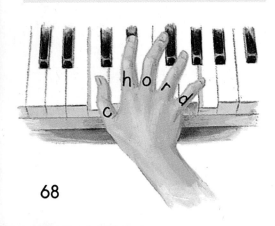

Harcourt Brace School Publishers

Spelling Practice

A. Follow the directions using the Unit words.

1. Write the word that has only the sounds /ôr/.

   _____

2. Write five more words that have /ôr/ spelled this way.

   _____   _____   _____

   _____   _____

3. Write the three words that have /ôr/ spelled *our.*

   _____   _____   _____

4. Write the three words that begin with consonant clusters.

   _____   _____   _____

5. Write the four two-syllable words that have /ôr/ spelled *or.*

   _____   _____

   _____   _____

6. Write the four words that begin with /k/.
   Underline the letters that spell /k/.

   _____   _____

   _____   _____

B. Add the letters that spell /ôr/ to write Unit words.

7. h __ se _____   8. n __ mal _____

9. ign __ _____   10. s __ ce _____

11. p __ tion _____   12. c __ t _____

C. Complete each sentence using a Unit word.

13. One of Karen's _____ is sweeping the sidewalk.

14. The ancient _____ is made of stone.

15. The orchestra held the final _____ for a full minute.

16. If the iron is too hot, you will _____ the shirt.

17. I am _____ from yelling during the game.

18. Your jacket has a very _____ texture.

Spelling and Language · Homophones

UNIT WORDS

court
sports
cord
encore
mourn
coarse
ore
normal
chores
source
restore
ignore
portion
hoarse
scorch
storm
adore
fortress
afford
chord

Homophones are words that sound alike but that have different spellings and different meanings. The words *chord* and *cord* are homophones.

Write the Unit word that is a homophone for each of these words.

1. course _____ 2. horse _____

3. morn _____ 4. oar _____

Write a third homophone for one of the homophone pairs above.

_____

Write a spelling word from Units 1–15 that is a homophone for each word below. Check your answers in the **Spelling Dictionary**.

5. sees _____ 6. isle _____

7. way _____ 8. foul _____

Writing on Your Own

Write a short research paper about your favorite game or sport. Tell about the history of the game or sport and describe how to play it. Find your information in several books in the library.

▸ **WRITER'S GUIDE**   For a sample research report, turn to page 279.

Using the Dictionary to Spell and Write

You can use the dictionary to check the correct spelling of a word. Suppose you want to spell the word *fortress*. Start by thinking of the possible initial spellings for /f/: *f* and *ph*. Since *f* is the more common spelling, look first under *f* in the dictionary. Then listen for the next sounds, /ôr/. You know that /ôr/ can be spelled *or, our, ore,* or *oar*. Check these spellings after *f* and you will soon find *fortress*.

Write the correct spelling for each pronunciation. Use the **Spelling Dictionary** to check your answers.

1. /sôrs/ _____ 2. /tôr′təs/ _____

3. /ôr·gan′ik/ _____ 4. /fôr′in/ _____

5. /kôrt/ _____ 6. /ôf′shôr′/ _____

▸ **SPELLING DICTIONARY** Remember to use your **Spelling Dictionary** when you write.

Harcourt Brace School Publishers

Spelling on Your Own

UNIT WORDS

Write all the Unit words in alphabetical order. Then make up some interesting or amusing titles for how-to books using the Unit words. Here is an example: **How to Avoid Going to Sports Court.**

MASTERY WORDS

order
form
shore
roar
force
orchard

Follow the directions using the Mastery words.

1. Write the word that has /ôr/ spelled *ore*. _____

2. Write the four words that have /ôr/ spelled *or*.

_____ _____

_____ _____

3. Write the word that has /ôr/ spelled as it is in *soar*. _____

Write the Mastery word that rhymes with each word.

4. border _____ 5. horse _____

6. more (2 words) _____ _____

Proofread this notice. Write the two misspelled words correctly.

> **TO ALL STUDENTS**
> Please leave oarder forums for new gym suits in Miss Alvarez's office.

7. _____ 8. _____

BONUS WORDS

cordial
pore
uniform
historian
pour
forgery
hoard
abnormal

Write the Bonus words that have these base words.

1. form   2. normal   3. forge   4. history

Complete the exercises using the Bonus words.

5. Write the words in four groups according to the letters that spell /ôr/.

6. Write the two words that are homophones. Then use each word in a sentence.

7. Write a short mystery story about a forgery. Use as many Bonus words as you can.

Harcourt Brace School Publishers

17 Science Words

UNIT WORDS

1. ecology
2. natural
3. wildlife
4. forestry
5. survival
6. resources
7. species
8. environment
9. conservation
10. energy
11. solar
12. nuclear
13. recycle
14. disposal
15. purify
16. antipollution
17. herbicide
18. pesticide
19. endangered
20. organic

The Unit Words

Ecology is the study of the relationship between living things and their environment. Your environment includes the places and things that affect your life—your home, school, friends, the weather where you live, and many other things. The words in this unit are often used in the study of the ecology of the earth.

Many of the Unit words also have other meanings not related to ecology. Are you part of a *nuclear* family? Are you full of *energy*? Do you use the library's *resources*?

Harcourt Brace School Publishers

Spelling Practice

A. Write the Unit word that is formed from each base word.

1. nature _____
2. survive _____
3. dispose _____
4. pollute _____
5. cycle _____
6. forest _____
7. organ _____
8. conserve _____

B. Follow the directions using the Unit words.

9. Write the two words with plural endings. Circle the word that can also be singular.

_____ _____

10. Write the word that is a compound word.

_____

11. The combining form *-cide* means "killing." An *insecticide* is something that kills insects. Write the two words that are made up of a base word + *i* + *cide*. Give the meaning for each word.

_____

_____

12. Write in alphabetical order the four words that begin with *e*.

_____ → _____

→ _____ → _____

13. Write the two words that end with *ar.*

_____ _____

C. Complete each sentence with a Unit word.

14. Kathleen spent last weekend at a wilderness _____ camp in the mountains.

15. Alone in the woods, she used all the _____ around her to survive.

16. She filtered lake water to _____ it.

17. She ate a _____ diet of foods that she found on the trail.

18. To save her _____ for hiking, she slept ten hours a day.

Spelling and Language · Analogies

An **analogy** shows the relationship between two pairs of words. For example: *Pollute* is to *pollution* as *nominate* is to *nomination.* In this analogy, *pollute* has the same relationship to *pollution* as *nominate* has to *nomination.* The suffix *-ion* is added to both verbs to form the nouns.

Complete these analogies with Unit words.

1. *Conserve* is to _____ as *reserve* is to *reservation.*

2. *Survive* is to _____ as *arrive* is to *arrival.*

3. *Angel* is to *angelic* as *organ* is to _____ .

4. *Comic* is to *comical* as *nature* is to _____ .

UNIT WORDS

- ecology
- natural
- wildlife
- forestry
- survival
- resources
- species
- environment
- conservation
- energy
- solar
- nuclear
- recycle
- disposal
- purify
- antipollution
- herbicide
- pesticide
- endangered
- organic

Writing on Your Own

For a school career booklet, write a paragraph comparing the work of a forest ranger and the work of an ecologist. You may want to use an encyclopedia or other reference books to learn about the two careers. Use as many Unit words as you can.

Proofreading

Ross made nine mistakes in the bibliography for his science report.

1. Circle each of the six misspelled words. Draw three lines under the letters that should be capitals.

Adams, Florence. Catch a Sunbeam: A Book of Soler Study and
    Experiment . New York: Harcourt Brace Jovanovich, Inc., 1978.
Evans, Robert G., and Humphrey, Clifford. what's Ecolagy? Northbrook,
    IL: Hubbard Scientific. 1972.
Leseem, Don. Life Is No Yuk for the Yak: A Book of Indangered animals .
    New York: Crane-Russak Co., 1977.
Pringle, Laurence. animals and Their Niches: How Specees Share
    Resorces . New York: William Morrow & Co., 1977.
Shuttlesworth, Dorothy E. Disappearing Enerjy: Can We End the Crisis?
    New York: Doubleday, 1974.

---

2. Write the six misspelled words correctly.

_____ _____ _____

_____ _____ _____

 WRITER'S GUIDE See the editing and proofreading marks on page 268.

Spelling on Your Own

PROTECT WILDLIFE

 UNIT WORDS

Make two columns. Label one *Do's* and the other *Don't's*. Write sentences using one or more Unit words that tell about the environment. Put each sentence in the proper column. Use all the Unit words. Use your science textbook for help. Here are two examples:

Do's	**Don't's**
Do protect wildlife.	*Don't hunt endangered animals.*

MASTERY WORDS

aid
replace
health
protection
farmer
hunter

Complete the exercises using the Mastery words.

1. Write the two words that have the sound /ā/. Underline the letters that spell /ā/.

_____   _____

2. Write the word that has the short vowel sound /e/ spelled *ea*.

_____

Add the suffix *-er* to each base word to spell a Mastery word.

3. farm _____   **4.** hunt _____

Complete the sentences using the Mastery words.

The chief enemy of many wild animals is the big-game __5__. The government of Tanzania came to the __6__ of its wildlife. The Serengeti National Park was created for the __7__ of wild animals.

5. _____   **6.** _____   **7.** _____

BONUS WORDS

organism
digestive
anatomy
lungs
circulation
algae
intestine
bacteria

Use the Bonus words to complete the exercises.

1. Write three words with the short vowel sound /a/.

2. Write two words that name parts of the body.

3. Write two words that name systems in the body.

Add a suffix to each base word to spell a Bonus word.

4. organ   **5.** digest   **6.** circulate

Review

Follow these steps when you are unsure of how to spell a word.

Say the word. Recall when you have heard the word used. Think about what it means.

Look at the word. Find any prefixes, suffixes, or other word parts you know. Think about other words that are related in meaning and spelling. Try to picture the word in your mind.

Spell the word to yourself. Think about the way each sound is spelled. Notice any unusual spelling.

Write the word while looking at it. Check the way you have formed your letters. If you have not written the word clearly or correctly, write it again.

Check your learning. Cover the word and write it. If you did not spell the word correctly, practice these steps until the word becomes your own.

UNIT 13 **Follow the directions using words from Unit 13.**

UNIT 13

occurred
picnicking
wondered
touching
preferred
appeared
referred
finished
offered
transferred

1. Write the word to which *k* was added before adding the ending. Then write the base word.

_____   _____

2. Write the four words that double the final *r* before adding an ending. Then write the base word for each word.

_____   _____

_____   _____

_____   _____

_____   _____

Finish each sentence.

3. My cousin _____ on a new TV series last night.

4. They _____ filming the series two weeks ago.

5. The first show was a _____ story about a lost dog.

WORDS IN TIME

The word *picnic* came into the English language during the 18th century. The original word *pique-nique* was probably a combination of two old French words: *piquer,* meaning "to pick," and *nique,* meaning "a small thing." The word *pique-nique* meant "a light social occasion that often took place in the countryside."

UNIT 14   Follow the directions using words from Unit 14.

6. Write the six words in which /ô/ is spelled *au*.

_____   _____   _____

_____   _____   _____

7. Write the word in which /ô/ is spelled *aw*. _____

8. Write the word that rhymes with *lost*. _____

Write a word that means the same as the underlined word or words in each sentence.

9. The wrestler was as <u>wide</u> as he was tall. _____

10. Elizabeth wanted to <u>put in</u> a new window. _____

UNIT 15   Follow the directions using words from Unit 15.

11. Write the three words that have /ûr/ spelled *our*.

_____   _____   _____

12. Write the word that rhymes with *perch*. _____

Write the letters in each word that spell /ûr/. Then write the words that have /ûr/ spelled with the same letters.

13. pearl _____ _____

14. hurl (two words) _____ _____ _____

15. serve (four words) _____

_____ _____

_____ _____

UNIT 14
awful
broad
frost
faucet
fault
laundry
pause
caution
daughter
install

UNIT 15
search
emergency
courage
journey
surface
courtesy
furnish
terminal
concern
deserve

WORDS IN TIME

In the Middle Ages, a journey was a day's trip over land. A day's trip, in that early time before cars and trains, usually covered about twenty miles. The word *journey* was originally French. *Jour* is the French word for *day.*

chord
sports
ignore
court
hoarse
coarse
source
chores
portion
storm

UNIT 16 Follow the directions using words from Unit 16.
Write the words that are homophones for the words below. Then circle the letters that spell /ôr/ in each word you wrote.

16. horse _____ **17.** cord _____

18. course _____

19. Write the words with two syllables.

_____ _____

Write the words to complete these sentences. Then circle the letters in the words you wrote that spell /ôr/.

20. Last Saturday we played tennis on the new _____.

21. Tennis is one of our favorite _____.

22. We played for an hour before the _____ hit.

23. After the game we went home to do

our _____.

24. Write the two words that have /ôr/ spelled *our*.

_____ _____

natural
energy
resources
wildlife
conservation
survival
environment
nuclear
recycle
disposal

UNIT 17 Follow the directions using words from Unit 17.
Write the word that is formed from each of these base words.

25. nature _____ **26.** source _____

27. conserve _____ **28.** dispose _____

29. survive _____ **30.** cycle _____

31. Write the word that is a compound word. _____

Complete these sentences.

32. Our community needs a new source of _____.

33. But the new plan presents some dangers to the

_____ in which we live.

34. A committee set up to protect the local _____
population had a meeting.

35. They agreed to the new plan, provided the engineers found a

safe _____ area for the _____
of wastes.

Spelling and Reading
A Biography

Read the following biography. Notice how the writer has ordered the events and details of the person's life.

Agatha Christie's first mystery novel appeared in 1920. The book proved she was a natural writer. Christie went on to become the world's most popular mystery writer. More than three hundred million copies of her books have been sold. Among English authors, only Shakespeare has been translated into more languages. Truly, Agatha Christie deserves the title she is often given: "the queen of mystery fiction."

Agatha Mary Clarissa Miller was born in 1890, in Devon, England. Her father died when she was very young, and she was raised by her mother. Mrs. Miller encouraged her daughter to write stories for her own amusement. Later Agatha studied singing in Paris. She wasn't a talented performer, however, and she wondered if she might not use her energy better in writing. Then she married an English Army officer named Archibald Christie. While he was away fighting in World War I, she wrote her first mystery novel. In this book she introduced one of the world's most famous fictional detectives—Hercule Poirot.*

Agatha Christie preferred writing to any other activity and wrote with scarcely a pause throughout her life. In fact, she finished at least one book a year until her death in 1976. Many of her ideas, she said, occurred to her while she was eating apples in the bathtub. Today her books are still a source of pleasure for many readers.

Write your answers to the questions.

1. According to the writer of this biography, what key event took place in Agatha Christie's life in 1920?
2. What did Christie's first book prove?
3. What clue does the writer give that Agatha Christie was probably a fast writer?
4. Will Agatha Christie's books continue to be popular in years to come? What makes you think as you do?

Underline the review words in your answers. Check to see that you spelled the words correctly.

*Hercule Poirot is pronounced /âr·kyool′ pwo·rō′/.

Spelling and Writing
A Biography

occurred
wondered
preferred
finished
broad
daughter
courage
source
chores
natural
energy
survival
environment

Think and Discuss

A biography is the life story of a person. In a biography, the writer describes the events in the person's life and provides the dates.

In a short biography, the opening sentence should introduce the subject. It should do this in a way that will catch the reader's interest. Look at the biography of Agatha Christie on page 79. What does the writer tell us in the first sentence? How does this sentence work to catch the reader's interest? Notice the other information in the first paragraph. Why do you think the writer presented this information here?

The body of a biography gives the key events in the subject's life. Usually these events are given in the order in which they happened. Look at the second paragraph of the biography on page 79. What do you learn about Agatha Christie's life? In what order are these events described?

In a good biography, a writer does more than list major events. The writer also presents details that reveal the character of the person. Reread the final paragraph of the biography on page 79. What amusing and revealing details does the writer give about Agatha Christie? What impression do these details give of her?

Apply

Write a short **biography** to read to your classmates. Think of someone your classmates will probably want to know about. Follow the writing guidelines on the next page.

Harcourt Brace School Publishers

Prewriting

Decide who you will write about. Choose a famous person whom you admire.

- Look up information about the person in the library. Take notes about the information.
- Make a three-column chart. Label the columns *Events, Dates,* and *Interesting Details.*
- Use your notes to fill in the chart.

Composing

Use your chart to write the first draft of your biography.

- Introduce your character and show what is special about him or her.
- Describe the important events of your character's life.
- Include details that reveal your character's personality.

 THESAURUS   For help finding exact words to describe your character, turn to page 205.

- Look back at your prewriting chart. Do you want to add any details to your draft?

Revising

Read your biography and show it to a classmate. Follow these guidelines to improve your work. Use the editing and proofreading marks on this page to indicate corrections.

 WRITER'S GUIDE   For help revising your work, see the checklist on page 267.

Editing

- Make sure you have described the major events of your character's life.
- Make sure your biography shows what is special about the person.

Proofreading

- Check your spelling, capitalization, and punctuation.

Copy your biography neatly onto clean paper.

Publishing

Read your biography to your classmates. Answer any questions they may have. Ask them what parts of the biography they found most interesting.

Editing and Proofreading Marks

≡	capitalize
⊙	make a period
∧	add something
∧,	add a comma
∀∀	add quotation marks
ℒ	take something away
◯	spell correctly
¶	indent the paragraph
/	make a lowercase letter
∼tr	transpose

19 "Silent" Letters

UNIT WORDS

1. limb
2. crumb
3. gnaw
4. plumber
5. tomb
6. foreign
7. column
8. campaign
9. hymn
10. salmon
11. design
12. palm
13. yolk
14. chalk
15. calm
16. assign
17. autumn
18. reign
19. resign
20. solemn

The Unit Words

All the Unit words contain letters that are not pronounced, or "silent" letters. At one time "silent" letters were sounded; people said /gnô'wə/, not /nô/, for *gnaw*.

Here are some common "silent" letters.

- the letter *b* after *m*, in words such as *limb*

- the letter *n* after *m*, in words such as *column*

- the letter *g* before *n*, in words such as *design*

- the letter *l* before *m* and *k*, in some words such as *salmon* and *yolk*

☐ In the words *palm* and *calm*, the letter *l* is usually not pronounced.

Harcourt Brace School Publishers

Spelling Practice

A. Follow the directions using the Unit words.

1. Write the two words in which the "silent" letter comes before the sound /k/.

_____   _____

2. Write the six words that end with the sound /n/ spelled *gn*.

_____   _____   _____

_____   _____   _____

3. Now write the one word that begins with the consonant sound /n/.

_____

4. Write the three words in which a "silent" letter comes before the sound /m/.

_____   _____   _____

5. Write the eight words in which the "silent" letter comes after the sound /m/. Underline the letter in each word that is not pronounced.

_____   _____   _____

_____   _____   _____

B. Write the Unit word that is the base word of each of these words. Then underline the letters that are "silent" in the Unit words.

6. /dez'ig·nā'shən/   /di·zīn'/

   designation _____

7. /ô·tum'nəl/   /ô'təm/

   autumnal _____

C. Complete the story with Unit words.

The __8__ day was cool and crisp. Peter sat alone on a park bench, eating his lunch. He watched a small gray squirrel scamper along the __9__ of a tree and down the trunk. Looking as __10__ as a judge, the squirrel began to __11__ at an acorn. Peter saved the last __12__ of his sandwich and tossed it to his lunch companion.

8. _____   9. _____

10. _____   11. _____

12. _____

Spelling and Language · Synonyms

UNIT WORDS

limb
crumb
gnaw
plumber
tomb
foreign
column
campaign
hymn
salmon
design
palm
yolk
chalk
calm
assign
autumn
reign
resign
solemn

Synonyms are words that mean the same thing or nearly the same thing. *Cheerful* and *pleasant* are synonyms.

Write the Unit word that is a synonym for the underlined word or group of words in each sentence below.

_____ 1. We sang a special <u>song</u> at the wedding.

_____ 2. In the <u>fall</u> the leaves look golden.

_____ 3. The water in the pond is very <u>still</u>.

_____ 4. A king and queen <u>rule</u> in Sweden.

_____ 5. Frank's dog began to <u>chew</u> on the bone.

Writing on Your Own

Imagine that you are writing a book of building projects for children eight to ten years old. Write directions for making and putting up a bird feeder. Use at least five of the Unit words.

 THESAURUS Do you need help finding vivid synonyms to replace some words in your directions? If so, turn to page 205.

Using the Dictionary to Spell and Write

The dictionary gives the pronunciation for each entry word. The pronunciation comes after the word. If a word has a "silent" letter, the pronunciation will not show that letter. Only sounds that are pronounced are shown. Look at the entry words below and their pronunciations. The *b* in *crumb* and *limb* is "silent." In the related words *crumble* and *limber*, the *b* is sounded.

crumb /krum/   **limb** /lim/
crum ble /krum'bəl/   **lim ber** /lim'bər/

Read the sentences below. One word in each sentence is written the way it is pronounced. Write the correct spelling for each word.

_____ 1. It is wise to /lim'bər/ up before exercising.

_____ 2. A /krum/ from the bread crust fell on the floor.

_____ 3. A /lim/ of the oak tree broke during the storm.

_____ 4. The old wall may start to /krum'bəl/.

 SPELLING DICTIONARY Remember to use your **Spelling Dictionary** when you write.

Harcourt Brace School Publishers

Spelling on Your Own

UNIT WORDS

The "silent" letters are missing in the Unit words below. Decide on the correct spelling. Then write each word on a separate sheet of paper.

1. pa __ m
2. autum __
3. lim __
4. rei __ n
5. colum __
6. __ naw
7. resi __ n
8. cha __ k
9. sa __ mon
10. solem __
11. hym __
12. crum __
13. tom __
14. forei __ n
15. plum __ er
16. desi __ n
17. ca __ m
18. assi __ n
19. yo __ k
20. campai __ n

MASTERY WORDS

whole
knob
hour
wrestle
doubtful
honest

Follow the directions using the Mastery words.

1. Write the two words that begin with vowel sounds. Underline the "silent" letter in each word.

   _____   _____

2. Write the word with a "silent" b. _____

3. Write the word that is a homophone for hole. _____

4. Write the word that has two "silent" letters. _____

Write the Mastery words that begin with these consonant sounds. Underline each "silent" letter.

5. /n/ _____
6. /h/ _____

7. /r/ _____

BONUS WORDS

pneumonia
heir
psychologist
knoll
khaki
psalm
condemn
rhinoceros

Write the Bonus word that is related to each word.

1. condemnation
2. psychology
3. pneumatic
4. heiress

Complete the exercises using the Bonus words.

5. Write the word that is a homophone for air.

6. Write the other seven words. Underline the "silent" consonant letter and the consonant letter next to it. Then write the symbol for the consonant sound you hear. Here is an example: <u>kh</u>aki /k/.

7. Write a paragraph using the words khaki, rhinoceros, and knoll.

20 Words with *er* and *est*

UNIT WORDS

1. coldest
2. thinner
3. saddest
4. livelier
5. loneliest
6. hottest
7. fatter
8. prettiest
9. steadier
10. earliest
11. cruelest
12. wealthier
13. creamier
14. paler
15. gravest
16. quieter
17. sharpest
18. simplest
19. sweetest
20. braver

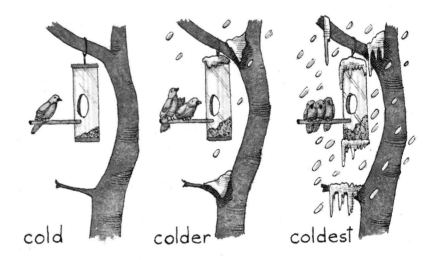

cold   colder   coldest

The Unit Words

An **adjective** describes a noun or limits its meaning in some way.

It was a *cold* day in November.

If you want to compare two things, you add the letters *er* to form a **comparative adjective.**

We have *colder* weather in December than in October.

To compare three or more things, you add the letters *est* to form a **superlative adjective.**

February is the *coldest* month of all.

Here are some rules for adding *er* and *est.*

1. When a word ends with one vowel letter and one consonant letter, double the consonant letter before you add *er* or *est.*

    thin   thinner   sad   saddest

2. When a word ends with *e,* drop the *e* before you add *er* or *est.*

    brave   braver   grave   gravest

3. When a word ends with *y,* change *y* to *i* before you add *er* or *est.*

    steady   steadier   pretty   prettiest

86 prettiest

Harcourt Brace School Publishers

Spelling Practice

A. Add *er* to each word to form a Unit word.

1. thin _____
2. quiet _____
3. steady _____
4. pale _____
5. lively _____
6. wealthy _____
7. fat _____
8. creamy _____
9. brave _____

B. Add *est* to each word to form a Unit word.

10. grave _____
11. hot _____
12. sweet _____
13. early _____
14. sad _____
15. lonely _____
16. pretty _____
17. cold _____
18. sharp _____
19. cruel _____
20. simple _____

C. Complete each sentence. Add *er* or *est* to the word in ( ).

21. The _____ desert in the world is the Sahara. (hot)
22. The _____ days of all were recorded in Antarctica. (cold)
23. Beige is a _____ color than orange. (pale)
24. This pudding is _____ than mine. (creamy)
25. Irene told the _____ story in the group. (sad)
26. This melon is the _____ of all. (sweet)
27. An elm has a _____ trunk than an oak. (thin)

D. Write a Unit word that is an antonym for each word.

28. dullest _____
29. poorer _____
30. latest _____
31. happiest _____

Write a synonym and an antonym for each word. Use Unit words.

32. iciest _____ _____
33. slimmer _____ _____

Spelling and Language •
Adding *er* and *est* to Adjectives

<table>
<tr><td>

UNIT WORDS

coldest
thinner
saddest
livelier
loneliest
hottest
fatter
prettiest
steadier
earliest
cruelest
wealthier
creamier
paler
gravest
quieter
sharpest
simplest
sweetest
braver

</td></tr>
</table>

Sometimes in your writing you may need to compare things or ideas. To most one-syllable words and a few two-syllable words, you add the endings *er* or *est*. To compare two things or ideas, add *er* to form the comparative of an adjective. Add *est* to form the superlative when you want to compare three or more things.

Complete each sentence by writing either the comparative or superlative form of the word in boldface.

wealthy **1.** This suburb is the _____ area in the state.

early **2.** I leave _____ this year than last.

simple **3.** Life was _____ one hundred years ago.

Writing on Your Own

Imagine that you have just gotten a kitten or puppy. You spent a day trying to decide between two animals. Write a letter to a friend about your experience. Use some of the Unit words to compare the two animals. Then explain how you decided which one to take home.

 WRITER'S GUIDE For a sample letter, turn to page 273.

Proofreading

When Evelyn wrote this letter to Frank, she misspelled six words.

1. Find Evelyn's six spelling mistakes. Then circle the misspelled words.

> Dear Frank,
>
> My vacation has been wonderful. It is quiter here than at home. The prettyest thing of all is the pond. It is a pailer blue than our lake at home. The earlyest we've gotten up has been eight o'clock. Then I have the simpilest breakfast meal. I'll feel the sadest of all when we leave here next week.

2. Write the six misspelled words correctly.

_____   _____   _____

_____   _____   _____

Spelling on Your Own

UNIT WORDS

Change the ending of each word to form a Unit word.

hottest
hotter
hot

cold
colder
coldest

1. hotter
2. colder
3. lonelier
4. prettier
5. palest
6. bravest
7. liveliest
8. graver
9. fattest
10. sweeter
11. steadiest
12. earlier
13. thinnest
14. sharper
15. crueler
16. sadder
17. creamiest
18. simpler
19. quietest
20. wealthiest

MASTERY WORDS

funniest
easier
nicer
happier
largest
safer

Add *er* to each word to spell a Mastery word.

1. nice _____

2. easy _____

3. happy _____

4. safe _____

Add *est* to each word to spell a Mastery word.

5. large _____

6. funny _____

Finish each sentence. Add *er* or *est* to the word in ( ).

7. Jem had the (large) _____ speaking part of all the actors.

8. She also had the (funny) _____ lines I have ever heard.

9. Jem makes acting look (easy) _____ than it really is.

BONUS WORDS

fiercest
friendlier
wittiest
severest
slimmer
greediest
bleakest
thriftiest

Write a synonym for each word. Use the base word of a Bonus word. Then write each word with *er* and *est*.

1. angry
2. skinny
3. kindly
4. chilly

Complete these exercises using the Bonus words.

5. Divide the words into four groups to show how the spelling changes when *er* or *est* is added. Write a heading for each group, such as "Drop final *e*."

6. Write a short children's story using the Bonus words. Use interesting comparisons to describe the main character. For example: The princess was *slimmer* than the *thinnest* reed.

The Sounds /ər/

UNIT WORDS

1. hangar
2. error
3. grammar
4. director
5. partner
6. consumer
7. burglar
8. cedar
9. monitor
10. rumor
11. whimper
12. vinegar
13. computer
14. vapor
15. author
16. prisoner
17. traitor
18. beggar
19. trader
20. lumber

YOU CAN KEEP AN AIRPLANE IN A
1. HANGER
2. HANGAR
3. HANGOR

YOU CAN KEEP AN AIRPLANE IN A HANGAR.

The Unit Words

Each Unit word has two or more syllables. Remember that a syllable has just one vowel sound. Say the word *hangar* to yourself. You can hear two syllables: /hang'ər/. The second syllable is the schwa sound /ə/ followed by the consonant *r*.

Schwa /ə/ is a weak vowel sound heard in unaccented syllables. Each Unit word ends with /ər/. The /ər/ is spelled three different ways in the Unit words.

* with **er** as in *trader*

* with **or** as in *vapor*

* with **ar** as in *cedar*

Harcourt Brace School Publishers

Spelling Practice

A. Follow the directions using the Unit words.

1. Write the word for this pronunciation: /trā'dər/. Then write the letters that spell /ər/.

_____   _____

2. Write six more words that have /ər/ spelled the same way.

_____ _____ _____

_____ _____ _____

3. Write the word for this pronunciation: /trā'tər/. Then write the letters that spell /ər/.

_____   _____

4. Write six more words that have /ər/ spelled the same way.

_____ _____ _____

_____ _____ _____

5. Write the word for this pronunciation: /beg'ər/. Then write the letters that spell /ər/.

_____   _____

6. Write five more words that have /ər/ spelled the same way.

_____ _____ _____

_____ _____

7. Write the six words that are formed by adding letters for /ər/ to a verb.

_____ _____ _____

_____ _____ _____

B. Complete this story using Unit words.

Mr. Schwarz works in an airplane __**8**__ . His job is to find and correct any __**9**__ in the way the plane functions. He uses a __**10**__ to check many of the instruments on the plane. The computer can __**11**__ the engine and detect problems.

8. _____   9. _____

10. _____   11. _____

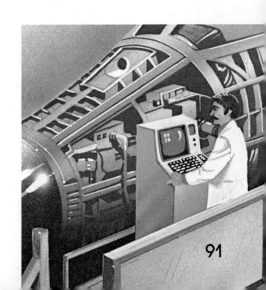

Spelling and Language · Possessive Nouns

UNIT WORDS

hangar
error
grammar
director
partner
consumer
burglar
cedar
monitor
rumor
whimper
vinegar
computer
vapor
author
prisoner
traitor
beggar
trader
lumber

A **possessive noun** shows ownership. To form the possessive of a singular noun, add an apostrophe and *s: one author's book.* Add just an apostrophe to a plural noun that ends with *s: many authors' books.*

Fill in each blank with the singular possessive form of the word in (   ).

1. The _____ choice for the play was a comedy.
      (director)

2. The _____ clothes were ragged but clean. (beggar)

Fill in each blank with the plural possessive form of the word in (   ).

3. Both _____ houses were near the airport. (partner)

4. There is a display of the _____ artwork. (prisoner)

Writing on Your Own

Pretend your grandparents gave you a computer for your birthday. Write them a thank-you note. Tell them how you use your computer and why it helps with your schoolwork. Use as many Unit words and possessive nouns as you can.

WRITER'S GUIDE For a sample letter, turn to page 273.

Using the Dictionary to Spell and Write

When a word does not fit at the end of a line, you can put part of the word on the next line. Use a hyphen to divide the word between syllables. Dictionary entry words show syllable divisions: **di·rec·tor.**

> All the actors relied on the direc-
> tor to help them learn their parts.

Some of the words in this paragraph don't quite fit on the line. Decide where to divide the underlined words. Then write the words in syllables below. Insert a hyphen to show where the words break.

> When Mr. Forbes gives us a grammar quiz, no one whimpers.
> The whole class likes Mr. Forbes's idea that we all have partners.
> We quiz our partners before the daily test. We also monitor
> our progress on a class chart. Now we know our grammar!

_____ _____

_____ _____

Harcourt Brace School Publishers

Spelling on Your Own

UNIT WORDS

Write each Unit word with the correct spelling for /ər/.

1. auth/ər/	**2.** burgl/ər/	**3.** ced/ər/	**4.** comput/ər/
5. begg/ər/	**6.** direct/ər/	**7.** err/ər/	**8.** consum/ər/
9. rum/ər/	**10.** monit/ər/	**11.** vineg/ər/	**12.** prison/ər/
13. trad/ər/	**14.** trait/ər/	**15.** whimp/ər/	**16.** gramm/ər/
17. hang/ər/	**18.** vap/ər/	**19.** lumb/ər/	**20.** partn/ər/

/ər/ = ar
er
or

MASTERY WORDS

1. Write the three Mastery words in which the sounds /ər/ are spelled *er.*

_____ _____ _____

2. Write the two words in which the sounds /ər/ are spelled *or.*

_____ _____

3. Write the word in which the sounds /ər/ are spelled *ar.*

_____

4. Write the word that means "one who visits." _____

5. Write the word that has a double consonant. _____

6. Proofread this notice. Circle the three misspelled words. Write them correctly below.

> MEMBIRS SIGN IN AT SENTER DESK
>
> NO VISITERS

fever
member
visitor
odor
center
collar

_____ _____ _____

BONUS WORDS

1. Make a chart of the Bonus words. List them according to the three spellings for /ər/.

2. The words *sculptor* and *inspector* refer to people who do something. Use each of these words in a sentence. The sentences you write should show the meanings of the words.

sculptor
regular
similar
cylinder
officer
disaster
inspector
suspenders

22 Prefixes

UNIT WORDS

1. invisible
2. repeat
3. insecure
4. companion
5. predict
6. reunite
7. remind
8. impatient
9. previous
10. consult
11. precaution
12. revenge
13. combine
14. prevent
15. impolite
16. impossible
17. reflect
18. confide
19. conference
20. preparation

The Unit Words

Sometimes you can change the meaning of a word by adding a prefix. A **prefix** is a word part that can be added to the beginning of a word to change the word's meaning. All of the Unit words have prefixes. Some of the prefixes are added to base words that you will recognize. Other prefixes are added to word parts that come from Latin.

The word *visible* means "capable of being seen," but *invisible* means "*not* capable of being seen." Adding the prefix *in-* gives the word the opposite meaning.

Here is a list of prefixes and the meanings they add to words.

PREFIX	MEANING	EXAMPLE
re-	"back" or "again"	*reunite*
con- or **com-**	"with"	*consult*
pre-	"before"	*precaution*
in- or **im-**	"not"	*impolite*

REMEMBER THIS

The sounds /m/, /p/, and /b/ are all said with the lips closed. That's why the prefixes *com-* and *im-* come before *m*, *b*, and *p*. It is easier to say the sounds together.

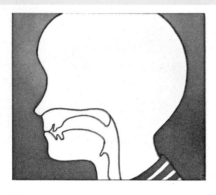

94

Spelling Practice

A. Follow the directions using the Unit words.

1. Write the five words that begin with the prefix that means "with." Underline the prefix in each word.

_____   _____   _____

_____   _____

2. Write the five words that begin with *pre-* in alphabetical order.

_____ → _____ → _____

→ _____ → _____

B. Add a prefix that means "not" to each of the words below to spell a Unit word.

3. secure _____   4. polite _____

5. visible _____   6. patient _____

7. possible _____

C. Write the Unit word for each definition.

8. to say or do again _____

9. to show back _____

10. getting back at someone _____

11. to bring back together again _____

12. to bring to mind again _____

D. Change the prefix of each word below to write a Unit word.

13. invent _____   14. result _____

15. contradict _____   16. obvious _____

17. reference _____   18. deflect _____

E. Write a Unit word from the same word family as each word below.

19. possibility _____   20. vision _____

21. confidence _____   22. unity _____

23. company _____   24. dictate _____

Spelling and Language · Noun-Forming Suffixes

UNIT WORDS

invisible
repeat
insecure
companion
predict
reunite
remind
impatient
previous
consult
precaution
revenge
combine
prevent
impolite
impossible
reflect
confide
conference
preparation

A **suffix** is a word part added to the end of a word. The suffixes *-ion*, *-tion*, and *-ation* can be added to verbs to form nouns. The noun *preparation* is formed by adding *-ation* to the verb *prepare*.

Add *-ion*, *-tion*, or *-ation* to the words in boldface. Write the nouns that complete each sentence. Remember to drop the final *e* when necessary.

reflect   **1.** Melissa saw her _____ in the mirror.

consult   **2.** Aaron visited the dentist for a _____ .

predict   **3.** The weather _____ is for colder weather.

prepare   **4.** The _____ for the play took weeks.

Writing on Your Own

Imagine this scene. A scientist has just invented a pill that makes people invisible. A newspaper reporter is interviewing the scientist about the amazing pill. Write a conversation in which the reporter asks the scientist about the invention. Use as many Unit words as you can. Add the suffixes *-ion*, *-tion*, and *-ation* to some verbs to form nouns. Read your conversation to the class.

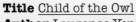 **WRITER'S GUIDE** For a sample conversation, turn to page 276.

Proofreading

This book report has six spelling errors.

1.   Read the book report and circle the six misspelled words.

> **Title** Child of the Owl
> **Author** Laurence Yep
> **Summary** This book tells the story of Casey, who is sent to live with her grandmother Paw-Paw in San Francisco's Chinatown. Casey is impatiant and finds it almost impossable to live there because she has had little preperation for the Chinese school. She doesn't like the noise and the crowds of city life. Casey and Paw-Paw learn to confied in each other and become close companians. Paw-Paw encourages Casey to learn to appreciate Chinatown. She says the people and customs refleck their Chinese culture and that it is their home.
> **Opinion** I liked this book because I enjoyed learning about a new place.

2.   Write the six misspelled words correctly.

_____   _____   _____

_____   _____   _____

Harcourt Brace School Publishers

Spelling on Your Own   in-/im- re- pre- con-/com-

UNIT WORDS

Copy and complete this chart using the Unit words. Write each word under the meaning of the prefix in the word.

"back" or "again"	"with"	"before"	"not"

Write a short paragraph using all the words in any one column.

MASTERY WORDS

Add one of these prefixes to each word. Write the Mastery words.

re-   in-   pre-

1. play _____   **2.** paid _____

3. complete _____   **4.** load _____

Write the Mastery word that has the same prefix as each of these words.

5. conflict _____   **6.** compact _____

7. prepare _____   **8.** inaccurate _____

Write the Mastery word that means the same thing as the underlined words in each sentence.

9. Lori had to <u>load</u> the video recorder <u>again</u>. _____

10. She wanted to <u>play</u> her favorite movie <u>again</u>. _____

reload
incomplete
replay
comfort
prepaid
contract

BONUS WORDS

Complete the exercises using the Bonus words.

1. Make a chart grouping the words by their prefixes.

2. Write one sentence for each of the two words that have the prefix meaning "not."

3. Two words begin with a prefix that means "again." Use both words in one sentence.

Write the Bonus word that fits each blank.
    "I have a __4__ to make," said Tim.
    "I entered the __5__ under false __6__."

revise
incapable
prehistoric
confession
reevaluate
competition
impersonal
pretense

Harcourt Brace School Publishers

23 Suffixes

UNIT WORDS

1. sheepish
2. mechanical
3. additional
4. beautifully
5. carefully
6. childish
7. easily
8. faithfully
9. foolish
10. medical
11. musical
12. national
13. nearly
14. peacefully
15. physical
16. practically
17. selfish
18. sensational
19. snobbish
20. usually

"It's true," Tom said sheepishly. "I ate all the lamb stew."

The Unit Words

Have you ever tried Tom Swifties? Tom Swifties are puns that use -ly adverbs, such as *sheepishly.* Here is another: "I think the gear is broken," Tom said mechanically.

The words in this unit are good for Tom Swifties because they can all be -ly adverbs.

Each Unit word has a suffix. **Suffixes** are word parts that are added to the end of a word. A suffix often changes the part of speech of the word. When you add -ish to the noun *child,* you form the adjective *childish.* When you add -ly to *childish,* you form the adverb *childishly.*

● The suffixes -ish and -al change nouns into adjectives.

sheep, *n.,* + -ish = sheepish, *adj.*

music, *n.,* + -al = musical, *adj.*

● The suffix -ly usually changes adjectives into adverbs.

beautiful, *adj.,* + -ly = beautifully, *adv.*

When you add suffixes, follow the usual rules for adding endings. Change *y* to *i* before adding -ly: *easy + -ly = easily.* Double the final consonant after short vowel sounds: *snob + -ish = snobbish.*

Harcourt Brace School Publishers

Spelling Practice

A. Add a suffix to each of these nouns to form adjectives. Write Unit words.

1. child _____   2. self _____

3. sheep _____   4. fool _____

5. snob _____

B. Add a suffix to make each word below an adverb.

6. practical _____   7. usual _____

8. easy _____   9. near _____

C. Follow the directions using Unit words.

10. Write the four words that end with the letters *ical.*

_____   _____

_____   _____

11. Write three more words that end with *-al.*

_____   _____   _____

D. Add the suffix *-ful* to each word to form an adjective. Then add *-ly* to form an adverb.

12. faith _____   _____

13. care _____   _____

14. peace _____   _____

15. beauty _____   _____

E. Complete the paragraph with Unit words.

Tom pushed the last __16__ control on the panel and waited while the computers took over. He watched __17__ as the numbers flashed across the control panel. One __18__ chore and he could settle down for the trip. Tom touched his hand to the health sensor for his __19__ checkup. A green "OK" on the panel told him all was well. He slipped __20__ out of his insulated suit and sat back __21__ for the trip.

16. _____   17. _____   18. _____

19. _____   20. _____   21. _____

Harcourt Brace School Publishers

Spelling and Language · Adverb Suffixes

UNIT WORDS

sheepish
mechanical
additional
beautifully
carefully
childish
easily
faithfully
foolish
medical
musical
national
nearly
peacefully
physical
practically
selfish
sensational
snobbish
usually

An **adverb** is a word that modifies a verb, an adjective, or another adverb. Many adverbs end with the suffix *-ly.*

Add *-ly* to each Unit word in boldface to make an adverb. Write the adverbs to complete the sentences.

foolish   1. Tracy _____ walked home in the downpour.

physical   2. Everyone in my family is _____ fit.

selfish   3. We _____ ate all the popcorn ourselves.

Writing on Your Own

Pretend you are a reporter for your school newspaper. You are reviewing a play written and performed by the fifth grade. Tell why you did or did not like the play. Use as many Unit words and adverbs as you can.

 WRITER'S GUIDE   For a sample opinion paragraph, turn to page 271.

Using the Dictionary to Spell and Write

Many dictionaries list prefixes and suffixes as entry words. The entries tell you the different meanings a prefix or suffix can add to a word. Knowing these meanings can help you check if you used a word correctly in your writing. Read the entries for *im-, in-,* and *-ish.*

> **im-**   *prefix* Form of *in-* (meaning "not") used before words beginning with *b, m,* and *p: improbable.*
>
> **in-**   *prefix* Not: *inadequate.*
>
> **-ish**   *suffix* **1** Like: *childish,* like a child. **2** Fond of or inclined to: *bookish,* fond of books.

Add *in-* or *im-* to each word. Then write the word.

1. practical _____   2. correct _____

3. personal _____   4. secure _____

Add the suffix *-ish* to each word in ( ). Then write the number of the meaning for *-ish* that fits the word you wrote.

5. Judd made a (fool) _____ mistake.

6. Paige is (self) _____ with her money.

Spelling On Your Own

UNIT WORDS

Make up a word search puzzle using all of the Unit words. The words can be written across, down, or diagonally. Fill in the empty spaces with other letters. When you finish your puzzle, let a classmate solve it.

```
S T V H Q U A Z
E A S I L Y W M
L P M N O A N E
F O O L I S H O
I N T S C A R F
S H E E P I S H
H O H M B A S T
```

MASTERY WORDS

several
likely
windy
lately
foggy
rainy

Do the "word math" to spell Mastery words.

1. fog + y = _____

2. rain + y = _____

3. wind + y = _____

Add the suffix -ly to each word to spell a Mastery word.

4. late _____   **5.** like _____

Follow the directions using the Mastery words.

6. Write the word that ends with -al. _____

7. Write the three words that have to do with weather.

_____   _____   _____

Complete this paragraph with Mastery words.

Wendy picked up __8__ stones and skipped one over the pond. A __9__ gust carried it over the waves. Sadly she thought, I'm __10__ to catch cold in this __11__ drizzle.

8. _____   **9.** _____

10. _____   **11.** _____

BONUS WORDS

feverish
immediately
vertical
traditional
stylish
occasionally
horizontal
gradually

1. Put the Bonus words into three groups of word endings: -al, -ly, and -ish. You may need to write some Bonus words twice.

2. Write the three words that have the suffix -ly. Then add the suffix -ly to the rest of the words.

3. Use each of the new words you formed in **2** in a sentence.

4. Draw a figure that has lines going up and down and lines going across. Then label the two kinds of lines correctly with Bonus words.

24 Review

Follow these steps when you are unsure of how to spell a word.

- **Say** the word. Recall when you have heard the word used. Think about what it means.
- **Look** at the word. Find any prefixes, suffixes, or other word parts you know. Think about other words that are related in meaning and spelling. Try to picture the word in your mind.
- **Spell** the word to yourself. Think about the way each sound is spelled. Notice any unusual spelling.
- **Write** the word while looking at it. Check the way you have formed your letters. If you have not written the word clearly or correctly, write it again.
- **Check** your learning. Cover the word and write it. If you did not spell the word correctly, practice these steps until the word becomes your own.

UNIT 19

chalk
calm
autumn
crumb
design
plumber
foreign
column
yolk
assign

UNIT 19 Follow the directions using words from Unit 19.

Write the word that rhymes with each of these words. Underline the silent letter in each word you wrote.

1. talk _____
2. refine _____
3. sum _____
4. palm _____
5. joke _____
6. line _____
7. summer _____

Complete the following sentences.

8. The words were written in one long _____ .

9. It was a warm day in early _____ .

10. Petri was born in a _____ country.

UNIT 20

quieter
simplest
earliest
hottest
livelier
coldest
thinner
prettiest
wealthier
braver

UNIT 20 Follow the directions using words from Unit 20.

Write the comparative or superlative adjective to complete each group of words.

11. simple, simpler, _____
12. early, earlier, _____
13. hot, hotter, _____
14. quiet, _____, quietest

Harcourt Brace School Publishers

Add *er* or *est* to the words in ( ) to complete these sentences.

15. My cat had kittens on the (cold) _____ night of the year.

16. It is the (pretty) _____ litter I have ever seen.

17. The gray female is (thin) _____ than the spotted one.

18. She is also (live) _____ .

19. The black male is (brave) _____ than most kittens.

20. Mom prefers the (quiet) _____ of the two males.

UNIT 21   Follow the directions using words from Unit 21.

21. Write four words that name people's job titles or occupations.

_____   _____

_____   _____

Write the words in which /ər/ is spelled with the letters shown

22. *ar* (3 words) _____   _____   _____

23. *or* (3 words) _____   _____   _____

24. *er* (4 words) _____   _____

_____   _____

UNIT 22   Add a prefix to each word to spell a word from Unit 22.

25. patient _____   26. possible _____

27. mind _____

Add a word part to each prefix below to spell a word or words from Unit 22.

28. re- (2 words) _____   _____

29. com- _____

30. pre- (3 words) _____   _____

_____

Complete the sentences below with Unit 22 words.

31. Most people _____ a doctor when they feel ill.

32. Some see a doctor to _____ personal problems.

UNIT 21
partner
trader
director
hangar
author
error
grammar
consumer
vinegar
computer

UNIT 22
repeat
combine
prevent
impossible
impatient
remind
previous
consult
confide
preparation

Follow the directions using words from Unit 23.

foolish
national
physical
easily
usually
selfish
mechanical
additional
medical
practically

Add a suffix to each word to change it to an adverb.

33. easy _____   34. usual _____

35. practical _____

Add a suffix to each word to change it to an adjective.

36. nation _____   37. addition _____

38. mechanic _____   39. self _____

40. fool _____   41. medic _____

Complete each sentence.

42. Helen has _____ therapy on her leg every week.

43. The therapist _____ comes to Helen's home to help her exercise.

44. Twice a month Helen meets her therapist

at the _____ clinic.

45. At the clinic she exercises with

_____ weight-lifting equipment.

46. Helen says this _____ exercise is making her leg much stronger.

47. In fact, she's _____ ready to walk without her leg brace.

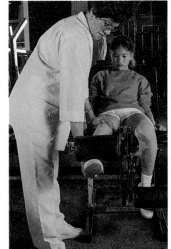

WORDS IN TIME

The word *foolish* has an interesting history. It comes from the Latin word *follis,* which meant "bellows," a device used to create a current of air. Informally, the word meant "windbag," or "an empty-headed person." The English adopted the Latin word and changed it to *fool.* A person who acted without sense was described as *foolis* or *foolish.* From this came other words such as *foolhasty,* to act with reckless speed; *foollarge,* to spend too much money; and *foolhardy,* which is still used today and means to act boldly but without thought.

Harcourt Brace School Publishers

Spelling and Reading
A News Story

Read the following news story from a school newspaper. Notice details in the story that answer the questions *who*, *what*, *where*, *when*, *why* and *how*.

CITY BANS SURFING

On Thursday, July 14, the City Council of Costa Corona banned wind surfing off city beaches. The ban was a move to prevent accidents, the council said.

Officer J.J. Higgens of the beach patrol defended the new law. "Wind surfing is dangerous," he said. "Someone could easily get hurt out there. Who's going to pay for the medical treatment?"

His partner Officer Thomas Matthews added that the ban would be eased in slowly. "We'll just remind people about the law the first few months," said Matthews. "By autumn, though, if people are still surfing out there, we'll start fining them — $250 for each offense."

The surfing ban promises to be one of the hottest issues of the summer in this small beach town. Wind-surfer Jessie Collins said, "How can they kick us out of the prettiest beach in this area? All this talk about accidents is foolish. There's more physical danger on the highway than out in the surf. It's so calm out there it's practically impossible to get hurt. I don't know who the author of this law was, but passing it was a major error. I hope they change that law soon, because I'm impatient to get back in the water."

Write the answers to the questions.

1. According to the news story, why did the city ban wind surfing?
2. What did Officer Higgens say in defense of the new law?
3. What does the writer say to show that people will probably be protesting the ban?
4. Is it practically impossible to get hurt while wind surfing, as Jessie Collins claims? Why do you think as you do?

Underline the review words in your answers. Check to see that you spelled the words correctly.

Harcourt Brace School Publishers

Spelling and Writing
A News Story

**Words to Help
You Write**

autumn
crumb
design
simplest
livelier
prettiest
partner
director
repeat
combine
previous
preparation
national
usually
practically

Think and Discuss

A news story gives information about an interesting or unusual event that has just happened or is still happening. News stories follow certain clear rules. Every news story begins with a title called a **headline**. The headline attracts the reader's attention by summing up the story in the fewest possible words. What is the headline of the news story on page 105?

After the headline comes the **lead paragraph.** In this paragraph the reporter covers the most important facts in the story. These facts tell *whom* the story is about, *what* happened, *when* it happened, *where* it happened, *why* it happened, and *how* it happened. Look back at the news story on page 105. Which of the six questions does the lead paragraph discuss and what are the answers?

All the paragraphs after the lead are called the **body** of the story. Additional details about the topic are presented here. In the body of the news story on page 105, the reporter tells what several people have to say about the ban on wind surfing. What information do you get from Officer Higgens's statement? What information do you get from Officer Matthews's statement? Why do you think the writer included Jessie Collins's comments?

Apply

Write a **news story** for a class newspaper about some recent event. Choose an interesting or unusual event that you can get information about. This can be an event in your home, in your neighborhood, or at your school. Follow the writing guidelines on the next page.

Prewriting

- Interview a person in your school, family, or neighborhood to whom something exciting and important has just happened.
- During the interview, be sure to write down the important facts: *who, what, when, where, why,* and *how.*
- Check your notes as you go along. Make sure you have spelled names correctly and have all the important facts accurately written down.

 THESAURUS   For help finding words to describe the event, turn to page 205.

Composing

Use your notes to write the first draft of your news story.

- Write a lead paragraph giving facts that answer the questions *who, what, where, when, why,* and *how.*
- Include in the body of your story details that support your topic. Also include direct quotations from the person you interviewed.
- Write a headline that sums up your main topic.

Revising

Read your news story and show it to a classmate. Follow these guidelines to improve your work. Use the editing and proofreading marks on this page to indicate corrections.

Editing

- Make sure you have answered the questions *who, what, where, when, why,* and *how* in your lead paragraph.
- Make sure all the details in your story relate to the topic.
- Check to make sure your quotations are accurate.
- Make sure your headline sums up your story correctly.

Proofreading

- Check your spelling, capitalization, and punctuation.

 WRITER'S GUIDE   For help punctuating quotations correctly, see page 283.

Copy your news story onto clean paper. Write carefully and neatly.

Publishing

Use your news story and those of your classmates to make up a class newspaper. Paste your articles on large sheets of paper. Then write the name of your newspaper at the top. Share your newspaper with your principal or another class.

Editing and Proofreading Marks	
≡	capitalize
⊙	make a period
∧	add something
⋀̦	add a comma
ᵛᵛ ᵛᵛ	add quotation marks
⟞	take something away
◯	spell correctly
⊓	indent the paragraph
/	make a lowercase letter
∼ tr	transpose

25 Noun Suffixes

UNIT WORDS

1. solution
2. navigation
3. location
4. instrument
5. activity
6. curiosity
7. gravity
8. astonishment
9. operation
10. celebration
11. electricity
12. development
13. appointment
14. charity
15. security
16. arrangement
17. decoration
18. equality
19. graduation
20. ability

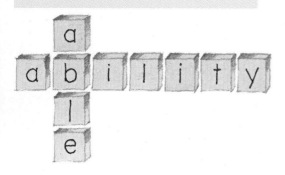

The Unit Words

Some suffixes can be added to words to make nouns. Each word in this unit has the noun suffix *-ment, -ion,* or *-ity.*

You add *-ment* and *-ion* to verbs to make nouns.

develop + -ment = development

navigate + -ion = navigation

You add *-ity* to some adjectives to make nouns.

equal + -ity = equality

Always drop *e* before you add a suffix that begins with a vowel: locate + -ion = location.

In some of the Unit words, other spelling changes are made when suffixes are added to base words.

curi<u>ous</u> + -ity = curi<u>os</u>ity
sol<u>ve</u> + -ion = sol<u>u</u>tion

Charity and *instrument* have no English base words. *Charity* comes from the Latin adjective *carus,* "dear, or valued." *Instrument* comes from the Latin verb *instruere,* "to equip, or to train."

Spelling Practice

A. Add a suffix to each verb to make a noun that is a Unit word.

1. locate _____

2. decorate _____

3. operate _____

4. graduate _____

5. navigate _____

6. celebrate _____

7. solve _____

B. Add a suffix to each adjective to make a noun that is a Unit word.

8. active _____

9. equal _____

10. electric _____

11. secure _____

12. curious _____

13. able _____

14. grave _____

C. Write the Unit word that begins with each of these word parts.

15. char _____

16. instru _____

D. Add a suffix to each verb to make a noun that is a Unit word.

17. arrange _____

18. develop _____

19. appoint _____

20. astonish _____

E. Drop the prefix in each word. Then add a suffix to spell a Unit word.

21. inactive _____

22. redevelop _____

23. insecure _____

24. redecorate _____

25. relocate _____

26. prearrange _____

F. Complete the paragraph with Unit words.

Last June, Sara attended an Apache Indian __27__ at a beautiful __28__ in New Mexico. In one of the shops, Sara met an artist who had a great __29__ for carving wood. Sara expressed her __30__ about a carved flute. To her great __31__, the artist replied by playing a haunting melody on the __32__. Sara will always remember that as her favorite moment during her visit to New Mexico.

27. _____

28. _____

29. _____

30. _____

31. _____

32. _____

Spelling and Language · Using Noun Suffixes

UNIT WORDS

solution
navigation
location
instrument
activity
curiosity
gravity
astonishment
operation
celebration
electricity
development
appointment
charity
security
arrangement
decoration
equality
graduation
ability

These two examples give the same information, but one uses a verb and the other uses a noun.

> We celebrated Kelly's birthday.
> We had a birthday celebration for Kelly.

Rewrite each of these sentences using a noun instead of the underlined verb. You may add details if necessary.

1. We decorated the room with balloons for the party.

_____

2. Kim graduated from college in June.

_____

3. The last act astonished us.

_____

Writing on Your Own

Pretend your class is planning a graduation party. You are on the Entertainment Committee. Write a paragraph explaining what you will do. Use these Unit words: *solution, location, operation, celebration, arrangement, decoration, graduation, ability.*

Proofreading

Milt's book report has six spelling mistakes. He also left out two periods.

1. Circle the spelling mistakes. Insert the periods and circle them.

> Last summer I read <u>Science Experiments You Can Eat</u>, by Vicki Cobb. The author of this book says that the kitchen is a good loction for a science laboratory. There is water available to prepare a solushun for an experiment, and you can use the regular kitchen measuring insturments As you do each activty in the book, you learn about science and you make something to eat. Did you know that mayonnaise is an emulsion? My curiosity was aroused by that, so I tried the opperation for making mayonnaise. I found out what an emulsion is and how to make one Then my family ate the results for dinner!

2. Write the six misspelled words correctly.

_____   _____   _____

_____   _____   _____

 WRITER'S GUIDE See the editing and proofreading marks on page 268.

Spelling on Your Own

UNIT WORDS

All the Unit words are nouns. Write an adjective that describes each one. Then use five of the pairs of adjectives and nouns in sentences.

The doctor performed a <u>difficult</u> <u>operation</u> this morning.

MASTERY WORDS

equipment
improvement
digestion
addition
fairness
likeness

Write the Mastery word for each of these base words. Underline the suffix that you add.

1. digest _____   **2.** add _____

3. like _____   **4.** improve _____

5. fair _____   **6.** equip _____

Synonyms are words that have the same or almost the same meaning. Write a Mastery word that is a synonym for each word below.

7. similarity _____   **8.** supplies _____

9. justice _____

Finish each of these sentences with a Mastery word.

10. Fruit is good for your _____.

11. For some people _____ is easier than subtraction.

12. The team has new baseball _____.

BONUS WORDS

popularity
relation
enlargement
humanity
attraction
adjustment
expedition
sincerity

1. Write three bonus words that are nouns formed by adding a suffix to an adjective.

2. Write the Bonus words that fit each of these patterns:

verb + *-ion* = noun
verb + *-ment* = noun

3. Write an opening paragraph for a newspaper story about any of these topics: a space expedition, a senator's popularity, a tax adjustment. Use as many Bonus and Unit words as you can in your paragraph.

26 Word Families

UNIT WORDS

1. performance
2. information
3. reform
4. promote
5. commotion
6. conductor
7. prospect
8. definition
9. produce
10. maintain
11. reduce
12. expect
13. confined
14. retain
15. respectful
16. emotional
17. remote
18. inspect
19. refined
20. contain

ex + spect = **expect**

/iks/ + /spekt/ = /ik·spekt'/

The Unit Words

Look at the words *performance, information,* and *reform.* All three words share the word part *form.* Different prefixes and suffixes have been added to *form.*

per- + form + -ance = performance
in- + form + -ation = information
re- + form = reform

Words with a common word part belong to the same **word family.** Other Unit words belong to word families that share these word parts.

WORD PARTS	EXAMPLES
duce	re*duce,* pro*duce*
fine	re*fined,* con*fined*
mote	re*mote,* e*motional*
spect	in*spect,* pro*spect*
tain	con*tain,* main*tain*

In some of the Unit words, the spelling of the word part changes when it is combined with prefixes, suffixes, and endings. The *s* in *spect* is dropped when the prefix *ex-* is added: *expect.* In *conductor,* the word part *duce* changes to *duct.*

Spelling Practice

A. Follow the directions using the Unit words.

1. Write the three words that belong to the same word family as the word *production*.

_____   _____   _____

2. Write the three words that have the word part *fine*.

_____   _____   _____

3. Write the three words that have the word part *tain*.

_____   _____   _____

4. Write the three words that belong to the same word family as the word *inform*.

_____   _____   _____

5. Write the four words that belong to the same word family as the word *spectacle*.

_____   _____

_____   _____

B. Start with the word part *mote* each time.

6. Add prefixes and write two Unit words.

_____   _____

7. Add a prefix and a suffix. Write another Unit word. _____

8. Add a prefix and two suffixes. Write a Unit word. _____

C. Add a suffix to each of these words. Write a Unit word.

9. perform _____   10. respect _____

11. inform _____   12. conduct _____

13. define _____   14. emotion _____

D. An **analogy** shows the relationship between two pairs of words. Finish each of these word analogies with a Unit word.

15. *Direct* is to *director* as *conduct* is to _____.

16. *Deliver* is to *deliverance* as *perform* is to _____.

17. *Compete* is to *competition* as *define* is to _____.

Spelling and Language · Noun Suffixes

The suffix *-er* or *-or* added to a verb makes a noun that names a person or thing that does something. For example, a person who *conducts* an orchestra is called a *conductor.*

Add *-or* to the verb in ( ) to complete each sentence.

1. The (prospect) _____ hiked through the canyon.

2. The (inspect) _____ comes once a month.

Add *-er* to the verb in ( ) to complete each sentence.

3. We will help the (produce) _____ advertise the play.

4. Mr. Briggs is the (promote) _____ for the circus.

Writing on Your Own

Imagine that a popular singer has come to town for one show. Write a story for your classmates about two friends who try to get tickets. Choose at least one word that has more than one meaning and use it at least once for each meaning. Use some Unit words in your story.

 WRITER'S GUIDE   For a sample of a story, turn to page 276.

Using the Dictionary to Spell and Write

Many words have more than one meaning and can be used as more than one part of speech. Each meaning given in a dictionary is numbered. The abbreviation after the number tells you the part of speech. This information will help you use words correctly when you write.

> **pros·pect** /pros′pekt/ **1** *n.* The act of looking ahead; expectation: The *prospect* of a vacation cheered us. **2** *n. (often pl.)* The possibility of future success: business *prospects.* **3** *n.* A possible buyer or candidate: a good *prospect* for the job. **4** *n.* A wide view ahead. **5** *v.* To explore or search out: *prospect* for gold.

Complete each sentence with the word *prospect.* Add an ending if one is needed. Then write the number of the meaning that fits the sentence and *n.* or *v.* to show its part of speech.

1. The miners _____ for gold in the river.   _____

2. The _____ of an airplane ride is exciting.   _____

3. Mrs. Field is a likely _____ for mayor.   _____

114

Spelling on Your Own

UNIT WORDS

-ation · re- · pro- · con- · de- · -ful · per- · -tion · in- · -al

Copy and complete this chart, listing the Unit words that share each word part. Then choose one group and use each word in a sentence.

form	mote	fine	duce	tain	spect

MASTERY WORDS

discount
counter
entry
entrance
remove
movable

Follow the directions using the Mastery words.

1. Write the two words that are related to *move*. Circle the word that has a prefix.

_____   _____

2. Write the two words that are related to *count*. Circle the word that has a suffix.

_____   _____

3. Write the two words that are related to the word *enter*. Then write the letter in *enter* that is dropped in the related words.

_____   _____

Write the Mastery word that means the opposite of each word or group of words.

4. exit (two words) _____   _____

5. increase the price _____

BONUS WORDS

prescription
scribble
dictate
contradict
extract
distraction
thermometer
thermos

Write two Bonus words that are related to each of these words.

1. describe   2. detract   3. predict   4. thermal

Complete the exercises using the Bonus words.

5. Write the two words that have to do with heat. Then use each word in a sentence.

6. The word *extract* can be used as a noun or a verb. Look up *extract* in the **Spelling Dictionary.** Use *extract* as a noun in a sentence. Then use it as a verb in a sentence.

7. Write a short description of a visit to a doctor's or dentist's office. Use as many Bonus words as you can.

27 Mathematics Words

UNIT WORDS

1. angle
2. average
3. capacity
4. compute
5. decimal
6. denominator
7. diameter
8. dividend
9. fraction
10. measurement
11. multiple
12. negative
13. numeral
14. numerator
15. percent
16. positive
17. radius
18. ratio
19. rectangle
20. triangle

The Unit Words

All of the words in this Unit have to do with mathematics. You probably use some kind of math almost every day. When you write words for math, you need to know how to spell them correctly.

Several of the Unit words end with the sounds /əl/. These sounds are spelled in two different ways in the Unit words.

● with **al** as in *decimal* /des'ə·məl/

● with **le** as in *angle* /ang'gəl/

Other words contain the sounds /ər/. These sounds are spelled three different ways in the Unit words.

● with **er** as in *diameter* /dī·am'ə·tər/

● with **ure** as in *measurement* /mezh'ər·mənt/

● with **or** as in *denominator* /di·nom'ə·nā'tər/

REMEMBER THIS

To help you spell *measurement,* remember that the letters that spell *sure* are in the middle of the word. Memorize this sentence:

Be *sure* of the mea*sure*ment.

Spelling Practice

A. Write a Unit word to name each shape or symbol.

1. _____
2. _____
3. _____
4. _____
5. _____
6. _____

B. Follow the directions using the Unit words.

7. Write the two words that are related to the word *number.*

_____   _____

8. Write the six words that end with the sounds /əl/. Circle the two words that have the base word *angle.*

_____   _____   _____

_____   _____   _____

9. Write the three words that end with the sounds /ər/.

_____   _____   _____

10. Write the word that has the suffix *-ment.* _____

11. Write the word that has the suffix *-ion.* _____

C. Write the Unit words that describe these numbers.

⁻3 **12** number   ⁺3 **13** number   3:2 **14**

12. _____   13. _____   14. _____

D. Write the Unit words that belong to the same word family as each of these words.

15. computer _____   16. multiply _____

17. fracture _____   18. radiate _____

19. divide _____   20. negate _____

E. Complete each sentence with a Unit word.

21. The _____ age of the students in this class is 12.

22. A liter bottle has a greater _____ than a quart bottle.

23. Can you _____ these figures without a calculator?

24. In the fraction $\frac{7}{8}$, 7 is the numerator and 8 is the _____ .

$$11 \times 4 = 44$$
$$12 \times 13 = 156$$
$$13 \times 2 = 26$$
$$14 \times 1 = 14$$
$$20 \overline{\smash{)}240}$$

$$20 \overline{\smash{)}240}^{\,12}$$

117

Spelling and Language · Multiple Meanings

UNIT WORDS

angle
average
capacity
compute
decimal
denominator
diameter
dividend
fraction
measurement
multiple
negative
numeral
numerator
percent
positive
radius
ratio
rectangle
triangle

Many of the Unit words have a general meaning as well as a specialized mathematical definition.

Write a Unit word to fit each pair of sentences. Then identify the way the word is used in each sentence as either **g**–general, or **m**–mathematical.

1. The _____ family watches television together. ____

2. The _____ of 6, 9, 11, and 14 is 10. ____

3. Number each _____ in the rectangle. ____

4. Let's approach the problem from a new _____ . ____

5. Is 36 a _____ of 4? ____

6. She received _____ injuries in the accident. ____

Writing on Your Own

Pretend a classmate was absent from math class this morning. Write a note explaining how to do the math problems you learned about. Use six or more Unit words to explain the steps. Choose at least one word with more than one meaning and use it at least once for each meaning.

Proofreading

When Rob wrote these definitions in his mathematics notebook, he made six spelling errors.

1. Read Rob's notes and circle the misspelled words.

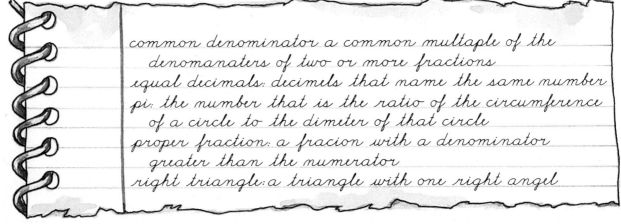

common denominator a common multaple of the
denomanaters of two or more fractions
equal decimals: decimels that name the same number
pi: the number that is the ratio of the circumfrence
of a circle to the dimeter of that circle
proper fraction: a fracion with a denominator
greater than the numerator
right triangle: a triangle with one right angel

2. Write the six misspelled words correctly.

_____   _____

_____   _____

Spelling on Your Own

UNIT WORDS

Write a glossary of mathematical terms using the Unit words. Give a definition or an illustration of each word. Use your math textbook and your dictionary for help.

decrease
doubled
equal
square
equation
product

MASTERY WORDS

Follow the directions using the Mastery words.

1. Write the three Mastery words with /kw/.

2. Write the word that names a shape.

Complete these sentences with Mastery words.

3. The number of mares will increase, but the number of stallions

   will _____ .

4. Last year, the herd _____ in size.

5. Nothing can _____ the thrill of owning a horse.

Write the word that can fill *both* the blanks.

6. By multiplying the numbers, we arrived at this _____ .

7. They inspected each item to make sure their _____ was the best on the market.

BONUS WORDS

Write a Bonus word for each definition.
1. the outside boundary
2. a branch of mathematics
3. the ratio or relative size of two things

Complete these exercises using the Bonus words.
4. Write three words with the root *gon*.
5. Write the adjective form of *triangle*.
6. Write the name of this figure.

triangular
polygon
perimeter
pyramid
diagonal
proportion
algebra
pentagon

UNIT WORDS

1. avenue
2. cabinet
3. policy
4. senator
5. tropical
6. paradise
7. comedy
8. delicate
9. magazine
10. elevator
11. recipe
12. definite
13. salary
14. medicine
15. benefit
16. violin
17. apology
18. tragedy
19. gasoline
20. dedicate

The Unit Words

The sound schwa /ə/ is a weak vowel sound heard in unaccented syllables. Schwa is the sound you hear at the beginning of *among* /ə·mung'/. This sound can be represented by any vowel letter. In the Unit words, the sound /ə/ is spelled with four different vowel letters.

- with **a** as in *salary* /sal'ər·ē/
- with **e** as in *comedy* /kom'ə·dē/
- with **i** as in *delicate* /del'ə·kit/
- with **o** as in *gasoline* /gas'ə·lēn/

Notice that in many of the Unit words, the sound /ə/ is the only sound in the syllable.

In three of the Unit words the schwa sound is heard twice. Two of these words have two different spellings for schwa. Pay careful attention to the letters that represent schwa in these words.

/med'ə·sən/ *medicine*
/el'ə·vā'tər/ *elevator*
/sen'ə·tər/ *senator*

Harcourt Brace School Publishers

Spelling Practice

A. Here are the accented first syllables of six Unit words. Add the second and third syllables. Then write the whole word.

1. trop _____
2. ben _____
3. par _____
4. av _____
5. cab _____
6. def _____

B. Follow the directions using the Unit words.

7. Write five words that have /ə/ spelled o.

_____ _____ _____

_____ _____

8. Write six words that end with the sound /ē/. Underline the word that does *not* end with the letter y.

_____ _____ _____

_____ _____ _____

C. Unscramble the syllables to write a Unit word. Underline the vowels that are pronounced /ə/.

9. cate i ded _____
10. i cine med _____
11. i del cate _____
12. mag zine a _____

D. Complete the following letter with Unit words. Capitalize two of the words.

Sixth Grade Class
Belmont School
39 Spender Street
Parker City, NH 03100

The President
1600 Pennsylvania ___13___
Washington, DC 20500

Dear Mr. President:

Our class is having a debate on the topic "Should schools stay open all year?" Some students are in favor of year-round school, but others cannot see any ___14___ from it. We are reading books and ___15___ articles to support our arguments.

We would like to know if you and the members of your ___16___ have come to a ___17___ decision about this subject. What is your official ___18___ ?

Sincerely,
The Sixth Grade Class, Belmont School

13. _____
14. _____
15. _____
16. _____
17. _____
18. _____

121

Spelling and Language · Word Families

UNIT WORDS

avenue
cabinet
policy
senator
tropical
paradise
comedy
delicate
magazine
elevator
recipe
definite
salary
medicine
benefit
violin
apology
tragedy
gasoline
dedicate

Words that belong to the same word family have the same **base word**. *Elevator* and *elevation* belong to the same word family. They have the same base word, *elevate.*

Write a Unit word that belongs to the same family as each word below.

1. police _____   2. apologize _____

3. senate _____   4. beneficial _____

5. tropics _____   6. dedication _____

 Writing on Your Own

Write a poem for your classmates about a person or team you admire. Try to make your classmates see why the person or team deserves praise. Use as many Unit words as you can.

WRITER'S GUIDE   For a sample poem, turn to page 279.

Using the Dictionary to Spell and Write

In a dictionary pronunciation, the accent mark shows you which syllable is said with more force: /sen'ə·tər/. The accented syllable in *senator* is /sen'/. Some words have two accented syllables. The syllable with the primary accent (') is said with the most force. The syllable with the secondary accent (') is not as strong. In the word *rectangle* /rek' tang'gəl/, the first syllable has a primary accent, the middle syllable has a secondary accent, and the last syllable is unaccented.

Write the correct spelling for each pronunciation below. Draw two lines under the letters that spell the accented (primary) syllable and one line under the letters that spell the syllable with secondary stress. Here is an example: rectangle.

act, āte, câre, ärt;	egg, ēven;	if, īce;	on, ōver, ôr;	bŏŏk, fŏŏd;	up, tûrn;
ə = a in *ago*, e in *listen*, i in *giraffe*, o in *pilot*, u in *circus*;		yōō = u in *music*;		oil;	out;
chair; sing; shop; thank; that; zh in *treasure*.					

1. /el'ə·vā'tər/ _____   2. /prə·nun' sē·ā'shən/ _____

3. /bak'ground'/ _____   4. /des'tə·nā'shən/ _____

5. /vī'ə·lin'/ _____   6. /graj'ōō·ā'shən/ _____

7. /trī'ang'gəl/ _____   8. /ben'ə·fish'əl/ _____

 SPELLING DICTIONARY Remember to use your **Spelling Dictionary** when you write.

Harcourt Brace School Publishers

Spelling on Your Own

UNIT WORDS

The Unit words below are missing the vowel letters that spell /ə/. Add the missing letters and write the words.

1. com ____ dy
2. pol ____ cy
3. med ____ c ____ ne
4. mag ____ zine
5. apol ____ gy
6. rec ____ pe
7. sal ____ ry
8. av ____ nue
9. cab ____ net
10. def ____ nite
11. vi ____ lin
12. el ____ vat ____ r
13. gas ____ line
14. ben ____ fit
15. sen ____ t ____ r
16. ded ____ cate
17. trag ____ dy
18. par ____ dise
19. del ____ cate
20. tropic ____ l

vowel
/vou'əl/

syllable
/sil'ə·bəl/

MASTERY WORDS

Follow the directions using the Mastery words.

1. Write the word that has double vowel letters. _____

2. Write the base word in *decoration*. _____

Write the three words that contain two /ə/ sounds. The /ə/ sounds are spelled with the letters given.

3. *i* and *e* _____ 4. *e* and *a* _____ 5. *i* and *a* _____

Write the Mastery words that have these first syllables.

6. en _____
7. pi _____
8. dec _____
9. an _____
10. el _____
11. cit _____

animal
enemy
elephant
decorate
pioneer
citizen

BONUS WORDS

1. The sound /ə/ is spelled five different ways in the Bonus words: *a, e, i, o,* and *u*. Write each Bonus word under the correct spelling for /ə/. You will use one word twice.

2. Look up the word *separate* in the **Spelling Dictionary.** Copy the pronunciations for *separate*. Then write two sentences using *separate*, first as an adjective and then as a verb.

3. Write a sentence describing the bird named by a Bonus word.

politics
pelican
diagram
coliseum
ceremony
separate
astronomy
imitate

123

UNIT WORDS

1. neon
2. create
3. slumber
4. common
5. cabbage
6. chapter
7. bullet
8. funnel
9. mammoth
10. rescue
11. blister
12. splendid
13. accent
14. trumpet
15. ruin
16. trial
17. poet
18. diet
19. fluid
20. triumph

The Unit Words

A **syllable** is a word or part of a word. Each syllable in a word has one vowel sound. When you divide a word into syllables, listen for the vowel sounds.

Say the words *beat* and *create.* In *beat,* the letters *ea* together have the vowel sound /ē/. The word *beat* has one vowel sound and one syllable. In *create,* there are two separate vowel sounds: /ē/ and /ā/. The word *create* has two vowel sounds and two syllables.

Each of the Unit words has two syllables. Here are some rules to help you divide the Unit words into syllables.

1. When a word has two vowel sounds between two consonants, divide the word *between* the two vowels.

   create   cre ate   neon   ne on

2. When a word has two consonant letters between two vowels, divide the word *between* the two consonants.

   mammoth   mam moth   splendid   splen did

Harcourt Brace School Publishers

Spelling Practice

A. Write the Unit words that have these double consonant letters. Draw a line between the two syllables of each word.

    1. bb _____

    2. cc _____

    3. ll _____

    4. nn _____

    5. mm (two words) _____   _____

B. Below are the first syllables of six words. Add the second syllables and write the Unit words.

    6. chap _____

    7. blis _____

    8. splen _____

    9. trum _____

    10. res _____

    11. slum _____

C. Write the Unit words that have these two vowel sounds together.

    12. /ē/ /ā/ _____

    13. /ō/ /i/ _____

    14. /ē/ /o/ _____

    15. /ī/ /u/ _____

    16. /ī/ /ə/ (two words) _____   _____

    17. /o͞o/ /i/ (two words) _____   _____

D. Write the Unit word that is a synonym for each word below.

    18. sleep _____

    19. magnificent _____

    20. spoil _____

    21. ordinary _____

    22. victory _____

    23. enormous _____

E. Write the Unit word that completes each analogy.

    24. *Syllable* is to *word* as _____ is to *book.*

    25. *Fruit* is to *orange* as *vegetable* is to _____.

    26. *Music* is to *composer* as *verse* is to _____.

    27. *Alto* is to *chorus* as _____ is to *band.*

    28. *Bruise* is to *injure* as _____ is to *burn.*

    29. *Break* is to *build* as *destroy* is to _____.

    30. *Judge* is to _____ as *teacher* is to *test.*

Spelling and Language · Noun and Verb Functions

UNIT WORDS

neon
create
slumber
common
cabbage
chapter
bullet
funnel
mammoth
rescue
blister
splendid
accent
trumpet
ruin
trial
poet
diet
fluid
triumph

Some words can be used as either nouns or verbs. The word *blister,* for example, can be a noun or a verb.

Noun: I have a *blister* on my hand from the shovel.
Verb: The paint *blistered* in the hot sun.

Complete each sentence with a Unit word. Add *ed* or *ing* to words used as verbs. The part of speech is given after each number.

1. *v.* Jerry _____ the stew by burning it.

2. *n.* But Mom came to the _____ .

3. *n.* Dinner was a _____ after all!

Writing on Your Own

Write a book report about a book you read recently and enjoyed. Use colorful words to tell about the characters and events in the story. Use as many Unit words as you can.

 WRITER'S GUIDE For help with the parts of a book report, turn to page 277.

Proofreading

Betty Ann wrote this letter to her friend Jeannie.

1. Circle the six misspelled words and insert the two missing apostrophes.

Dear Jeannie,
I'm finally getting used to living here, but it hasn't been easy. At first I didn t think I had anything in comon with the girls in my class. They all laughed at my acsent. Then Dad came to my resque. He suggested that I have a slummber party. He made mamoth bowls of popcorn for us and his famous stuffed cabbige. Everyone had a great time. It turns out they all wish they had an accent like mine!

Love,
Betty Ann

2. Write the six misspelled words correctly.

_____   _____

_____   _____

Spelling on Your Own

UNIT WORDS

Make a "word chain" with the Unit words. Use a letter in one word to write another one of the words. Words may go across or down, as in a puzzle. Make as many chains as necessary to use all the words, or try to fit all the words into one chain.

MASTERY WORDS

narrow
seldom
practice
swallow
public
mirror

Follow the directions using the Mastery words.

1. Write the three words that have double letters.

_____   _____

Write the Mastery words that have these first syllables.

2. sel _____   **3.** pub _____

4. prac _____

Finish the paragraph with Mastery words.

Almost every afternoon I __5__ the piano for an hour or so. I __6__ miss a day. Our piano is in a long, __7__ hallway. Sometimes I watch myself in the __8__ while I play. I want to look right when I'm ready to play in __9__.

5. _____   6. _____   7. _____

8. _____   9. _____

BONUS WORDS

pliers
riot
brilliant
fabric
liar
fuel
fungus
villain

1. Write the four Bonus words that have two vowel sounds together. Draw a line between the two syllables of each word.

2. Write the word that has only a plural form, as *scissors* does. Use the word in a sentence.

3. Write the four Bonus words that have two consonant letters together in the middle. Write sentences using the two words that have double consonant letters.

4. Write a short paragraph about one kind of fungus. Use the encyclopedia or a science book for help.

30 Review

Follow these steps when you are unsure of how to spell a word.

- **Say** the word. Recall when you have heard the word used. Think about what it means.
- **Look** at the word. Find any prefixes, suffixes, or other word parts you know. Think about other words that are related in meaning and spelling. Try to picture the word in your mind.
- **Spell** the word to yourself. Think about the way each sound is spelled. Notice any unusual spelling.
- **Write** the word while looking at it. Check the way you have formed your letters. If you have not written the word clearly or correctly, write it again.
- **Check** your learning. Cover the word and write it. If you did not spell the word correctly, practice these steps until the word becomes your own.

UNIT 25 Follow the directions using words from Unit 25.

Write the noun form of these verbs; circle the suffix in each answer.

1. decorate _____
2. locate _____
3. operate _____
4. solve _____
5. develop _____
6. arrange _____

Write the noun form of these adjectives; circle the suffix in each answer.

7. active _____
8. able _____
9. electric _____

Complete the following sentence.

10. My sister wanted to learn how to play a musical _____

UNIT 26 Write the Unit 26 word that belongs to the same word family as each of these words.

11. informative _____
12. definitive _____
13. product _____
14. expectation _____
15. container _____
16. performer _____
17. conduct _____
18. refinery _____
19. inspection _____
20. reduction _____

UNIT 25

activity
instrument
decoration
ability
operation
solution
location
electricity
development
arrangement

UNIT 26

information
produce
expect
contain
definition
performance
conductor
reduce
inspect
refined

UNIT 27   Follow the directions using words from Unit 27.

Write the word for each definition. The first letter is given to help you.

21. three-sided shape (t) _____

22. symbol for a number (n) _____

23. ordinary; common (a) _____

24. based on the number for 10 (d) _____

25. determination of size (m) _____

Complete each definition.

26. A _____ is a word, symbol, or group of symbols that represents a number.

27. A _____ is a part of a whole.

28. A _____ number is a number less than zero.

Complete the paragraph.

The __29__ of the planetary circle was only a __30__ of the length that the captain had originally thought. She decided to go through the circle and save almost fifty __31__ of the rocket's fuel. Unfortunately, her decision had __32__ as well as __33__ aspects.

29. _____   30. _____

31. _____   32. _____

33. _____

UNIT 28   Follow the directions using words from Unit 28.

34. Write the two words that end in /ər/.

_____   _____

35. Write four words that have a one-letter syllable with /ə/ spelled *e*.

_____   _____

_____   _____

Write the words that have /ə/ spelled with each of the following letters. Then circle the letter in each word.

36. *i* (three words) _____ _____ _____

37. *a* (two words) _____ _____

38. *o* (three words) _____ _____ _____

UNIT 27

average
decimal
triangle
measurement
numeral
diameter
fraction
negative
percent
positive

UNIT 28

avenue
definite
gasoline
elevator
medicine
senator
comedy
magazine
recipe
tragedy

UNIT 29

poet
create
rescue
common
splendid
chapter
accent
ruin
trial
diet

39. Write two words that have double consonant letters. Then draw a line between the syllables of each word.

_____   _____

40. Write five words that have two vowels together that stand for two different sounds. Draw a line between the two sounds.

_____   _____

_____

Write the word that is an antonym for each of these words.

41. awful _____   **42.** unusual _____

43. save _____   **44.** abandon _____

Complete each analogy using words from Unit 29.

45. *Play* is to *playwright* as *poem* is to _____

46. *Scene* is to *play* as _____ is to *novel*.

47. *Umpire* is to *game* as *judge* is to _____

Write the word that belongs to each word family.

48. creation   creator   _____

49. splendiferous   splendor   _____

50. accentuate   accentual   _____

Write the word that completes each sentence.

51. My friend is a talented _____ .

52. He can _____ beautiful pictures with words.

53. He once wrote a _____ poem about an abandoned shack.

54. Nothing seems _____ or ordinary in the eyes of my friend.

WORDS IN TIME

The word *common* has a long history. It comes from the Latin word *communis*, which means "things that go together." In English the word was abbreviated to *commun*. The definition was also altered to mean "shared by all or many." Today, this is still the definition of our word *common*.

Spelling and Reading
Story Conversation

Read the following scene from a story. Notice how the writer uses conversation to tell the story.

"This pyramid is beautiful. It looks like a big three-dimensional triangle — don't you think?" Kyo asked her friend Wally.

"It really does. The Egyptians created some amazing things," answered Wally.

"Wally, look at this door. Let's go in."

"Are you kidding? The rest of the tour group is heading around the other way."

"So what? This is a shortcut. We'll meet them back at the same location anyway."

"Are you sure?" Wally asked uncertainly.

"I'm positive," Kyo replied confidently.

"It's getting darker, Kyo."

"Well, what do you expect? We're in a pyramid."

"I don't want to get lost and ruin the whole day."

"Don't turn this into a tragedy! It's an adventure."

"Wait! What's that funny green glow?"

"Don't worry. Sometimes dust can produce a strange glow like that."

"Oh, no!" shrieked Wally. "There goes the electricity."

"Okay," Kyo whispered. "Now you can worry."

Write the answers to the questions.

1. In this conversation, what does Kyo say the pyramid looks like?
2. How does Kyo explain the "funny green glow" to Wally?
3. How do Kyo's and Wally's feelings about going inside the pyramid differ?
4. What might the "funny green glow" actually be?

Underline the review words in your answers. Check to see that you spelled the words correctly.

Spelling and Writing
Story Conversation

Think and Discuss

Story conversation tells the exact words spoken by characters. These words are written between quotation marks. A new paragraph begins each time the speaker changes. Conversation may serve many different purposes in a story. Writers often use conversation to make a story seem realistic. Look back at the story conversation on page 131. What words does the writer use to make the story seem more realistic?

Writers may also use conversation to develop plot. They may use it to build the reader's curiosity about what will happen next. What do you learn about the plot from the conversation on page 131? A story is usually built around some main conflict or problem. What do you think the main conflict in the story of Wally and Kyo might be? How does the writer use conversation to reveal this conflict?

Writers also use conversation to show what their characters are feeling. What does Kyo appear to be feeling at the beginning of the conversation on page 131? What does Wally appear to be feeling? Whose feelings have changed by the end of the conversation? How does the writer reveal these changes?

Apply

Now you will write a scene using **story conversation**. Write the story to entertain your classmates. Follow the writing guidelines on the next page.

Words to Help You Write
activity
ability
location
expect
contain
reduce
average
negative
positive
avenue
magazine
recipe
poet
create
rescue
splendid
ruin
diet

Prewriting

Look at the picture. Imagine that it shows a scene from a story about two characters named Reid and Paula.

- Write the following questions about the characters: Who are they? What are they like? How do they know each other? What is happening in the scene?
- Under each question write details that answer the question.

 THESAURUS For help finding vivid words to describe your characters, turn to page 205.

Composing

Use your notes to help you write the first draft of your conversation.

 WRITER'S GUIDE For help punctuating conversation, see pages 276 and 282.

- Write a conversation with Reid and Paula that tells a story.
- Use words that reveal each character's thoughts and feelings.
- Look over your prewriting notes. Do you want to add anything?

Revising

Read your conversation and show it to a classmate. Follow these guidelines to improve your work. Use the editing and proofreading marks on this page to indicate corrections.

Editing

- Make sure your conversation tells a story.
- Check that your conversation sounds real.

Proofreading

- Check your spelling, capitalization, and punctuation.

Copy your story neatly onto clean paper.

Publishing

Have two classmates take the parts of your two characters and read the conversation to the class.

Harcourt Brace School Publishers

Editing and Proofreading Marks

≡	capitalize
⊙	make a period
∧	add something
⅄	add a comma
ᵛⱽ ᵛⱽ	add quotation marks
℮	take something away
◯	spell correctly
¶	indent the paragraph
/	make a lowercase letter
∼ tr	transpose

31 More Syllable Patterns

UNIT WORDS

1. balance
2. salute
3. marine
4. govern
5. talent
6. pretend
7. mature
8. patent
9. melon
10. spirit
11. career
12. severe
13. merit
14. tenor
15. perish
16. famine
17. maroon
18. plateau
19. weapon
20. topic

The Unit Words

Each of the words in this unit has two syllables. Listen for the accented syllable in each word. The middle consonant in each word is part of the accented syllable. Divide the words so that the consonant letter is with the accented syllable.

bal'ance
pre tend'

REMEMBER THIS

A *plateau* is a high, flat, plate-like plain. Remember that there is a *plate* in *plateau* and it will be easier to spell.

Harcourt Brace School Publishers

Spelling Practice

A. Write the Unit words with these pronunciations. Then draw a line between the syllables of each word.

1. /mə·rēn′/ _____

2. /mə·rōōn′/ _____

3. /kə·rir′/ _____

4. /si·vir′/ _____

B. Follow the directions using the Unit words.

5. Write four more words that have accented second syllables. If you need help, use your **Spelling Dictionary.**

_____   _____

_____   _____

6. Write three words that begin with consonant clusters. Circle the word that also ends with a consonant cluster.

_____   _____   _____

7. Write three more words that end with consonant clusters.

_____   _____   _____

C. Write the Unit words that have these vowel-consonant-vowel letter combinations in the middle. Draw a line between the syllables. Then write **1** or **2** to show which syllable is accented in the word.

8. atu _____ __

9. ala _____ __

10. alu _____ __

11. ami _____ __

D. Rearrange the letters in these words to write Unit words.

12. lemon _____

13. timer _____

14. noter _____

15. optic _____

E. Write the Unit word that fits each clue.

16. /e/ is spelled *ea* _____

17. ends with /sh/ _____

18. begins and ends with the same letter _____

19. every other letter is *e* _____

20. /ō/ is spelled *eau* _____

21. ends with /s/ but not with *s* _____

Spelling and Language · Using Verbs

UNIT WORDS

UNIT WORDS
balance
salute
marine
govern
talent
pretend
mature
patent
melon
spirit
career
severe
merit
tenor
perish
famine
maroon
plateau
weapon
topic

Half of the Unit words can be used as verbs. You add *ed* to verbs to show action in the past. Add *ing* to verbs used with forms of *be*. When a verb ends with *e*, drop the *e* before you add *ed* or *ing*.

Add *ed* or *ing* to each base word below to complete the sentences.

salute   1. We _____ the flag.

pretend   2. Carl is _____ to be a juggler.

balance   3. He is _____ a plate on his head.

perish   4. The fish _____ from lack of food.

Writing on Your Own

Pretend you have just finished a long talk with an adult you admire. Your conversation was about what career you might have someday. Write an entry in your journal to help you remember the conversation. Use some of these words: *talent, pretend, spirit, career, topic.* Add *ed* and *ing* to some verbs.

WRITER'S GUIDE   For a sample journal entry, see page 275.

Using the Dictionary to Spell and Write

You can use the dictionary to check if you used homographs correctly in your writing. **Homographs** are words that are spelled the same but that have different meanings and different word histories. The dictionary shows a separate entry word for each homograph. Read the two entries for *maroon*.

> **ma·roon**[1] /mə·ro͞on'/ *n., adj.* A dark red color: Lilia's shoes are *maroon*.
> **ma·roon**[2] /mə·ro͞on/ *v.* **1** To leave someone or something on a deserted island or coast. **2** To leave someone helpless: The tourist felt *marooned* when he missed the bus.

Write *maroon* to complete each sentence. Add an ending if it is needed. Then write the entry number (and definition number, if there is one).

1. The stray cat was _____ on the ice. ___ ___

2. Let's paint the car _____ . ___ ___

Spelling on Your Own

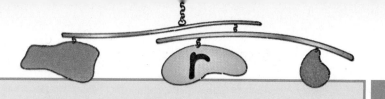

UNIT WORDS

Copy and complete this chart with Unit words grouped according to the middle consonant letter in each word. The number of words to be included in each column is given to help you.

r(6)	l(4)	t(4)	p(2)	v(2)	m(1)	n(1)

MASTERY WORDS

divide
cabin
habit
shadow
cement
prepare

Here are the first syllables of Mastery words. Add the second syllables and write the words. Then underline the accented syllable in each word.

1. hab _____

2. shad _____

3. ce _____

4. di _____

5. pre _____

Complete this paragraph using the Mastery words.

The first week in July my family rents a __6__ at Lime Lake. We __7__ our time between the nearby mountains and the beach. We all like to go hiking, but Dad has a __8__ of walking too fast. We usually __9__ a picnic basket with sandwiches and fruit for the hike. Guess who always seems to end up carrying the basket? Me, of course.

6. _____ 7. _____

8. _____ 9. _____

BONUS WORDS

pivot
senate
panel
clinic
precede
minute
rebel
propel

1. Make a list of the Bonus words in which the first syllable is accented. Then make another list of the Bonus words in which the second syllable is accented. Two words have two different pronunciations and belong in both lists.

2. Look up *minute* and *rebel* in the **Spelling Dictionary**. Write a sentence using each pronunciation and meaning of each word.

32 Words from Latin and Greek

UNIT WORDS

1. television
2. transportation
3. apartment
4. telegram
5. automatic
6. report
7. portable
8. compartment
9. telescope
10. telegraph
11. import
12. partial
13. autograph
14. apart
15. televise
16. automotive
17. export
18. autobiography
19. departure
20. automobile

The Unit Words

New inventions need new names. Often these names are made up from familiar Greek and Latin word parts. For example, the word *television* was created by adding the Greek root *tele,* which means "at a distance," to the word *vision.* So *television* means "seeing at a distance."

Each of the Unit words has one of these four Greek or Latin roots.

ROOTS	EXAMPLES
tele, "at a distance"	*telegraph,* "writing sent over a distance"
port, "carry"	*import,* "carry into a country"
auto, "self"	*autograph,* "signature by oneself"
part, "divide"	*apart,* "divided in pieces"

REMEMBER THIS

The suffix in *portable* means "to be able." Remember the *able* as in "able to carry" when spelling *portable.*

Harcourt Brace School Publishers

Spelling Practice

A. Complete these exercises using the Unit words.

1. Write the five words that begin with the word part that means "self."

_____   _____   _____

_____   _____

2. Add *tele* to each of these words to write a Unit word.

scope   gram   vision

_____   _____   _____

3. Write the word with /īz/ spelled *ise.* _____

4. The Greek root *graph* means "writing." Write three Unit words with *graph*.

_____   _____   _____

B. Follow the directions to write Unit words.

5. Add a one-letter prefix to *part*. _____

6. Add a suffix to the word you wrote for **5.** _____

7. Change the prefix of the word you wrote for **6.** _____

8. Add a three-letter suffix to *part*. _____

9. Add a three-letter suffix to *depart*. _____

10. Write two words that are opposites.

_____   _____

11. Write the word with the prefix *re-*. _____

12. Write the word with the suffix *-able*. _____

13. Write the word that has four syllables and the root *port*. _____

C. Complete this sign with Unit words.

14. _____

15. _____

16. _____

17. _____

18. _____

19. _____

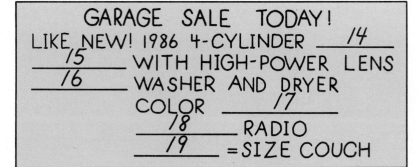

GARAGE SALE TODAY!
LIKE NEW! 1986 4-CYLINDER ___14___
___15___ WITH HIGH-POWER LENS
___16___ WASHER AND DRYER
COLOR ___17___
___18___ RADIO
___19___ =SIZE COUCH

Spelling and Language · Prefixes

UNIT WORDS

television
transportation
apartment
telegram
automatic
report
portable
compartment
telescope
telegraph
import
partial
autograph
apart
televise
automotive
export
autobiography
departure
automobile

A **prefix** is a word part that comes before a word or root. The two prefixes *re-* and *de-* often occur with the same roots. The prefix *re-* adds the meaning "back," or "again." The prefix *de-* adds the meaning "away, or off." Look at the words *refer* and *defer*.

> They will *refer* the case to the judge.
> She will *defer* a decision until next week.

Change the prefix of each word in boldface to *re-* or *de-*. Complete the sentence with the new word.

deceive   **1.**   I think Leon will _____ the prize.

reserve   **2.**   Does he _____ to win?

deflect   **3.**   Tilt the mirror to _____ the light.

Writing on Your Own

Write an opinion paragraph to answer this question: Which invention has affected your life the most—television or the automobile? Use four or more Unit words and give facts and examples to support your ideas.

 WRITER'S GUIDE   For help, turn to the sample opinion paragraph on page 271.

Proofreading

Karen listed the television programs she watched one weekend.

1. Read Karen's log and circle the six misspelled words. Draw three lines under the three letters that should be capitals.

Friday night	8:00-9:00	"Apartmen 4Z"
	9:00-10:30	"Telscope on mars"
Saturday night	7:00-7:30	"Sports Riport"
	7:30-8:00	"Life on Telegraff hill"
	8:00-9:00	"Animals in Space"
sunday night	7:30-9:00	"Autobigraphy of a Telavision Star"

2. Write the six misspelled words correctly.

_____   _____   _____

_____   _____   _____

Spelling on Your Own

This chart shows the Greek and Latin roots found in the Unit words. Copy the chart and complete it with Unit words. Then write a short definition for each word.

part	tele	auto	port

MASTERY WORDS

handicraft
handy
careless
leader
carefree
mislead

Follow the directions using the Mastery words.

1. Write the two words that have the base word *lead*.

_____ _____

2. Write the two words that have the base word *hand*.

_____ _____

3. Write the two words that have the base word *care*.

_____ _____

An **analogy** is a statement that compares the relationship between two pairs of words. Finish each of these analogies with a Mastery word. Here is an example: *Teach* is to *teacher* as *sing* is to *singer*.

4. *Spell* is to *misspell* as *lead* is to _____ .

5. *Painful* is to *painless* as *careful* is to _____ .

BONUS WORDS

suspense
dispenser
manuscript
manual
photocopy
geography
photogenic
geology

Write the Bonus words that share a root word with each of these words. You will use one word twice.

1. photograph   **2.** geophysics   **3.** manufacture   **4.** suspenders

Complete these exercises using the Bonus words.

5. The words *graph* and *graphy* mean "something written." Write the Bonus Word that contains one of these word parts. Then write as many words as you can that contain *graph* or *graphy*.

6. The word part *photo* means "light." Write the two Bonus words that begin with this word part. Then write at least four other words that begin with *photo*.

33 Synonyms and Antonyms

The Unit Words

Words that mean the same or nearly the same thing are called **synonyms.** The words *rival* and *foe* are synonyms; they both mean "someone in competition."

Words that mean the opposite are called **antonyms.** *Backward* and *forward* are antonyms because they refer to opposite directions.

You can improve your writing by substituting a precise synonym for a more general word. For example, even though *rival* and *foe* have almost the same meaning, the slight difference may make one word a better choice in a particular sentence. Read these sentences to help you see the difference in meaning between synonyms.

My sister Amy is my *rival* on the tennis court.
Britain was a *foe* of America in 1776.

You use antonyms in writing when you want to compare two different things. For example, you could compare a job someone held for a short time with a job that continued for a long time using the antonyms *temporary* and *permanent.*

Spelling Practice

A. Write the two Unit words that are synonyms for each of these words.

1. hide   _____   _____

2. enough   _____   _____

3. opponent   _____   _____

4. acknowledged   _____   _____

B. Write a Unit word that is a synonym for each word. Then write the Unit word that is an antonym for the word.

5. lasting   _____   _____

6. penny-pinching _____   _____

7. usual   _____   _____

8. end   _____   _____

9. praise   _____   _____

10. ahead   _____   _____

C. Write the two Unit words that are synonyms for the underlined word in each of these sentences.

11. I said I was late because I had overslept.

_____   _____

12. They tried to hide their tracks in the snow.

_____   _____

13. On Friday we play our biggest competitor.

_____   _____

14. The sunlight in the room was enough for the plants.

_____   _____

D. Write the Unit word that belongs in each group of synonyms.

15. thrifty, mean, skimpy, _____

16. rare, uncommon, extraordinary, _____

17. regular, common, usual, _____

18. close, finish, ending, _____

Spelling and Language · Adding -ly

UNIT WORDS

UNIT WORDS

adequate
admitted
approval
backward
conceal
conclusion
confessed
criticism
disguise
exceptional
foe
forward
generous
introduction
permanent
rival
stingy
sufficient
temporary
typical

An **adverb** is a word that modifies a verb, an adjective, or another adverb. An adverb answers the question *How? When?* or *Where?* You can often form an adverb by adding *-ly* to an adjective.

Add *-ly* to each of the Unit words in boldface. Then write the word in each sentence. Remember that the spelling of some words changes when *-ly* is added.

permanent 1. The puzzle was glued _____ to the cardboard.

adequate 2. Erica felt _____ prepared for the test.

typical 3. It was a _____ foggy morning.

generous 4. Mike watered the garden _____ .

Writing on Your Own

Write a conversation you might have with a foreign student. Tell what the student asks you about your school and country and what you tell the student. Use as many Unit words and adverbs as you can.

 WRITER'S GUIDE For a sample of conversation, turn to page 276.

Using the Dictionary to Spell and Write

Many dictionaries give the history of words and explain their origin. In the **Spelling Dictionary** this symbol ▶ marks a word history. Knowing the origin of a word can often help you remember its meaning. This can be very useful when you want to be sure you used a word correctly in your writing. Read the entry for *temporary* and its word history.

> **tem·po·rar·y** /tem'pə·rer'ē/ *adj.* Lasting only for a short time; not permanent.
> ▶ *Temporary* comes from the Latin word *tempus,* "time."

Look up these words in the **Spelling Dictionary**. Write a sentence that explains the origin of each word.

1. rival _____

_____

2. generous _____

_____

Spelling on Your Own

UNIT WORDS

Write the four pairs of Unit words that are synonyms and the six pairs of Unit words that are antonyms. Then use each pair of antonyms in a sentence.

MASTERY WORDS

Follow the directions using the Mastery words.

sleepy
rely
damage
depend
drowsy
repair

1. Write the word that is a synonym for *fix*. Then write the word that is an antonym for *fix*.

_____   _____

2. Write the two words that are synonyms for *tired*.

3. Write the two words that are synonyms for *count on*.

_____   _____

4. Write the six words in alphabetical order.

_____ → _____ → _____

→ _____ → _____ → _____

Add the suffix *-able* to each of these Mastery words to form an adjective. Write the new word. You will need to change *y* to *i* in one word.

5. repair _____   6. depend _____

7. rely _____

BONUS WORDS

corridor
vigorous
complicate
energetic
simplify
passage
soothe
irritate

1. Write the two pairs of words that are synonyms and the two pairs of words that are antonyms. Then use each synonym in a sentence.

2. Write the Bonus word that means "to make more difficult."

3. Use the Bonus word that means "to make easier" in a sentence.

4. Write the two words that are synonyms for *active*. Then write the base word for each word.

5. Add *ed* to the four words that are verbs. Then use each verb with *ed* in a sentence.

34 Three-Syllable Words

UNIT WORDS

1. barbecue
2. mineral
3. property
4. century
5. assignment
6. determine
7. remainder
8. insulate
9. capital
10. industry
11. monument
12. mystery
13. interest
14. carpentry
15. violet
16. circular
17. colonist
18. athletics
19. creative
20. appetite

athletic equipment

The Unit Words

Restaurant signs often use "Bar B Q" for the word *barbecue.* The made-up spelling can help you remember the correct spelling. First it shows you that the word has three syllables. Also, when you see the letter *B,* you see the beginning letter of the second syllable. Finally, the name for the letter *Q* is a homophone for the word *cue.*

Each of the Unit words has three syllables. Remember that each syllable in a word has one vowel sound.

☐ The word *interest* can be said with three syllables: /in'ter·ist/, or with two syllables: /in'trist/. Pronouncing all three syllables in *interest* will help you remember the correct spelling.

REMEMBER THIS

There is only one *e* in *athletics.* You can hear it in the middle syllable, *let.*

Harcourt Brace School Publishers

Spelling Practice

A. Follow the directions using the Unit words.

1. Write the five words that end with the sound /ē/. Circle the word that has the sound /i/ spelled y.

_____   _____

_____   _____

2. Write the two words that end with /əl/.

_____   _____

3. Write the two words that end with /ər/. Underline the letters that spell /ər/.

_____   _____

4. Write the six words that begin with vowel letters.

_____   _____

_____   _____

5. Write the four words that have two vowel letters together. Circle the two words that have only one vowel sound for the two letters.

_____   _____

B. Write the Unit words with these definitions. Then draw a vertical line between the syllables of each word.

6. settler of a colony _____

7. thing built in memory of a person _____

8. money paid for the use of money _____

C. Complete the paragraph with Unit words.

   Is there really a monster in the waters of Loch Ness? The __9__ of Loch Ness in Scotland has fascinated scientists throughout this __10__. For years, __11__ in the "monster" has grown. Scientists cannot __12__ if the creature exists for sure, but they believe it is possible. Because high mountains __13__ Loch Ness on all sides, the lake is warm enough for "Nessie" to exist. Nessie's large __14__ could easily be satisfied by the great variety of fish in the lake.

9. _____   **10.** _____   **11.** _____

12. _____   **13.** _____   **14.** _____

Spelling and Language · Adding Suffixes

<table>
<tr><td>

UNIT WORDS

barbecue
mineral
property
century
assignment
determine
remainder
insulate
capital
industry
monument
mystery
interest
carpentry
violet
circular
colonist
athletics
creative
appetite

</td></tr>
</table>

Suffixes are added to the end of a base word to change the part of speech of the word. You can add more than one suffix to some base words.

Add the suffix in ( ) to the word in boldface to complete the first sentence in each pair. Then add the second suffix to the word you wrote in the first sentence to complete the second sentence.

capital

1. We learned to _____ (-ize) the names of cities.

2. In fact, the whole lesson was on _____ . (-ation).

create

3. Making the kite was a _____ (-ive) experience.

4. It takes _____ (-ity) to design kites.

Writing on Your Own

Pretend you are entering a contest to design a monument to industry in the United States. Draw a picture of the best monument you can imagine. Then write a paragraph that describes your drawing. Use as many Unit words as you can. Add the suffixes *-ize, -ation, -ive, -al,* or *-ity* to some words.

 WRITER'S GUIDE   For help revising your descriptive paragraph, turn to the checklist on page 267.

Proofreading

Scott helped type this announcement for school. When he proofread it, he found six spelling errors.

1. Circle each misspelled word.

> What's your special intrest? Join a club today!
>
> The Health Club. Learn to control your apetite.
> The Computer Club. You will learn to use our own school computer.
> The Mineral Club. Take weekly hikes to look for minerels.
> The Booster Club. Support our school athletics program.
> Creaitive Writing. Help put together the Lincoln magazine.
> The Builders' Club. Learn beginning carpentery.

2. Write the six misspelled words correctly.

_____   _____   _____

_____   _____   _____

Spelling on Your Own

UNIT WORDS

Write the Unit word that has each syllable below as its middle syllable.

1. main
2. tu
3. dus
4. su
5. a
6. cu
7. pe
8. be
9. sign
10. pen
11. i
12. u
13. let
14. o (two words)
15. er (two words)
16. ter (three words)

MASTERY WORDS

Write the Mastery word that:

1. means "full of danger." _____

2. ends with -ful. _____

3. has double letters. _____

4. is the noun form of invent. _____

5. has four letters and three syllables. _____

6. means "call to mind." _____

remember
area
wonderful
dangerous
invention
wilderness

Proofread this notice. Write the four misspelled words correctly.

> Next week the hiking club will go backpacking in a wileress airea. The hike will not be dangerious if you rember to stay with the group.

7. _____   8. _____

9. _____   10. _____

BONUS WORDS

Write a Bonus word for each meaning.

1. a race of more than 26 miles
2. a place to live
3. a place to get prescriptions filled
4. a useful book

triumphant
marathon
pharmacy
gymnastics
nutritious
strenuous
residence
almanac

Complete these exercises using the Bonus words.

5. Write the three words that can be used only as adjectives. Then use each word in a sentence.
6. Write the word that begins with /f/ and another word that has the same spelling for /f/.
7. Use the word with /i/ spelled y in a sentence.

UNIT WORDS

1. invitation
2. population
3. necessary
4. evaporate
5. patriotic
6. arithmetic
7. gymnasium
8. necessity
9. material
10. scientific
11. petroleum
12. naturally
13. imitation
14. variety
15. aviator
16. hibernation
17. machinery
18. appreciate
19. conversation
20. experience

The Unit Words

A Rhyme Styme is a riddle with two rhyming words for the answer. Here are two examples with words from this unit:

What do you call the people who fly in airplanes? The aviation population.

What is a telephone call asking someone to a party? An invitation conversation.

Each of the words in this unit has four syllables. Remember that a syllable has just one vowel sound. Pronounce each syllable in the Unit words to help you remember to spell each word correctly.

Try to make up your own Rhyme Stymes with the Unit words. The rhyming words you use must have four syllables, and they must have the accent on the same syllable.

Spelling Practice

A. Write the Unit word with each of these suffixes.

1. -or _____

2. -ence _____

3. -ity _____

4. -ly _____

B. Follow the directions using the Unit words.

5. Write the five words that end with *-ion*.

_____ _____ _____

_____ _____

6. Write the three words that end with *ic*.

_____ _____ _____

7. Write the two words that end in vowel-consonant-*e*.

_____ _____

8. Write the five words that end with the sound /ē/ spelled *y*.

_____ _____ _____

_____ _____

9. Write the two words with these vowel sounds together: /ē/ /ā/.

_____ _____

10. Write the four words with these two vowel sounds together: /ē/ /ə/.
Underline the letters that spell the two sounds.

_____ _____

_____ _____

C. The following well-known sayings include Unit words. Write the word
that completes each saying. Capitalize the word you write.

11. _____ is the spice of life.

12. _____ is the mother of invention.

13. _____ is the best teacher.

14. _____ is the sincerest form of flattery.

D. Answer this Rhyme Styme with two Unit words.
What do you call what bears say to each other while talking
in their sleep?

_____ _____

Spelling and Language · Noun Suffixes

UNIT WORDS

UNIT WORDS

invitation
population
necessary
evaporate
patriotic
arithmetic
gymnasium
necessity
material
scientific
petroleum
naturally
imitation
variety
aviator
hibernation
machinery
appreciate
conversation
experience

The suffixes *-ion* and *-ation* are added to some verbs to form nouns.

dedicate   dedication   restore   restoration

Finish each sentence with a noun form of the verb in boldface.

appreciate   1.   We showed our _____ by clapping.

evaporate   2.   Did you notice any _____ of the liquid from the dish?

converse   3.   We can't have a _____ with this noise.

invite   4.   Send Reggie an _____ to the party.

populate   5.   The _____ of our area will double in five years.

Writing on Your Own

Imagine that you have been asked to write a poem for the dedication of a new aviation museum. Use as many of the Unit words as you can. Add the suffixes *-ion* and *-ation* to some verbs to form nouns.

 WRITER'S GUIDE   For a sample poem, turn to page 279.

Using the Dictionary to Spell and Write

Knowing how to pronounce a word can help you remember how to spell a word. In a word with two or more syllables, there may be more than one accented syllable. The syllable that receives the primary stress has a heavy accent mark. The syllable that receives the secondary stress has a light accent mark.

Primary Stress		Secondary Stress

a·vi·a·tor /ā′vē·ā′tər/ *n.* A person who flies airplanes; pilot.

Write the Unit word for each pronunciation. Draw two lines under the syllable that receives primary stress. Draw one line under the syllable with secondary stress.

1.   /sī′ən·tif′ik/   _____

2.   /hī′bər·nā′shən/   _____

3.   /pop′yə·lā′shən/   _____

4.   /pā′trē·ot′ik/   _____

5.   /kon′vər·sā′shən/   _____

 **SPELLING DICTIONARY**   Remember to use your **Spelling Dictionary** when you write.

Harcourt Brace School Publishers

Spelling on Your Own

nouns	verbs	adjectives	adverb

UNIT WORDS

Write the Unit words in four groups according to their parts of speech. There will be three verbs, at least four adjectives, one adverb, and fourteen nouns. Some words can be listed in two groups.

MASTERY WORDS

> dissatisfy
> underwater
> constitution
> experiment
> humidity
> political

Write the Mastery word that has each of these suffixes.

1. -al _____

2. -ment _____

3. -ion _____

4. -ity _____

Write the Mastery word that:

5. begins with the prefix meaning "not." _____

6. is a compound word. _____

Complete each sentence with a Mastery word.

7. The _____ in the jungle is very high.

8. A _____ outlines the rules of a government.

9. The chemist conducted a lab _____ .

BONUS WORDS

> democratic
> independent
> mysterious
> legislature
> intermission
> nomination
> eligible
> artificial

Write the Bonus word that has the same adjective-forming suffix as each of these words.

1. official   **2.** allergic   **3.** suspicious   **4.** divisible

Complete each sentence with a Bonus word.

5. Mr. Chavez accepted the ____ for president.

6. Sandy Doud is ____ for the office of vice president.

Follow the directions. Use Bonus words in your answers.

7. Write the three Bonus words that end with noun-forming suffixes. Then use one of the words in a sentence.

8. Write a paragraph on the importance of voting on Election Day. Use at least three Bonus words.

Review

Follow these steps when you are unsure of how to spell a word.

- **Say** the word. Recall when you have heard the word used. Think about what it means.
- **Look** at the word. Find any prefixes, suffixes, or other word parts you know. Think about other words that are related in meaning and spelling. Try to picture the word in your mind.
- **Spell** the word to yourself. Think about the way each sound is spelled. Notice any unusual spelling.
- **Write** the word while looking at it. Check the way you have formed your letters. If you have not written the word clearly or correctly, write it again.
- **Check** your learning. Cover the word and write it. If you did not spell the word correctly, practice these steps until the word becomes your own.

UNIT 31 **Follow the directions using words from Unit 31.**

UNIT 31
govern
topic
pretend
mature
career
balance
salute
spirit
severe
talent

1. Write the two words that end with *u*-consonant-*e*. Then draw a line between the syllables of each word.

_____   _____

2. Write the word that ends with /k/. _____

3. Write the word that ends with /s/. _____

Write 1 or 2 to show which syllable is accented in each word.

4. career ____   5. pretend ____   6. talent ____   7. spirit ____

Write the base word for each of these words.

8. severity _____   9. government _____

10. maturity _____

Complete these sentences.

11. Shira wants a _____ in theater.

12. Shira used to _____ that she was a great actress.

13. Now that she is more _____, she knows it will take a lot of work.

14. Shira has a lot of _____ for acting, however.

15. She knows how to get into the _____ of a character.

Harcourt Brace School Publishers

UNIT 32 Follow the directions using words from Unit 32.

Write the words that have each of these Greek or Latin roots.

UNIT 32

apartment
television
automobile
report
transportation
automatic
portable
telescope
partial
televise

16. part (two words) _____ _____

17. tele (three words) _____ _____

_____

18. port (three words) _____ _____

_____

19. auto (two words) _____ _____

Complete each sentence below.

20. I saw Halley's comet through my brother's _____ .

21. I had only a _____ view of it, due to clouds.

22. My sister said she would wait and see it on _____ .

23. My brother said the station might not _____ the comet.

UNIT 33 Follow the directions using words from Unit 33.

Write the word that is an antonym for each word below.

UNIT 33

forward
generous
approval
admitted
conclusion
backward
criticism
introduction
permanent
temporary

24. backward _____   25. beginning _____

26. stingy _____   27. criticism _____

28. praise _____   29. forward _____

Write the word that is a synonym for each word below.

30. forever _____   31. confessed _____

32. brief _____   33. beginning _____

Complete each sentence.

34. Our class made a _____ donation to the paper drive.

35. The principal gave her _____ for the drive.

WORDS IN TIME

The word *automobile* first appeared in France around 1890. The Greek root *auto,* meaning "self," was combined with the French word *mobile,* meaning "moving."

UNIT 34
mystery
interest
colonist
determine
capital
property
remainder
industry
circular
athletics

UNIT 34   Follow the directions using words from Unit 34.

36. Write the two words that begin with /k/.

_____   _____

37. Write the three words with the middle syllable *ter.*

_____   _____   _____

38. Write the word that begins with /s/. _____

Write a word to complete each sentence. Then draw a line between the syllables of each word you wrote.

39. Bailey is interested in tennis, running, and other _____.

40. In the _____ of her time, she studies ballet.

41. Bailey's parents take a big _____ in her activities.

42. Bailey's dad works in the dairy products _____.

43. Her mom writes popular _____ books.

44. It's difficult to _____ where Bailey gets her talent.

UNIT 35   Follow the directions using words from Unit 35.

45. Write the five words that begin with vowel sounds. Then draw a line between the syllables of each word you wrote.

_____   _____   _____

_____   _____

46. Write the three words with double consonants.

_____   _____   _____

Write the word that comes from the same word family as each of these words.

47. popular _____   **48.** expert _____

49. science _____

50. necessitate (two words) _____   _____

Write the word that is a synonym for each of these words.

51. fabric _____   **52.** essential _____

Write the word that is the antonym for each of these words.

53. appear _____   **54.** luxury _____

UNIT 35
experience
necessary
population
appreciate
material
invitation
evaporate
arithmetic
necessity
scientific

Harcourt Brace School Publishers

Spelling and Reading
A Letter of Opinion

Read this letter of opinion. Notice how the writer expresses and supports her opinion.

34 Kelly Avenue   **Heading**
Fuller, New York 10701
May 17, 20--

Editor   **Inside**
Fuller News   **Address**
Fuller, New York 10701

Dear Editor: **Greeting**

     It's a mystery to me why the City Commission
decided to build a garage instead of a park on the city's
north side. Here is why I disagree with this decision.   **Body**
     A park would give children a safe place to play.
Adults would appreciate a quiet spot where they could
take a partial break from the hectic pace of the city.
Finally, a park would provide the city with some
necessary natural beauty.
     In conclusion, I urge the City Commission to recon-
sider its decision. The citizens of Fuller need a park —
not a garage!

Yours truly,   **Closing**
Diane Anderson
Diane Anderson   **Signature**

Write your answers to the questions.

1. With what decision does the writer of the letter disagree?

2. Who are the two groups of citizens Diane believes would
appreciate a park?

3. Why does Diane believe that a park is necessary in the city?

4. If you were a member of the City Commission, would you vote
for the garage or the park? Why?

**Underline the review words in your answers. Check to see that
you spelled the words correctly.**

Spelling and Writing
A Letter of Opinion

Harcourt Brace School Publishers

Words to Help You Write

govern
pretend
salute
spirit
report
partial
admitted
approval
conclusion
mystery
interest
determine
experience
necessary
appreciate
scientific

Think and Discuss

As in all persuasive writing, the purpose of a letter of opinion is to convince an audience to share the writer's opinion on an issue. Before writing a letter of opinion, the writer should first know who the audience will be. Who will be the audience of Diane's letter on page 157?

A letter of opinion has the same form as a business letter. It has a **heading, inside address, greeting, body, closing,** and **signature.** The first paragraph in the body of the letter introduces the issue and the writer's opinion about it. The topic sentence of this paragraph explains the writer's opinion. What is the topic sentence in the first paragraph of Diane's letter on page 157? The first paragraph of a letter of opinion might also contain a general statement about the writer's reasons for his or her opinion. What general statement does Diane give for her readers that explains how she will support her opinion?

The other paragraphs in the body of the letter should state a specific reason for the writer's opinion and provide facts to support it. What reasons does Diane give to persuade the city commission that a park should be built instead of a garage?

Look at the last paragraph of Diane's letter. Notice that it contains a statement that summarizes reasons for her opinion. Why might this be an effective way to end a letter of opinion?

Apply

Write a **letter of opinion** to your school newspaper that states your opinion on some issue. Follow the writing guidelines on the next page.

Prewriting

Choose an issue you are concerned about. Decide how you feel about it. Be sure to consider issues related to events at your school.

- Make a two-column chart. Label the columns *Feelings* and *Facts*.
- Fill in your chart with notes about your opinion on the issue and facts that support your opinion.

 THESAURUS For help finding exact words to express and support your opinion, turn to page 205.

Composing

Use your chart to write your letter.

- Identify the issue you want to discuss and express your opinion about.
- Explain the reasons for your opinion. Then offer facts to support your belief.
- In the last paragraph, summarize your stand on the issue.

Revising

- Look over your prewriting chart. Have you left out any points you wanted to make?

Editing

- Make sure you stated your opinion and your reasons for having it.
- Make sure that you have presented the most persuasive facts to support your opinion.
- Check that your letter is clear and convincing to your audience.

 WRITER'S GUIDE For information on the correct form for your letter, turn to page 273.

Proofreading

- Check your spelling and correct any mistakes.
- Check your capitalization and punctuation.

Copy your letter onto clean paper. Write carefully and neatly.

Publishing

Share your letter with your class. Ask your classmates if they agree with you. If they do, ask whether it is because they found your letter convincing. If they do not, ask them to give you at least one reason you did not give that might convince them to support your opinion.

Editing and Proofreading Marks

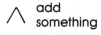

≡	capitalize
⊙	make a period
∧	add something
⋏	add a comma
❛❜	add quotation marks
ℯ	take something away
◯	spell correctly
¶	indent the paragraph
/	make a lowercase letter
tr	transpose

SPELLING DICTIONARY

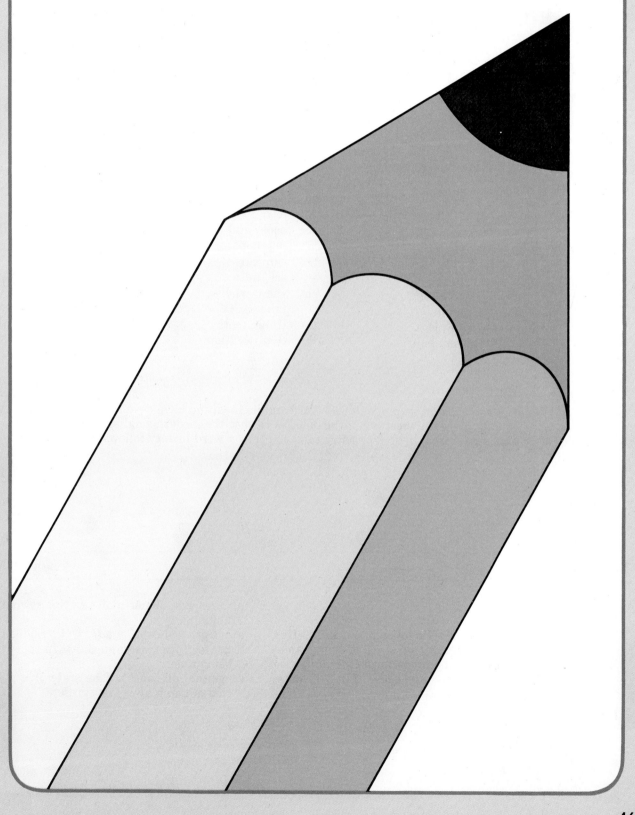

PRONUNCIATION KEY

Remember these things when you read pronunciations:

- When you see parentheses around a sound, it means that the sound is not always pronounced. /mə·shēn′(ə·)rē/
- This mark ′ comes after the syllable you say with the most force. This lighter mark ′ comes after the syllable you say with a little less force. /rek′tang′gəl/

/a/	act, cat	/m/	mother, room	/u/	up, come
/ā/	ate, rain	/n/	new, can	/û/	early, hurt
/â/	care, bear	/ng/	sing, hang	/yo͞o/	mule, few
/ä/	car, father	/o/	on, stop	/v/	very, five
/b/	bed, rub	/ō/	over, go	/w/	will
/ch/	chair, watch	/ô/	or, saw	/y/	yes
/d/	duck, red	/oi/	oil, toy	/z/	zoo, buzz
/e/	egg, hen	/ou/	out, cow	/zh/	treasure
/ē/	even, see	/o͞o/	food, too	/ə/	The schwa
/f/	fish, off	/o͝o/	book, pull		is the sound
/g/	go, big	/p/	pig, hop		these letters
/h/	hat, hit	/r/	ran, car		stand for:
/i/	if, sit	/s/	see, miss		a in ago
/ī/	ice, time	/sh/	show, wish		e in listen
/j/	jump, bridge	/t/	take, feet		i in giraffe
/k/	cat, look	/th/	thing, tooth		o in pilot
/l/	lost, ball	/t͟h/	that, weather		u in circus

Word Histories

A word history explains how a word and its meaning have developed. A word history usually gives the meaning of the older word that the modern English word comes from. This sign ► in a dictionary entry tells you that a word history follows.

ability   absence

A

a·bil·i·ty /ə·bil′ə·tē/ *n., pl.* **a·bil·i·ties**
1 The quality or state of being able; power to do or perform: the *ability* to speak three languages. **2** (*pl.*) Talents. **3** Special natural gift.

ab·nor·mal /ab·nôr′məl/ *adj.* Not normal; unusual.

a·brupt /ə·brupt′/ *adj.* **1** Sudden. **2** Steep. **3** Hasty; quick. **4** In speech, being rude.

ab·sence /ab′səns/ *n.* The state or a period of being away; not present.

Harcourt Brace School Publishers

abuse

album

a·buse /v. ə·byōōz′, n. ə·byōōs′/ v. **a·bused, a·bus·ing,** n. **1** v. To make improper use of; to misuse. **2** n. An improper use; a misuse. **3** v. To treat roughly or cruelly; to mistreat. **4** n. Rough and cruel treatment: This chair can't take any more *abuse*.

ac·cent /n. ak′sent, v. ak′sent or ak·sent′/ **1** n. Greater force used in pronouncing some syllables or words; stress. **2** v. To pronounce with greater force. **3** n. A pronunciation mark showing where stress is located in a word. **4** v. To pronounce or mark the stressed syllables in a word. **5** n. A manner of speaking characteristic of a region or a foreign country.

a·chieve /ə·chēv′/ v. **a·chieved, a·chiev·ing** To accomplish.

ac·quaint /ə·kwānt′/ v. To help someone get to know something or someone.

ac·tion /ak′shən/ n. **1** The act of doing something. **2** Something done.

ac·tiv·i·ty /ak·tiv′ə·tē/ n., pl. **ac·tiv·i·ties** **1** Movement: There was a great deal of *activity* on the field. **2** Something that is done. **3** Work or pastime.

ad·di·tion /ə·dish′ən/ n. **1** The act or process of adding. **2** Something added.

ad·di·tion·al /ə·dish′ən·əl/ adj. Added to; extra: *additional* help.

ad·dress /ə·dres′/ n., pl. **ad·dress·es,** v. **1** n. A speech. **2** v. To deliver a speech. **3** n. /also ad′res/ The writing on an envelope or package that tells where and to whom it is to be sent. **4** v. To write this information on a letter or package: to *address* a letter.

ad·e·quate /ad′ə·kwit/ adj. Enough; sufficient: We had an *adequate* amount of time. —**ad′e·quate·ly** adv.

ad·just /ə·just′/ v. **1** To change something so it fits or matches. **2** To arrange or regulate the order, position, or relation of something for a specific reason: to *adjust* a camera lens. **3** To get used to; to adapt oneself.

ad·just·ment /ə·just′mənt/ n. The process of changing or fixing something to make it fit or work properly.

ad·mit /ad·mit′/ v. **ad·mit·ted, ad·mit·ting** **1** To allow or permit to enter or join: to *admit* to a club. **2** To confess; to acknowledge: to *admit* one is wrong.

a·dopt /ə·dopt′/ v. **1** To become the legal parent of another person's child. **2** adj. use: an *adopted* daughter. **3** To take on or use as one's own. **4** To vote to accept.

a·dore /ə·dôr′/ v. **a·dored, a·dor·ing** **1** To worship. **2** To love and admire greatly: I *adore* my parents. **3** To like very much.

af·fec·tion·ate /ə·fek′shən·it/ adj. Expressing warmth or love: He is a very *affectionate* puppy.

af·ford /ə·fôrd′/ v. **1** To be able to pay for. **2** To be able to manage, spare, or have without difficulty, risk, etc.

a·gainst /ə·genst′/ prep. **1** In the opposite direction of. **2** In contact with. **3** In opposition to.

a·gree /ə·grē′/ v. **a·greed, a·gree·ing** **1** To be willing; to consent. **2** To have the same ideas or opinions.

aid /ād/ **1** v. To help. **2** n. Help. **3** n. A person or thing that helps: a visual *aid* used in teaching.

ail·ment /āl′mənt/ n. An illness of the mind or body: a heart *ailment*.

air·mail /âr′māl′ or er′māl′/ **1** n. Mail carried by airplanes. **2** adj. Having to do with mail sent by airplanes: an *air-mail* letter.

aisle /īl/ n. A passageway between sections of seats, as in a theater.

-al suffix **1** Of or having to do with something: *logical*. **2** The act or process of doing something: *refusal*.

al·bum /al′bəm/ n. **1** A book used for keeping stamps, pictures, etc.: a photograph *album*. **2** A long-playing record or set of records.

Abbreviations

n. = noun;   *pron.* = pronoun;   *v.* = verb;   *adj.* = adjective;   *adv.* = adverb;
prep. = preposition;   *conj.* = conjunction;   *interj.* = interjection

al·gae /al'jē/ *n., pl.* A large group of simple plants that grow in water and damp places and lack true roots, stems, or leaves.

al·ge·bra /al'jə·brə/ *n.* A branch of mathematics that deals with the relations between numbers, and uses letters and other symbols to represent specific numbers.

al·low·ance /ə·lou'əns/ *n.* An amount of money usually given at regular intervals or periods of time: Tom gets a weekly *allowance*.

al·ma·nac /ôl'mə·nak/ *n.* A booklike calendar published every year that gives information about many subjects; a reference book.

al·read·y /ôl·red'ē/ *adv.* Before or by this time.

al·ter /ôl'tər/ *v.* **al·tered, al·ter·ing** To change.

a·mong /ə·mung'/ *prep.* **1** With. **2** One of many. **3** Surrounded by; in the midst of. **4** Between.

a·muse /ə·myōōz'/ *v.* **a·mused, a·mus·ing** To entertain.

a·nat·o·my /ə·nat'ə·mē/ *n., pl.* **a·nat·o·mies** **1** The structure of an animal or plant. **2** The human body; skeleton. **3** The science dealing with the structure of organisms.

an·gle /ang'gəl/ *n., v.* **an·gled, an·gling** **1** *n.* A geometric shape formed by two lines that have the same end point. **2** *v.* To move or turn at an angle. **3** *n.* A point of view.

an·i·mal /an'ə·məl/ **1** *n.* A living being that is not a plant. **2** *n.* Any such creature other than humans. **3** *adj.* Of or having to do with animals.

an·nounce·ment /ə·nouns'mənt/ *n.* A public or formal declaration or notice: The teacher made an *announcement* to the class.

an·noy /ə·noi'/ *v.* **1** To bother; to make slightly angry. **2** *adj. use:* an *annoying* sound.

an·ti·pol·lu·tion /an'ti·pə·lōō'shən/ *adj.* Designed to reduce or eliminate pollution: *antipollution* devices.

a·part /ə·pärt'/ *adv.* **1** In pieces or to pieces: to take a puzzle *apart*. **2** Separated away from each other.

a·part·ment /ə·pärt'mənt/ *n.* A room or set of rooms that make up a dwelling.

a·pol·o·gize /ə·pol'ə·jīz/ *v.* **a·pol·o·gized, a·pol·o·giz·ing** To ask pardon or say one is sorry for a fault, offense, or mistake.

a·pol·o·gy /ə·pol'ə·jē/ *n.* **a·pol·o·gies** Words saying that one is sorry for an offense, fault, or accident.

ap·pear /ə·pir'/ *v.* **ap·peared, ap·pear·ing** **1** To come into sight. **2** To look as if; to seem likely. **3** To come before the public.

ap·pe·tite /ap'ə·tīt/ *n.* **1** A desire for food. **2** Any strong desire or liking.

ap·plaud /ə·plôd'/ *v.* To show approval by clapping hands, cheering, etc.

ap·point /ə·point'/ *v.* **1** To choose, select, or name for a position. **2** To fix or set: to *appoint* a time to meet.

ap·point·ment /ə·point'mənt/ *n.* **1** The act of selecting, choosing, or naming for an office or position not filled by an election. **2** The office or position. **3** A meeting with someone at a certain place and time.

ap·pre·ci·ate /ə·prē′shē·āt/ *v.* **ap·pre·ci·at·ed, ap·pre·ci·at·ing** **1** To recognize the value or quality of something: *appreciate* music. **2** To be thankful or grateful.

ap·prov·al /ə·prōō′vəl/ *n.* **1** Formal permission. **2** A favorable or positive feeling or opinion; praise.

a·quar·i·um /ə·kwâr′ē·əm/ *n., pl.* **a·quar·i·ums** **1** A tank, pond, etc., in which fish, water animals, and water plants are kept. **2** The place where such a collection is exhibited.

ar·e·a /âr′ē·ə/ *n.* **1** Region; section of land. **2** The size of a surface.

a·rith·me·tic /ə·rith′mə·tik/ *n.* The study of numbers in terms of addition, subtraction, multiplication, and division.

ar·range·ment /ə·rānj′mənt/ *n.* **1** A putting or placing in proper order. **2** The way or order in which a person or thing is placed: the *arrangement* of flowers in a vase. **3** (*usually pl.*) Plans; preparations.

ar·ti·fi·cial /är′tə·fish′əl/ *adj.* **1** Made synthetically rather than by nature. **2** Not genuine: an *artificial* smile.

as·sign /ə·sīn′/ *v.* **1** To give something to someone as a responsibility. **2** To put to a task or job.

as·sign·ment /ə·sīn′mənt/ *n.* **1** The act of assigning or giving out to do. **2** Something assigned or given out to be done, as a lesson or project.

as·ton·ish·ment /ə·ston′ish·mənt/ *n.* Great surprise; amazement.

as·tron·o·my /ə·stron′ə·mē/ *n.* The scientific study of the stars, planets, and other heavenly bodies.

ath·let·ics /ath·let′iks/ *n., pl.* Sports and games, as football, baseball, etc.

at·las /at′ləs/ *n.* A book of maps.

at·ten·tion /ə·ten′shən/ *n.* **1** Careful looking or listening. **2** Care or thought; consideration: to give *attention* to one's hygiene.

at·trac·tion /ə·trak′shən/ *n.* **1** The act or power of attracting, causing interest, or drawing someone or something near: magnetic *attraction*. **2** Something that attracts or interests.

auc·tion /ôk′shən/ **1** *n.* A public sale at which things are sold to the highest bidder. **2** *v.* To sell something at an auction.

au·di·to·ri·um /ô′də·tôr′ē·əm/ *n.* A building or large room or hall in which people gather: The meeting was held in the *auditorium*.

au·then·tic /ô·then′tik/ *adj.* Genuine; real.

au·thor /ô′thər/ *n.* A person who writes original stories, books, etc.: William Shakespeare was the *author* of many poems and plays.

au·thor·i·ty /ə·thôr′ə·tē/ *n., pl.* **au·thor·i·ties** **1** The power to command, make decisions, judge, etc. **2** (*usually pl.*) Persons having the legal right to enforce the law. **3** A person with special knowledge.

au·to /ô′tō/ *n., pl.* **au·tos** An automobile.

au·to·bi·og·ra·phy /ô′tə·bī·og′rə·fē/ *n., pl.* **au·to·bi·og·ra·phies** The story of someone's life written by that person.

au·to·graph /ô′tə·graf/ **1** *n.* A person's signature. **2** *v.* To write one's own name.

au·to·mat·ic /ô′tə·mat′ik/ *adj.* **1** Operating by itself, as machinery. **2** Done without conscious thought.

---

act, āte, câre, ärt;   egg, ēven;   if, īce;   on, ōver, ôr;   bŏŏk, fōōd;   up, tûrn;
ə = a in *ago*, e in *listen*, i in *giraffe*, o in *pilot*, u in *circus*;   yōō = u in *music*;   oil;   out;
chair;   sing;   shop;   thank;   that;   zh in *treasure*.

au·to·ma·tion /ô′tə·mā′shən/ *n.* The automatic or self-moving operation or control of a process, machine, etc., by electronic or mechanical means instead of by human beings.

au·to·mo·bile /ô′tə·mə·bēl′/ *n.* A car.

au·to·mo·tive /ô′tə·mō′tiv/ *adj.* Of or for automobiles, trucks, etc.

au·tumn /ô′təm/ *n.* **1** The season of fall. **2** *adj. use: autumn* colors.

a·vail·a·ble /ə·vā′lə·bəl/ *adj.* Readily used or obtained.

av·e·nue /av′ə·n(y)ōō/ *n.* A street, especially a wide one.

av·er·age /av′rij/ *adj., n., v.* **av·er·aged, av·er·ag·ing** **1** *adj.* Typical; common; ordinary: *average* height. **2** *n.* The sum of the elements in a set of numbers divided by the number of elements in the set. **3** *v.* To calculate an average.

a·vi·a·tor /ā′vē·ā′tər/ *n.* A person who flies planes or other aircraft; a pilot.

aw·ful /ô′fəl/ *adj.* Very bad; unpleasant; terrible: an *awful* meal.

ax·le /ak′səl/ *n.* The bar or shaft that goes through the center of a wheel, on or with which a wheel or wheels turn.

B

back·ground /bak′ground′/ *n.* **1** The area or surface upon which things are made or placed. **2** The part of a scene or picture that appears in the distance or toward the back. **3** A person's past experience.

back·ward /bak′wərd/ **1** *adv.* Toward the back. **2** *adv.* With the back facing to the front. **3** *adj.* Directed toward the back: a *backward* glance.

bac·te·ri·a /bak·tir′ē·ə/ *n., pl.* Microscopic organisms that can be helpful or harmful to people.

bal·ance /bal′əns/ *v.* **bal·anced, bal·anc·ing,** *n.* **1** *v.* To keep something in position without letting it fall. **2** *n.* The ability to keep one's body in a certain position without falling.

ban·quet /bang′kwit/ *n.* A large feast.

bar·be·cue /bär′bə·kyōō/ *n., v.* **bar·be·cued, bar·be·cu·ing** **1** *n.* In the United States, a social gathering where food is roasted over an open fire. **2** *n.* A grill or pit used for outdoor cooking. **3** *v.* To roast food over an open fire. **4** *n.* Food cooked with a highly seasoned sauce.

bas·ket·ball /bas′kit·bôl′/ *n.* **1** A large, round ball. **2** A team game played by tossing such a ball into the opponent's basket. **3** *adj. use:* a *basketball* team.

batch /bach/ *n., pl.* **batch·es** **1** A number of things taken together. **2** An amount of something made at one time.

beau·ti·ful /byōō′tə·fəl/ *adj.* Lovely; pretty. —**beau′ti·ful·ly** *adv.*

beg /beg/ *v.* **begged, beg·ging** **1** To ask for charity, as food, money, etc. **2** To ask earnestly.

beg·gar /beg′ər/ A person who lives by begging for food, money, etc.

beige /bāzh/ *n., adj.* Grayish tan color.

be·lieve /bi·lēv′/ *v.* **be·lieved, be·liev·ing** **1** To think or accept something as being real or true. **2** To think or accept as having told the truth. **3** To have faith or trust in. **4** To think or suppose.

ben·e·fi·cial /ben′ə·fish′əl/ *adj.* Useful; helpful; worthwhile.

ben·e·fit /ben′ə·fit/ *n., v.* **ben·e·fit·ed, ben·e·fit·ing** **1** *n.* Advantage; help. **2** *v.* To be helpful to. **3** *v.* To gain from.

bewilder

be·wil·der /bi·wil′dər/ v. To baffle or confuse; to puzzle.

bill·board /bil′bôrd′/ n. A very large outdoor board or sign on which advertisements are printed.

bind /bīnd/ v. **bound, bind·ing** 1 To tie. 2 To fasten in a cover. 3 To hold or unite by a promise, duty, etc.

bleak /blēk/ adj. **bleak·er, bleak·est** 1 Cold and piercing; chilly. 2 Gloomy.

blis·ter /blis′tər/ 1 n. A small swelling on the skin filled with watery matter. 2 v. To raise or develop a blister.

blow /blō/ v. **blew, blown, blow·ing** 1 To move with force. 2 To push by blowing. 3 To send air out through the mouth. 4 To make a sound by blowing. 5 To clear by blowing.

bor·row /bor′ō or bôr′ō/ v. To take something with the promise to return it. **—borrow trouble** To worry before there is a problem.

boss·y /bôs′ē or bos′ē/ adj. **boss·i·er, boss·i·est** Tending to be a boss or tell others what to do; domineering.

bound /bound/ 1 v. Past tense and past participle of *bind.* 2 adj. Having a cover or binding: a *bound* book. 3 adj. Certain. 4 adj. Determined.

bound·a·ry /boun′də·rē or boun′drē/ n., pl. **bound·a·ries** Something that indicates an outer limit or edge.

bowl·ing /bō′ling/ n. A game in which balls are rolled down a wooden alley in an attempt to knock down ten bottle-shaped wooden pins at the other end.

boy·cott /boi′kot/ 1 v. To refuse to buy from, sell to, or associate with. 2 n. An act of boycotting.

brain /brān/ n. The part of the central nervous system, located in the skull of humans and other vertebrate animals, that controls and coordinates mental and physical actions.

brain·storm /brān′stôrm′/ n. A sudden bright idea or inspiration.

branch /branch/ n., pl. **branch·es** A woody part of a tree growing out from the trunk.

brave /brāv/ adj. **brav·er, brav·est** Courageous; not afraid.

breathe /brēth/ v. **breathed, breath·ing** 1 To draw air in and let it out through the mouth or nose. 2 To live or be alive. 3 To whisper.

brief /brēf/ adj. 1 Not lasting a long time; short. 2 Using few words.

bril·liant /bril′yənt/ adj. 1 Shining brightly; glowing; sparkling. 2 Demonstrating great intelligence, skill, or talent: a *brilliant* lawyer. 3 Splendid: a *brilliant* performance.

bris·tle /bris′(ə)l/ n., v. **bris·tled, bris·tling** 1 n. One of the stiff hairs found on a hog's back. 2 n. Anything made with stiff hairs. 3 v. To have the bristles stand up straight, as in anger.

broad /brôd/ adj. 1 Wide. 2 Open and clear. 3 Having wide range; extensive. 4 Not narrow or limited; liberal. 5 Not detailed; general.

bron·co /brong′kō/ n., pl. **bron·cos** A small, wild or partly broken horse of western U.S.

bronze /bronz/ 1 n. A hard, reddish-brown metal made by mixing copper and tin. 2 adj. use: a *bronze* statue. 3 n., adj. Reddish-brown in color.

broth /brôth or broth/ n. A thin soup made by boiling meat, fish, vegetables, etc., in water and then straining.

browse /brouz/ v. **browsed, brows·ing** To look around or to look through.

browse

act, āte, câre, ärt;   egg, ēven;   if, īce;   on, ōver, ôr;   bŏŏk, fōod;   up, tûrn;
ə = a in *ago,* e in *listen,* i in *giraffe,* o in *pilot,* u in *circus;*   yōō = u in *music;*   oil;   out;
ch in *chair;* sing; shop; thank; that; zh in *treasure.*

budge /buj/ *v.* **budged, budg·ing** To move even slightly or a little.

bulb /bulb/ *n.* **1** The ball-shaped part of a plant from which leaves and roots grow. **2** Any object with this shape: electric light *bulb*.

bul·let /bŏŏl′it/ *n.* A cone-shaped piece of metal that can be fired from a gun.

bur·glar /bûr′glər/ *n.* A person who breaks into a building to steal.

bur·ro /bûr′ō/ *n., pl.* **bur·ros** A small donkey, used for riding or for carrying packs.

burst /bûrst/ *v.* **burst, burst·ing,** *n.* **1** *v.* To break apart suddenly. **2** *v.* To break out: to *burst* into tears. **3** *n.* A sudden outbreak. **4** *v.* To appear suddenly.

c

cab·bage /kab′ij/ *n.* A vegetable with folded leaves that form a round head.

cab·in /kab′in/ *n.* **1** A small house made of wood. **2** A room equipped for sleeping on a ship.

cab·i·net /kab′ə·nit/ *n.* **1** A piece of furniture, usually with shelves and doors. **2** (*sometimes written* **Cabinet**) A group of official advisers chosen by the head of state to lead different departments of a government.

calm /käm/ **1** *adj.* Quiet; still; peaceful. **2** *n.* Quietness; stillness. **3** *v.* To make quiet: to *calm* a crying child.

cam·paign /kam·pān′/ **1** *n.* An organized series of events or activities aimed at achieving some particular result: a presidential *campaign*. **2** *v.* To participate in a campaign.

ca·pac·i·ty /kə·pas′ə·tē/ *n., pl.* **ca·pac·i·ties** **1** The amount of room or space inside. **2** The largest amount that can be contained, held, or done: The bus was filled to *capacity*. **3** Ability or skill to learn or do.

cap·i·tal /kap′ə·təl/ *n.* **1** The city or town where the government of a country or state is located. **2** *adj. use:* a *capital* city. **3** A capital letter.

ca·reer /kə·rir′/ *n.* A person's lifework; profession: a *career* in law.

care·free /kâr′frē′/ *adj.* Without worries; happy: a *carefree* day.

care·ful /kâr′fəl/ *adj.* Cautious; done with care or effort —**care′ful·ly** *adv.*

care·less /kâr′lis/ *adj.* Reckless; done without care or effort.

car·go /kär′gō/ *n., pl.* **car·goes** The freight carried by a ship, train, etc. *Alternate plural:* **cargos.**

car·pen·try /kär′pən·trē/ *n.* The trade or work of a carpenter, a person who builds and repairs the wooden parts of houses, buildings, etc.

cause /kôz/ *n., v.* **caused, caus·ing** **1** *n.* A person or thing that makes something occur. **2** *v.* To make something happen; to bring about. **3** *n.* A reason for action.

cau·tion /kô′shən/ **1** *n.* Great care to avoid accidents, harm, etc.; watchfulness. **2** *n.* A warning. **3** *v.* To warn; to urge to be careful.

cease /sēs/ *v.* **ceased, ceas·ing** To come to an end or put an end to; to stop.

ce·dar /sē′dər/ *n.* **1** A large, broad evergreen tree related to the pine family, with a fragrant, durable, reddish wood. **2** The wood of this tree. **3** *adj. use:* a *cedar* closet.

ceil·ing /sē′ling/ *n.* The top of a room as seen from inside the room.

cel·e·bra·tion /sel′ə·brā′shən/ *n.* **1** Special activities held to express joy, honor, or respect for a particular person, event, time, or day. **2** The act of celebrating.

ce·ment /si·ment′/ **1** *n.* A substance made from limestone and clay burned together. **2** *n.* This substance mixed with water and sand or gravel, used in making concrete. **3** *n.* Any gluelike substance that will bind or glue objects together. **4** *v.* To join or bind with or as if with cement.

center

circular

cen·ter /sen′tər/   **1** *n.* The middle.   **2** *v.* To put or place in or at the middle. **3** *n.* The main point of interest or attraction.   **4** *v.* To concentrate or direct toward one place.

cen·tu·ry /sen′chə·rē/ *n., pl.* **cen·tu·ries** A period of 100 years that begins on a particular date.

cer·e·mo·ny /ser′ə·mō′nē/ *n., pl.* **cer·e·mo·nies** A formal service or series of actions performed in a certain manner.

chalk /chôk/ *n.*   **1** A soft, white or gray limestone, made up largely of very small seashells.   **2** A substance made from this or a similar matter, used for writing or drawing on a chalkboard.

chap·ter /chap′tər/ *n.*   **1** A main division of a book, usually numbered and often having a title.   **2** An important portion or division of anything: a *chapter* in your life.   **3** A branch or division of a society, etc.

charge /chärj/ *v.* **charged, charg·ing,** *n.* **1** *v.* To ask for as a price.   **2** *n.* Cost. **3** *v.* To buy something and pay for it later.   **4** *v.* To attack or run toward suddenly: The lion *charged* its prey.   **5** *v.* To accuse.

char·i·ty /char′ə·tē/ *n., pl.* **char·i·ties** **1** Good will and love toward others. **2** Kindness in judging people's faults. **3** The giving of help to the poor, sick, or helpless.   **4** An organization or fund for helping those in need.

chess /ches/ *n.* A game of skill played on a board by two players. Each player has sixteen pieces including one king. The object of the game is to checkmate, or trap, the other player's king.

chief /chēf/   **1** *n.* A person highest in command or authority.   **2** *adj.* Possessing the highest command or authority. **3** *adj.* Most important: Jill's *chief* concern is passing her history test.

child·ish /chīl′dish/ *adj.*   **1** Of, like, or proper for a child.   **2** Not suitable for an adult; foolish; silly: *childish* behavior. —**child′ish·ly** *adv.*

choice /chois/   **1** The act of choosing; selection.   **2** The person or thing picked or chosen.   **3** A variety of things from which to choose: This paint store offers a wide *choice* of colors.

chop /chop/ *v.* **chopped, chop·ping** **1** To cut with a sharp tool, as a saw or ax.   **2** To cut into small pieces: The chef used a special knife to *chop* vegetables for the stew.

chord /kôrd/ *n.* A combination of three or more musical notes sounded together.

chore /chôr/ *n.*   **1** A job or task: Taking out the garbage is Daniel's only *chore.*   **2** An unpleasant or disagreeable thing to do.

chow·der /chou′dər/ *n.* A thick soup or stew, made with vegetables, clams or fish, and often milk.

cir·cu·lar /sûr′kyə·lər/   **1** *adj.* Having the shape of or moving in a circle. **2** *n.* A notice or advertisement distributed to many people.

---

act, āte, câre, ärt;   egg, ēven;   if, īce;   on, ōver, ôr;   bŏŏk, fŏŏd;   up, tûrn;

ə = a in *ago*, e in *listen*, i in *giraffe*, o in *pilot*, u in *circus*;   yōō = u in *music*;   oil;   out;

chair;   sing;   shop;   thank;   that;   zh in *treasure.*

cir·cu·la·tion /sûr'kyə·lā'shən/ *n.* **1** A moving around or through of something back to where it started. **2** The continuous movement of the blood through the body. **3** The passage of anything from one person or place to another.

cit·i·zen /sit'ə·zən/ *n.* A person who is a native of a particular country or becomes a member of a country by passing a special test.

claim /klām/ *v.* **1** To demand what is one's own or one's right. **2** To state something that one thinks is true.

clin·ic /klin'ik/ *n.* A facility, sometimes attached to a hospital, where medical or psychological treatment is provided.

coach /kōch/ **1** *n.* A teacher of those who play sports. **2** *n.* A teacher of acting, dancing, or singing. **3** *v.* To teach.

coarse /kôrs/ *adj.* **coars·er, coars·est** Rough; not fine or smooth: *coarse* salt.

coast /kōst/ **1** *n.* Land by or near the ocean. **2** *v.* To ride or slide down a slope with little or no effort.

coil /koil/ **1** *n.* Anything formed by winding or twisting around and around in a circular or spiral shape. **2** *v.* To wind into a coil.

cold /kōld/ *adj.* **cold·er, cold·est** **1** Having a low temperature; lacking warmth. **2** *n.* The lack of heat. **3** *adj.* Feeling chilled. **4** *adj.* Lacking the usual heat: Eat your dinner before it gets *cold.* **5** *adj.* Lacking friendly affection. **6** *n.* A mild illness.

col·i·se·um /kol'ə·sē'əm/ *n.* **1** A large building or stadium used for public entertainment, such as exhibitions, sports, events, etc. **2** (*written* **Coliseum**) A spelling of *Colosseum,* a stadium in Rome built in A.D. 69-80.

col·lar /kol'ər/ *n.* **1** A fold of cloth that goes around one's neck. **2** A band put on an animal's neck.

col·o·nist /kol'ə·nist/ *n.* A person who begins, settles, or lives in a colony.

col·umn /kol'əm/ *n.* **1** A vertical post shaped like a cylinder and used for support or decoration in a building. **2** Something shaped like a column. **3** A long, narrow section of a page, set off from the rest of the text on a page. **4** A feature article in a newspaper or magazine, usually written by one person, that appears regularly.

com- *prefix* With or together: *compound.* Used before words beginning with *b, m,* or *p.*

com·bine /kəm·bīn'/ *v.* **com·bined, com·bin·ing** To bring or come together; to unite. —**com'bi·na'tion** *n.*

com·e·dy /kom'ə·dē/ *n., pl.* **com·e·dies** **1** A play, movie, or TV show that is humorous or has a happy ending. **2** Any experience that is amusing or humorous.

com·fort /kum'fərt/ **1** *v.* To make someone feel better, especially in a time of trouble or sorrow. **2** *n.* Anything that eases trouble or sorrow.

com·mon /kom'ən/ *adj.* **1** Usual; ordinary. **2** Widespread; general. **3** Belonging to or shared by all: This park is for *common* use. **4** Of, for, from, by, or to all: the *common* good. **5** *n.* An area of land that is public property, a park.

com·mo·tion /kə·mō'shən/ *n.* Great confusion or excitement; disturbance.

com·mu·ni·ty /kə·myōō'nə·tē/ *n., pl.* **com·mu·ni·ties** **1** A group of people living together in one area. **2** The public.

com·mut·er /kə·myōō'tər/ *n.* A person who travels a long distance to and from work.

com·pan·ion /kəm·pan'yən/ *n.* A person who goes with or accompanies someone else; one who shares in what another is doing.

com·part·ment /kəm·pärt'mənt/ *n.* A separate section of an enclosed area.

competition

contain

com·pe·ti·tion /kom′pə·tish′ən/ *n.* **1** The effort to do better than others. **2** A contest between two or more people.

com·plain /kəm·plān′/ *v.* **1** To find fault with; to grumble. **2** To report something wrong to a person in authority. **3** To talk about one's troubles or pain.

com·pli·cate /kom′plə·kāt/ *v.* **com·pli·cat·ed, com·pli·cat·ing** To make more difficult or complex.

com·pute /kəm·pyo͞ot′/ *v.* **com·put·ed, com·put·ing** To figure or calculate by using mathematics.

com·put·er /kəm·pyo͞o′tər/ *n.* An electronic machine that can solve problems when given certain coded information and can store and recall this information for future use.

con- *prefix* Form of *com-* (meaning "with or together"): *condense.*

con·ceal /kən·sēl′/ *v.* To hide; to keep secret.

con·ceit·ed /kən·sē′tid/ *adj.* Having a high opinion of oneself; vain.

con·cern /kən·sûrn′/ **1** *v.* To have to do with. **2** *n.* Anything that has to do with someone or something. **3** *v.* To be interested in. **4** *v.* To worry. **5** *n.* Something important. **6** *n.* A worry.

con·clu·sion /kən·klo͞o′zhən/ *n.* **1** The close, end, or completion of something. **2** A closing part, as the final remarks in a speech. **3** The result of an act or process; outcome. **4** An opinion or judgment arrived at by reasoning.

con·demn /kən·dem′/ *v.* **1** To judge as being wrong. **2** To convict or sentence to punishment. **3.** To declare unfit or unsafe for use or service: The inspector *condemned* the building.

con·di·tion /kən·dish′ən/ *n.* **1** The state in which a person or thing is. **2** Good health. **3** A requirement.

con·duct /*n.* kon′dukt, *v.* kən·dukt′/ **1** *n.* Personal behavior; way of acting. **2** *v.* To act or behave oneself. **3** *v.* To direct or manage an action. **4** *v.* To direct, guide, or lead. **5** *v.* To serve as a channel, as for electricity.

con·duc·tor /kən·duk′tər/ *n.* **1** A person who conducts; leader; guide. **2** A person in charge of a train, streetcar, or bus. **3** The director of an orchestra, chorus, etc.

con·fer·ence /kon′fər·əns *or* kon′frəns/ *n.* A meeting held for discussion or consultation on a particular subject: My parents had a *conference* with my teachers.

con·fess /kən·fes′/ *v.* **con·fessed, con·fess·ing** To admit or acknowledge guilt, love, shame, etc.

con·fes·sion /kən·fesh′ən/ *n.* **1** The act of admitting something, especially faults or guilt. **2** That which is admitted or confessed.

con·fide /kən·fīd′/ *v.* **con·fid·ed, con·fid·ing** **1** To tell something in trust or confidence; to share a secret: Sarah *confided* her fear to Jim. **2** To have trust or place confidence. —**con′fi·dence** *n.*

con·fine /kən·fīn′/ *v.* **con·fined, con·fin·ing** To keep from going out; to limit: She was *confined* to bed.

con·fu·sion /kən·fyo͞o′zhən/ *n.* A mixed-up state of mind or things: Moving turned into a day of *confusion.*

con·ser·va·tion /kon′sər·vā′shən/ *n.* The act of protecting or preserving from loss, injury, decay, or waste.

con·sti·tu·tion /kon′stə·t(y)o͞o′shən/ *n.* **1** The basic laws by which a country is governed. **2** (*written* **the Constitution**) The basic law of the United States.

con·sult /kən·sult′/ *v.* To turn to or seek information, advice, or aid from: to *consult* a map. —**con′sul·ta′tion** *n.*

con·sum·er /kən·so͞o′mər/ *n.* A person who uses goods and services.

con·tain /kən·tān′/ *v.* **1** To have inside; to include or hold. **2** To be able to hold. **3** To control or restrain.

---

act, āte, câre, ärt;   egg, ēven;   if, īce;   on, ōver, ôr;   bo͝ok, fo͞od;   up, tûrn;
ə = **a** in *ago,* **e** in *listen,* **i** in *giraffe,* **o** in *pilot,* **u** in *circus;*   **yo͞o** = **u** in *music;*   oil;   out;
chair; si**ng**; **sh**op; **th**ank; **th**at; **zh** in *treasure.*

contract

curious

con·tract /n. kon′trakt, v. kən·trakt′ *or in def.* 2 kon′trakt/ **1** *n.* A binding agreement between two or more people, usually a written one. **2** *v.* To form an agreement. **3** *v.* To get, acquire, or catch: to *contract* a cold. **4** *v.* To draw or pull together; to shrink or become smaller.

con·tra·dict /kon′trə·dikt′/ *v.* **1** To say the opposite of. **2** To be the opposite of or contrary to.

con·trib·ute /kən·trib′yoot/ *v.* **con·trib·ut·ed, con·trib·ut·ing** To join others in giving money or help to some cause; to donate. —**con·trib′u·tor** *n.*

con·ver·sa·tion /kon′vər·sā′shən/ *n.* An informal discussion; a talk.

cord /kôrd/ *n.* **1** A rope or string made of several strands twisted or braided together. **2** A pair of insulated wires used to connect an appliance, etc., to an electric outlet: a telephone *cord*.

cor·dial /kôr′jəl/ *adj.* Friendly; warm.

cor·du·roy /kôr′də·roi/ *n., pl.* **cor·du·roys** **1** A strong cloth with velvety stripes or ridges close together on one side. **2** (*pl.*) A pair of pants made of corduroy.

cor·rec·tion /kə·rek′shən/ *n.* **1** The act of correcting or making right. **2** A change made or suggested to correct an error or make an improvement.

cor·ri·dor /kôr′ə·dər/ *n.* A long hallway with rooms opening onto it.

count /kount/ *v.* **count·ed, count·ing** **1** *v.* To total; to add up. **2** *v.* To name numbers in order. **3** *v.* To be sure of.

coun·ter /koun′tər/ *n.* A long table on which things are put.

cour·age /kûr′ij/ *n.* Bravery.

court /kôrt/ *n.* **1** An open area enclosed by buildings or walls. **2** An area marked off for a game: a basketball *court*. **3** A palace. **4** Those who serve a king or queen or other ruler. **5** A place where law cases are tried.

cour·te·ous /kûr′tē·əs/ *adj.* Considerate; respectful; polite.

cour·te·sy /kûr′tə·sē/ *n., pl.* **cour·te·sies** Polite manners; consideration for other people.

cow·er /kou′ər/ *v.* To crouch, as in fear, pain, etc.; to tremble.

cream·y /krē′mē/ *adj.* **cream·i·er, cream·i·est** **1** Full of cream. **2** Like cream; smooth, soft, and rich in consistency, appearance, etc.

cre·ate /krē·āt′/ *v.* **cre·at·ed, cre·at·ing** **1** To bring into being or existence; to make. **2** To be the cause of or to cause.

cre·a·tive /krē·ā′tiv/ *adj.* **1** Having the ability or power to bring into existence, originate, or make. **2** Resulting from originality of thought, expression, etc.: *creative* thinking.

crit·i·cism /krit′ə·siz′əm/ *n.* **1** The making of judgments or opinions. **2** Unfavorable comments or judgments; the pointing out of faults.

cru·el /kroo′əl/ *adj.* **1** Willing to give pain to others. **2** Showing a mean disposition. **3** Causing or resulting in pain and suffering: a *cruel* winter.

crumb /krum/ *n.* **1** A small piece of bread or cake. **2** A bit or scrap.

crum·ple /krum′pəl/ *v.* **crum·pled, crum·pling** To crush something so as to form wrinkles: to *crumple* paper.

cube /kyoob/ *n.* A solid object with six equal square sides: an ice *cube*.

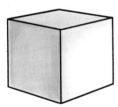

curb /kûrb/ **1** *v.* To control or restrain. **2** *n.* The raised edge of a sidewalk.

cure /kyoor/ *v.* **cured, cur·ing,** *n.* **1** *v.* To make well; to restore to good health. **2** *v.* To get rid of: to *cure* a cold. **3** *n.* Something that cures, as a medicine or treatment; a remedy.

cu·ri·os·i·ty /kyoor′ē·os′ə·tē/ *n., pl.* **cu·ri·os·i·ties** **1** An eager desire to know or find out. **2** Too much interest in other people's affairs. **3** A strange, rare, or unusual object.

cu·ri·ous /kyoor′ē·əs/ *adj.* **1** Eager to learn. **2** Unusual; odd; strange.

cylinder

cy·lin·der /sil′in·dər/ *n.* **1** A geometric figure bounded by two circles and the parallel surfaces that connect them. **2** Any object having this shape.

D

dam·age /dam′ij/ *n., v.* **dam·aged, dam·ag·ing** **1** *n.* Harm or injury. **2** *v.* To do or cause damage.

damp /damp/ *adj.* Slightly wet; moist.

dan·ger·ous /dān′jər·əs/ *adj.* Not safe.

daugh·ter /dô′tər/ *n.* A female child.

dawn /dôn/ **1** *n.* The first appearance of light in the morning. **2** *v.* To begin to grow light in the morning. **3** *n.* A beginning. **4** *v.* To begin to grow clear to the mind: It *dawned* on me that I had forgotten to return the book to Frank.

de- *prefix* Away, or off: *detour.*

de·ceive /di·sēv′/ *v.* **de·ceived, de·ceiv·ing** To trick into accepting something as true that is not true.

dec·i·mal /des′ə·məl/ **1** *n.* A fraction whose denominator is ten or a multiple of ten, as .04 = 4/100, .28 = 28/100. **2** *adj.* Of or based on the number 10.

de·ci·sion /di·sizh′ən/ *n.* **1** A making up of one's mind. **2** A judgment reached or given.

dec·o·rate /dek′ə·rāt/ *v.* **dec·o·rat·ed, dec·o·rat·ing** **1** To make something beautiful; to trim: to *decorate* a tree. **2** To paint, paper, or add new furniture to a room, house, etc.

dec·o·ra·tion /dek′ə·rā′shən/ *n.* **1** The act of decorating or making fancy or attractive by adding ornaments. **2** Things used to decorate; ornaments.

de·crease /*v.* di·krēs′, *n.* dē′krēs *or* di·krēs′/ *v.* **de·creased, de·creas·ing,** *n.* **1** *v.* To make or become less: to *decrease* the amount of salt in a recipe; Their influence *decreased.* **2** *n.* A lessening; reduction: a *decrease* in population. **—de·creas′ing·ly** *adv.*

depend

ded·i·cate /ded′ə·kāt/ *v.* **ded·i·cat·ed, ded·i·cat·ing** **1** To set apart for a special purpose; to devote. **2** To write or state publicly that one has written a book, song, etc., as a sign of affection, respect, or gratitude for a person named.

def·i·nite /def′ə·nit/ *adj.* **1** Having specific limits. **2** Not vague; known for certain; exact: a *definite* answer.

def·i·ni·tion /def′ə·nish′ən/ *n.* A statement that gives the meaning of a word.

del·i·cate /del′ə·kit/ *adj.* **1** Fine or fragile in design or structure. **2** Pleasing in taste, smell, or color; mild or soft. **3** Easily hurt or injured: a *delicate* child. **4** Sensitive; responding quickly to slight changes. **5** Requiring careful treatment, skill, or tact: a *delicate* question.

de·li·cious /di·lish′əs/ *adj.* Tasty; very good: a *delicious* meal.

de·liv·er /di·liv′ər/ *v.* **de·liv·ered, de·liv·er·ing** **1** To hand over; to give to: to *deliver* a package. **2** To carry and give out; to distribute: to *deliver* mail. **3** To speak or give forth in words.

dem·o·crat·ic /dem′ə·krat′ik/ *adj.* **1** Of or relating to a political system in which power is held by the people. **2** Treating all people as equals.

de·nom·i·na·tor /di·nom′ə·nā′tər/ *n.* The bottom or second number in a fraction, as 3 in $\frac{2}{3}$ or 2/3. It is the number by which the numerator is divided.

de·par·ture /di·pär′chər/ *n.* A going away; a leaving.

de·pend /di·pend′/ *v.* To put trust in; to rely on. **—de·pend′a·ble** *adj.*

---

act, āte, câre, ärt;　　egg, ēven;　　if, īce;　　on, ōver, ôr;　　bŏŏk, fōod;　　up, tûrn;
ə = a in *ago*, e in *listen*, i in *giraffe*, o in *pilot*, u in *circus*;　　yōō = u in *music*;　　oil;　　out;
chair; sing; shop; thank; that; zh in *treasure.*

de·pos·it /di·poz′it/ *n., v.* **de·pos·it·ed, de·pos·it·ing** **1** *v.* To put or set down. **2** *n.* A store of minerals. **3** *v.* To put money into a bank. **4** *n.* Money put into a bank. **5** *n.* Money given as a partial payment.

depth /depth/ *n.* **1** How deep something is. **2** The distance from front to back.

de·serve /di·zûrv′/ *v.* **de·served, de·serv·ing** To be worthy of; to merit.

de·sign /di·zīn′/ **1** *n.* A plan or sketch used as a pattern for making something. **2** *v.* To plan, work out, or sketch a pattern for making something. **3** *n.* A decorative pattern.

des·ti·na·tion /des′tə·nā′shən/ *n.* The place to which someone or something is going or is being sent.

de·tail /di·tāl′ *or* dē′tāl/ *n., v.* **de·tailed, de·tail·ing** **1** *n.* A small or unimportant part of something. **2** *n.* A dealing with small things one by one. **3** *v.* To tell item by item about something.

de·ter·mine /di·tûr′min/ *v.* **de·ter·mined, de·ter·min·ing** **1** To decide very firmly. **2** To settle or come to a decision. **3** To find out: I used a map to *determine* the best route.

de·vel·op·ment /di·vel′əp·mənt/ *n.* **1** The process of growing larger or better; growth. **2** The outcome or result of such growth. **3** An outcome; a new event. **4** The planning or working out of something in greater and greater detail. **5** A group of similar houses or apartment buildings built on an area of open land.

de·vour /di·vour′/ *v.* **1** To eat or consume hurriedly. **2** To destroy.

di·ag·o·nal /dī·ag′ə·nəl/ *adj.* Extending in a slanting direction from one edge of a solid figure to an opposite edge.

di·a·gram /dī′ə·gram/ *n., v.* **di·a·gramed, di·a·gram·ing** **1** *n.* A line drawing that shows or explains the parts, operation, etc., of something; illustration. **2** *v.* To make such an outline or drawing. *Alternate spellings:* **diagrammed, diagramming.**

di·am·e·ter /dī·am′ə·tər/ *n.* **1** A line segment joining two points on a circle and

passing through the center of the circle. **2** The measure of this line segment.

dic·tate /dik′tāt/ *v.* **dic·tat·ed, dic·tat·ing** **1** To say something aloud for a person to write or for a machine to record. **2** To give orders.

di·et /dī′ət/ **1** *n.* The foods a person or animal regularly eats. **2** *n.* A special selection of foods prescribed for health reasons, etc. **3** *v.* To eat foods according to a special diet.

di·ges·tion /di·jes′chən *or* dī·jes′chən/ *n.* The breaking down of food in the mouth, stomach, and intestines into a form that can be used by the body.

di·ges·tive /di·jes′tiv *or* dī·jes′tiv/ *adj.* Having to do with the process of changing food chemically into a form that can be used by the body.

di·rec·tor /di·rek′tər *or* dī·rek′tər/ *n.* **1** A person who directs or is in charge, as one in charge of the production of a play or movie. **2** One of a group of people selected to direct or manage the operation of a corporation or club.

dis·as·ter /di·zas′tər/ *n.* An event causing great distress or damage.

dis·count /dis′kount/ **1** *n.* An amount subtracted from the price. **2** *v.* To subtract a part of the cost.

dis·ease /di·zēz′/ *n.* An illness.

dis·guise /dis·gīz′/ *v.* **dis·guised, dis·guis·ing,** *n.* **1** *v.* To change in appearance or manner so as not to be recognized. **2** *n.* Something that disguises, as a costume or mask. **3** *v.* To hide or conceal.

dis·loy·al /dis·loi′əl/ *adj.* Not loyal, faithful, or trustworthy.

dis·pen·ser /dis·pen′sər/ *n.* A person or thing that dispenses, or gives out.

Harcourt Brace School Publishers

disposal

dis·po·sal /dis·pō′zəl/ *n.* A getting rid of something, as by throwing away, etc.

dis·sat·is·fy /dis·sat′is·fī/ *v.* **dis·sat·is·fied, dis·sat·is·fy·ing** To fail to satisfy or please.

dis·trac·tion /dis·trak′shən/ *n.* The act of distracting or diverting; that which draws away or diverts attention.

di·vide /di·vīd′/ *v.* **di·vid·ed, di·vid·ing** 1 To split or separate into parts or groups. 2 To separate numbers into equal parts. 3 To cause to be separated. 4 To distribute.

div·i·dend /div′ə·dend/ *n.* In mathematics, a number that is divided by another number.

di·vi·sion /di·vizh′ən/ *n.* 1 The act of dividing. 2 A sharing or dividing into parts. 3 In math, the dividing of one number by another. 4 Something that divides, as a boundary line or partition. —**di·vi′sion·al** *adj.*

dock /dok/ 1 *n.* A platform built on the shore or out from the shore where ships or boats load, unload, etc.; wharf; pier. 2 *v.* To bring or come into a dock.

dodge /doj/ *v.* **dodged, dodg·ing,** *n.* 1 *v.* To move quickly to get out of the way. 2 *v.* To avoid by using tricks. 3 *n.* A trick used to avoid or deceive.

dom·i·no /dom′ə·nō/ *n., pl.* **dom·i·noes** 1 A small, flat, rectangular piece of wood, plastic, etc., that is either blank or marked with dots. 2 (*pl., used with a singular verb*) A game played with these pieces where players try to match pieces having the same number of dots. *Alternate plural:* **dominos.**

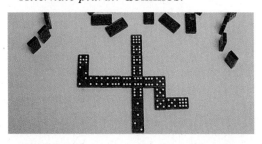

electricity

dou·ble /dub′əl/ *adj., v.* **dou·bled, dou·bling,** *n., adv.* 1 *adj.* Twice as large, as many, or as much: a *double* portion; *double* fare. 2 *v.* To make or become twice as much or as great.

doubt·ful /dout′fəl/ *adj.* Unsure.

drench /drench/ *v.* **drenched, drench·ing** To wet completely; to soak.

drown /droun/ *v.* 1 To die or kill by suffocating with water or another liquid. 2 To cover or wet with a liquid. 3 To keep from being heard.

drow·sy /drou′zē/ *adj.* **drow·si·er, drow·si·est** Sleepy.

E

ear·ly /ûr′lē/ *adj.* **ear·li·er, ear·li·est,** *adv.* 1 *adj.* Happening near the beginning. 2 *adv.* At or near the beginning. 3 *adv., adj.* Before the usual time.

earn /ûrn/ *v.* 1 To receive in return for work or service; to be paid. 2 To gain through effort; to deserve.

earth·quake /ûrth′kwāk′/ *n.* A shaking or vibration of the earth's surface.

eas·i·ly /ē′zə·lē/ *adv.* 1 Without a great deal of effort or difficulty. 2 Without a doubt; by far.

eas·y /ē′zē/ *adj.* **eas·i·er, eas·i·est** 1 Not difficult. 2 Not strict.

eaves·drop /ēvz′drop′/ *v.* **eaves·dropped, eaves·drop·ping** To listen in on a conversation secretly.

ech·o /ek′ō/ *n., pl.* **ech·oes,** *v.* **ech·oed, ech·o·ing** 1 *n.* The repetition of a sound caused by sound waves striking an object and bouncing back. 2 *v.* To sound again or be repeated. 3 *v.* To be sounded again like an echo.

e·col·o·gy /i·kol′ə·jē *or* ē·kol′ə·jē/ *n.* The study of the relationships between living things and their environment.

e·lec·tric·i·ty /i·lek′tris′ə·tē/ *n.* 1 A form of energy that can produce light, heat, motion, and magnetic force. 2 Electric current.

---

act, āte, câre, ärt; egg, ēven; if, īce; on, ōver, ôr; bŏŏk, fo͞od; up, tûrn;
ə = a in *ago*, e in *listen*, i in *giraffe*, o in *pilot*, u in *circus*; yo͞o = u in *music*; oil; out;
chair; sing; shop; thank; that; zh in *treasure*.

el·e·phant /el′ə·fənt/ *n.* The largest of all land animals, having a very long trunk and two ivory tusks.

el·e·va·tor /el′ə·vā′tər/ *n.* A moving platform, cage, or enclosed room that carries people or things up and down from one level to another.

el·i·gi·ble /el′ə·jə·bəl/ *adj.* Able to qualify for something.

e·mer·gen·cy /i·mûr′jən·sē/ *n., pl.* **e·mer·gen·cies** A serious, unexpected event that requires quick action.

e·mo·tion·al /i·mō′shən·əl/ *adj.* **1** Having to do with the emotions. **2** Appealing to or arousing the emotions.

em·ploy·er /im·ploi′ər/ *n.* An individual or company that hires or employs one or more persons; a boss.

en·core /än(g)′kôr/ **1** *interj.* Once more; again. **2** *n.* A demand by an audience for the repetition of a song, performance, etc. **3** *n.* The repetition of the song, performance, etc., in response to such a demand.

en·dan·gered /in·dān′jərd/ *adj.* Threatened with becoming extinct.

en·e·my /en′ə·mē/ *n., pl.* **en·e·mies** **1** A person or country who tries to harm or fight another. **2** Anything that harms.

en·er·get·ic /en′ər·jet′ik/ *adj.* Full of energy; lively; vigorous.

en·er·gy /en′ər·jē/ *n., pl.* **en·er·gies** **1** Vigorous activity; power. **2** (*often pl.*) Power used in an effective way. **3** The power to do work.

en·gine /en′jin/ *n.* **1** A machine that burns fuel to make something move: bus *engine*. **2** A locomotive.

en·large·ment /in·lärj′mənt/ *n.* **1** The act of increasing the size of something. **2** Something made bigger.

en·trance /en′trəns/ *n.* **1** A door, gate, or other opening for entering. **2** The act of entering.

en·try /en′trē/ *n., pl.* **en·tries** **1** The place where a door, gate, or other opening is located. **2** A word and its meaning in the dictionary. **3** A thing or person in a contest.

en·vi·ron·ment /in·vī′rən·mənt/ *n.* All the surroundings and conditions that have an effect on the development of a person, animal, or plant.

e·qual /ē′kwəl/ *adj., v.* **e·qualed** *or* **e·qualled, e·qual·ing** *or* **e·qual·ling,** *n.* **1** *adj.* Having the same measure or amount: *equal* portions. **2** *adj.* Having the same rights, privileges, or rank. **3** *v.* To be equal to: 10 × 2 *equals* 20.

e·qual·i·ty /i·kwol′ə·tē/ *n., pl.* **e·qual·i·ties** Sameness in amount, size, value, position, etc.

e·qua·tion /i·kwā′zhən/ *n.* **1** In math, a statement that two or more quantities are equal. **2** In chemistry, a statement using chemical formulas and symbols to show the substances used and produced in a chemical reaction.

e·qua·tor /i·kwā′tər/ *n.* An imaginary line around the earth's center, located halfway between the North Pole and the South Pole.

e·quip·ment /i·kwip′mənt/ *n.* Things needed for a special use or purpose; supplies: office *equipment*.

-er *suffix* **1** A person or thing that does something: *swimmer*. **2** A person who lives in or comes from: *Southerner*. **3** A person practicing a trade or profession: *oceanographer*.

er·ror /er′ər/ *n.* **1** A mistake. **2** The condition of being incorrect.

e·vap·o·rate /i·vap′ə·rāt/ *v.* **e·vap·o·rat·ed, e·vap·o·rat·ing** **1** To turn into vapor. **2** To remove moisture or liquid from. **3** To disappear.

eve·ry·day /ev′rē·dā′/ *adj.* **1** Taking place each day: an *everyday* chore. **2** Suitable for ordinary or common use.

ex·act /ig·zakt′/ *adj.* Accurate; correct; precise. —**ex·act′ness** *n.*

ex·am·ine /ig·zam′in/ *v.* **ex·am·ined, ex·am·in·ing** **1** To look at closely and carefully; to investigate. **2** To ask questions of in order to gain information or to test an individual's knowledge, etc. —**ex·am′in·er** *n.*

ex·am·ple /ig·zam′pəl/ *n.* **1** Something used to represent a whole group; a sample. **2** A pattern or model of something to be copied or avoided. **3** A sample problem that is already worked out.

excellent

ex·cel·lent /ek′sə·lənt/ *adj.* Very good.

ex·cept /ik·sept′/ *prep.* Leaving out; other than; but.

ex·cep·tion·al /ik·sep′shən·əl/ *adj.* Not ordinary; unusual; extraordinary. —**ex·cep′tion·al·ly** *adv.*

ex·cuse /*v.* ik·skyōōz′, *n.* ik·skyōōs′/ *v.* **ex·cused, ex·cus·ing,** *n.* **1** *v.* To forgive or pardon. **2** *v.* To be a reason or explanation for. **3** *n.* A reason or explanation. **4** *v.* To free someone from a duty. **5** *v.* To allow to leave.

ex·ert /ig·zûrt′/ *v.* To put into use or put forth.

ex·haust /ig·zôst′/ **1** *v.*To make or become very tired. **2** *v.* To use up or consume completely. **3** *n.* The fumes or the gases that escape from an engine.

ex·ile /eg′zīl *or* ek′sīl/ *v.* **ex·iled, ex·il·ing,** *n.* **1** *v.* To force someone to leave his or her native country. **2** *n.* A person who cannot return to his or her native country.

ex·ist /ig·zist′/ *v.* **1** To have actual being; to be. **2** To live.

ex·is·tence /ig·zis′təns/ *n.* **1** The state of being. **2** Life. **3** A manner, style, or mode of living.

ex·it /eg′zit *or* ek′sit/ **1** *n.* A way out of an enclosed place, as a door. **2** *n.* A departure, especially of an actor from a stage. **3** *v.* To leave.

ex·pect /ik·spekt′/ *v.* **1** To look forward to; to regard as likely to happen. **2** To look for with reason or justification: to *expect* good work.

ex·pe·di·tion /ek′spə·dish′ən/ *n.* An organized journey made for a specific purpose: a military *expedition.*

ex·pe·ri·ence /ik·spir′ē·əns/ *n., v.* **ex·pe·ri·enced, ex·pe·ri·enc·ing 1** *n.* Something that happens to an individual or what an individual has seen, done, or lived through. **2** *n.* Knowledge or skill gained by seeing, doing, or living through: work *experience.* **3** *v.* To undergo or feel.

famine

ex·per·i·ment /*n.* ik·sper′ə·mənt, *v.* ik·sper′ə·ment/ **1** *n.* A test or trial performed or research conducted to gain knowledge or try out a theory. **2** *v.* To make an experiment.

ex·pert /*n.* ek′spûrt, *adj.* ek′spûrt *or* ik·spûrt′/ **1** *n.* A person who is very knowledgeable or skillful in some special area. **2** *adj.* Very skillful. **3** Of or done by an expert.

ex·plo·sion /ik·splō′zhən/ *n.* **1** A blowing up. **2** A loud noise caused by this blowing up. **3** A noisy outburst.

ex·port /*v.* ik·spôrt′ *or* eks′pôrt, *n.* eks′pôrt/ **1** *v.* To send goods out of one country for sale and use in another. **2** *n.* Something that is exported. **3** *n.* The act of exporting.

ex·po·sure /ik·spō′zhər/ *n.* **1** The act or condition of being exposed, uncovered, or unprotected. **2** The position or direction of something with regard to the sun, weather, etc. **3** A section of film that makes a single picture.

ex·tinct /ik·stingkt′/ *adj.* No longer living, in existence, or active.

ex·tract /*v.* ik·strakt′, *n.* eks′trakt/ **1** *v.* To take, pull, or draw out: to *extract* a tooth. **2** *n.* A solid or liquid substance pressed or taken from a plant, drug, etc.: orange *extract.*

F

fab·ric /fab′rik/ *n.* A material made of woven, knitted, or matted fibers.

fail·ure /fāl′yər/ *n.* **1** Something that has not been successful. **2** An act of neglect: *failure* to obey the law.

fair·ness /fâr′nis/ *n.* Not favoring one group or person over another; the act of being fair or just.

faith·ful /fāth′fəl/ *adj.* Loyal; true. —**faith′ful·ly** *adv.*

fam·ine /fam′in/ *n.* **1** A widespread lack of food; a time of starving. **2** Starvation. **3** Any serious scarcity.

---

act, āte, câre, ärt;   egg, ēven;   if, īce;   on, ōver, ôr;   bŏŏk, fōŏd;   up, tûrn;
ə = a in *ago,* e in *listen,* i in *giraffe,* o in *pilot,* u in *circus;*   yōō = u in *music;*   oil;   out;
chair; si**ng**; **sh**op; **th**ank; **th**at; **zh** in *treasure.*

farmer

forgery

farm·er /fär′mər/ *n.* A person who owns, manages, or works on a farm.

fat /fat/ *n., adj.* **fat·ter, fat·test** **1** *n.* Any of a large group of greasy substances found in plant and animal tissues. **2** *n.* Any such substance used in cooking, as oil, butter, etc. **3** *adj.* Containing much grease, oil, etc.: *fat* meat. **4** *adj.* Having too much weight on the body; plump.

fau·cet /fô′sit/ *n.* A device containing a valve for turning on or off the flow of a liquid, as from a pipe.

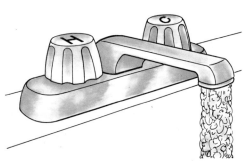

fault /fôlt/ *n.* **1** Defect; failing: His only *fault* is that he is careless. **2** A mistake. **3** Responsibility for failure; blame: It was not her *fault* that she was late. **4** A break in the earth's crust that causes rock layers to shift. **—at fault** In the wrong. **—to a fault** To an almost excessively favorable degree. **—find fault with** To complain about or criticize.

fe·ver /fē′vər/ *n.* **1** A high body temperature, usually indicating illness. **2** A sickness, usually indicated by a high temperature. **3** An extremely excited or eager condition.

fe·ver·ish /fē′vər·ish/ *adj.* **1** Having a fever. **2** Showing signs of a fever. **3** Excited; eager. **—fe′ver·ish·ly** *adv.*

field /fēld/ **1** *n.* A large area of open land. **2** *n.* A region of land that produces natural resources. **3** *n.* An area of land used for sports events. **4** *v.* To catch and throw back a baseball. **5** *n.* An occupation or area of specialization.

fierce /firs/ *adj.* **fierc·er, fierc·est** Cruel, violent, savage, or angry.

fil·ter /fil′tər/ *n., v.* **fil·tered, fil·ter·ing** **1** *n.* A material such as paper, sand, etc., through which a liquid or air is passed to strain out dirt or other matter. **2** *v.* To remove by means of a filter.

fin·ish /fin′ish/ *n., v.* **fin·ished, fin·ish·ing** **1** *v.* To end or bring to an end. **2** *n.* The end. **3** *v.* To use up.

floun·der[1] /floun′dər/ *v.* To struggle or move about clumsily.

floun·der[2] /floun′dər/ *n.* A flatfish used as food.

flour·ish /flûr′ish/ *v.* To grow or develop well; to thrive.

flu·id /floo′id/ **1** *n.* Any substance, as a liquid or gas, that is able to flow or pour easily. **2** *adj.* Able to flow or pour easily; not solid.

flur·ry /flûr′ē/ *n., pl.* **flur·ries** A light, brief rain or snowfall, often with wind.

foam /fōm/ **1** *n.* A mass of suds or small bubbles. **2** *v.* To form or produce masses of suds or small bubbles.

foe /fō/ *n.* An enemy or rival; opponent.

fog·gy /fog′ē/ *adj.* **fog·gi·er, fog·gi·est** **1** Full of fog or mist. **2** Confused.

fool·ish /foo′lish/ *adj.* Silly or unwise; showing a lack of good sense. **—fool′ish·ly** *adv.*

for·bid /fər·bid′/ *v.* **for·bade, for·bid·den, for·bid·ding** Not to allow.

for·bid·ding /fər·bid′ing/ *adj.* Unfriendly; threatening.

force /fôrs/ *n., v.* **forced, forc·ing** **1** *n.* Power. **2** *v.* To break open; to take by strength. **3** *v.* To make someone do something. **4** *n.* A group of people who do a particular job.

for·eign /fôr′in/ *adj.* **1** Not native to a country. **2** Having to do with other countries. **3** Not belonging normally: a *foreign* object in the eye.

for·est·ry /fôr′is·trē/ *n.* The science of developing and managing forests.

for·ev·er /fôr·ev′ər/ *adv.* To the end of time; always.

for·ger·y /fôr′jər·ē/ *n., pl.* **for·ger·ies** **1** The act of making or writing something false, as a signature, to be passed off as genuine. **2** Something made or written falsely to deceive.

forget

generous

for·get /fər·get′/ *v.* **for·got, for·got·ten, for·get·ting** **1** To fail to remember. **2** To leave behind.

form /fôrm/ **1** *n.* Shape. **2** *v.* To shape: They will *form* the dough into a circle. **3** *n.* A document with blanks to be filled in: an insurance *form.*

for·tress /fôr′tris/ *n.* A very large fort built with walls and defenses for resisting attack.

for·ward /fôr′wərd/ **1** *adj.* Toward, at, or near the front. **2** *adv.* To or toward the front; ahead. **3** *v.* To send onward. **4** *adv.* To the future.

fowl /foul/ *n., pl.* **fowl** **1** A bird, such as a chicken, duck, or turkey, used as food. **2** Any bird.

frac·tion /frak′shən/ *n.* **1** Part of a whole. **2** A tiny amount. **3** A rational number that is more than zero and less than 1, or the sum of a whole number and such a rational number.

freight /frāt/ *n.* Goods transported by train, truck, ship, or plane.

fric·tion /frik′shən/ *n.* The rubbing of one thing against another.

friend·ly /frend′lē/ *adj.* **friend·li·er, friend·li·est** Like a friend; pleasant; helpful; neighborly; kindly: Melissa is a *friendly* girl.

friend·ship /frend′ship/ *n.* **1** The condition or fact of being friends. **2** Warm feelings.

fringe /frinj/ *n., v.* **fringed, fring·ing** **1** *n.* A decorative border made of threads, cords, etc. **2** *v.* To trim or border with a fringe.

frol·ic /frol′ik/ *n., v.* **frol·icked, frol·ick·ing** **1** *n.* A time or occasion of fun; merriment. **2** *v.* To have fun.

frost /frôst *or* frost/ **1** *n.* Dew or water vapor frozen into delicate white crystals. **2** *n.* Cold weather that freezes things. **3** *v.* To cover with frost. **4** *v.* To cover with icing: to *frost* a cake.

fu·el /fyoo′(ə)l/ *n., v.* **fu·eled, fu·el·ing** **1** *n.* A substance that is burned to produce heat energy. **2** *v.* To supply something with fuel: *fuel* a fire. *Alternate spellings:* **fuelled, fuelling.**

-ful *suffix* Full of: *cheerful.*

fun·gus /fung′gəs/ *n., pl.* **fun·gi** /fun′jī/ A plant that has no chlorophyll, flowers, or leaves, such as mold, a mushroom, mildew, etc. *Alternate plural:* **fun·guses.**

fun·nel /fun′əl/ *n., v.* **fun·neled, fun·nel·ing** **1** *n.* A cone-shaped object used to pour liquids into a small opening without spilling. **2** *v.* To pour through or as if through a funnel. *Alternate spellings:* **funnelled, funnelling.**

fun·ny /fun′ē/ *adj.* **fun·ni·er, fun·ni·est** Able to cause laughter; amusing.

fu·ri·ous /fyoor′ē·əs/ *adj.* Very angry.

fur·nish /fûr′nish/ *v.* **1** To fill with furniture. **2** To supply.

fuse /fyooz/ *n.* **1** A slow-burning wick or other device used to set off an explosive charge. **2** A wire or strip of metal inserted in an electrical circuit that melts and breaks the connection when the electric current becomes too strong.

fu·ture /fyoo′chər/ **1** *n.* The time to come. **2** *adj.* Having to do with or happening in the future. **3** *adj.* The future tense.

G

gar·bage /gär′bij/ *n.* Trash.

gas·o·line /gas′ə·lēn/ *n.* An almost colorless liquid made from petroleum and used mainly as a fuel for cars, boats, etc. *Alternate spelling:* **gasolene.**

geese /gēs/ Plural of *goose.*

gene /jēn/ *n.* In plants and animals, a part within a cell that determines the characteristics an offspring will inherit from its parents.

gen·er·ous /jen′ər·əs/ *adj.* **1** Sharing; unselfish. **2** Large: a *generous* amount. —**gen′er·ous·ly** *adv.* ▸*Generous* comes from the Latin word *generosus,* "noble, free in giving."

act, āte, câre, ärt; egg, ēven; if, īce; on, ōver, ôr; bŏŏk, fŏŏd; up, tûrn; ə = a in *ago,* e in *listen,* i in *giraffe,* o in *pilot,* u in *circus;* yŏŏ = u in *music;* oil; out; chair; sing; shop; thank; that; zh in *treasure.*

gen·ius /jēn′yəs/ *n., pl.* **gen·ius·es**   1 An extremely high degree of mental ability or creative talent.   2 A person who possesses such ability.

gen·u·ine /jen′yo͞o·in/ *adj.*   1 Real; authentic.   2 Sincere.

ge·og·ra·phy /jē·og′rə·fē/ *n.*   1 The science that studies the earth's surface and its life.   2 The natural features of an area.

ge·ol·o·gy /jē·ol′ə·jē/ *n.* The science that studies the earth's physical history through its rocks and minerals.

germ /jûrm/ *n., pl.* **germs** A microscopic animal or plant that can cause disease.

gi·gan·tic /jī·gan′tik/ *adj.* Huge; giant.

gla·cier /glā′shər/ *n.* A large mass of ice that moves slowly down a mountain or over a large area of land.

glimpse /glimps/ *n., v.* **glimpsed, glimps·ing**   1 *n.* A quick look or view.   2 *v.* To catch a short, quick view of.   3 *v.* To glance.

glow /glō/   1 *v.* To shine because of intense heat, especially without a flame.   2 *n.* Brightness.

gnaw /nô/ *v.* **gnawed, gnawed** *or* **gnawn** /nôn/, **gnaw·ing** To bite or chew away little by little.

goal /gōl/ *n.*   1 Aim.   2 In games, as soccer, the place where a score can be made.   3 A score made in these games.

goose /go͞os/ *n., pl.* **geese** /gēs/   1 A tame or wild swimming bird, similar to a duck but larger and with a longer neck.   2 The female of this kind of bird. The male is called a gander.

gov·ern /guv′ərn/ *v.* To rule or guide.

gra·cious /grā′shəs/ *adj.*   1 Kind and polite.   2 Elegant; refined: *gracious* living. —**gra′cious·ly** *adv.*

grad·u·al /graj′o͞o·əl/ *adj.* Slowly; little by little. —**grad′u·al·ly** *adv.*

grad·u·a·tion /graj′o͞o·ā′shən/ *n.*   1 A graduating from a school, college, or university.   2 The ceremony of graduating: *graduation* exercises.

grain /grān/ *n.*   1 The seeds of certain cereal grasses, as wheat, rye, etc.   2 The natural patterns or markings of wood, marble, etc.   3 A tiny bit of something: a *grain* of sand. —**with a grain of salt** With some doubt.

gram·mar /gram′ər/ *n.* The study of words and sentences and how they are used in speaking and writing.

grape /grāp/ *n.* A juicy berry that grows in bunches on vines.

grave¹ /grāv/ *adj.* **grav·er, grav·est** Very important; serious.

grave² /grāv/ *n.* A burial place for a body.

grav·i·ty /grav′ə·tē/ *n., pl.* **grav·i·ties**   1 The natural force that pulls or tends to pull objects toward the center of the earth.   2 Weight or heaviness.   3 Seriousness.

greed·y /grē′dē/ *adj.* **greed·i·er, greed·i·est** Wanting much more than one needs.

grief /grēf/ *n.* Extreme sorrow.

grouch·y /grouch′ē/ *adj.* **grouch·i·er, grouch·i·est** Bad-tempered; sulky.

growth /grōth/ *n.*   1 The process of growing; development.   2 The amount grown.   3 Something that has grown.

gum·bo /gum′bō/ *n., pl.* **gum·bos**   1 A thick soup or stew containing okra.   2 The okra.   3 A soil that gets very sticky when wet.

gym·na·si·um /jim·nā′zē·əm/ *n., pl.* **gym·na·si·ums** A building or large room equipped for physical exercise or training and for certain indoor athletic sports. *Alternate plural:* **gymnasia** /jim·nā′zē·ə/.

gym·nas·tics /jim·nas′tiks/ *n., pl.*   1 Physical exercises that develop muscular strength, control, and agility.   2 The practice or art of such physical exercises.

H

hab·it /hab′it/ *n.* An act done so often that one does it almost automatically without thinking.

hallway

hunter

hall·way /hôl′wā′/ *n.* A corridor or passageway.

hand·i·craft /han′dē·kraft′/ *n.* **1** Skill in working with the hands. **2** An art or job requiring skillful hands.

hand·y /han′dē/ *adj.* **hand·i·er, hand·i·est 1** Within easy reach. **2** Skillful with the hands.

han·gar /hang′ər/ *n.* A storage building for aircraft.

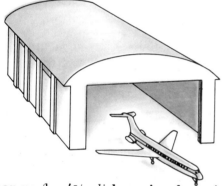

hap·py /hap′ē/ *adj.* **hap·pi·er, hap·pi·est** Showing joy or pleasure.

haunt /hônt/ **1** *v.* To visit frequently. **2** *n.* A place visited frequently: That diner is a favorite *haunt*.

hawk¹ /hôk/ *n.* A bird of prey with a strong, hooked beak, long claws, broad wings, and keen sight.

hawk² /hôk/ *v.* To carry goods about and offer them for sale by shouting.

health /helth/ *n.* **1** Freedom in body and mind from illness. **2** Condition of the body and mind.

heat /hēt/ **1** *n.* The condition of being hot; warmth; high temperature. **2** *v.* To cause to become warm or hot.

hedge /hej/ *n., v.* **hedged, hedg·ing 1** *n.* A border or fence formed by a row of bushes planted closely together. **2** *v.* To avoid giving a direct answer.

height /hīt/ *n.* **1** Measurement from top to bottom; tallness. **2** How high or how far up something or someone is. **3** The highest point; greatest degree.

heir /âr/ *n.* A person who inherits or is entitled to inherit the position or property of another.

her·bi·cide /(h)ûr′bi·sīd′/ *n.* A substance used to destroy plants, as weeds.

he·ro /hir′ō *or* hē′rō/ *n., pl.* **he·roes 1** A person known for his or her courage and great deeds. **2** The main character, as in a play or story.

hi·ber·na·tion /hī′bər·nā′shən/ *n.* The act of hibernating or spending the winter sleeping or in a dormant state.

his·to·ri·an /his·tôr′ē·ən/ *n.* A person who writes about historic events and is an authority on history.

hoard /hôrd/ **1** *v.* To save and store away for preservation or future use, often in a greedy way. **2** *n.* A pile or stock of something hoarded.

hoarse /hôrs/ *adj.* **hoars·er, hoars·est** Having a rough, deep sound: Karen's voice is *hoarse* because of her cold.

hoist /hoist/ *v.* To rise or lift up, especially with a mechanical device.

hon·est /on′ist/ *adj.* Truthful; fair.

hor·i·zon·tal /hôr′ə·zon′təl/ *adj.* Parallel to the ground or horizon. —**hor′i·zon′tal·ly** *adv.*

hot /hot/ *adj.* **hot·ter, hot·test 1** Very warm; having a high temperature. **2** Showing great excitement, anger, etc.

hour /our/ *n.* **1** One of 24 parts of a day in time; 60 minutes. **2** A certain time: George starts his lunch *hour* at noon.

huge /(h)yōōj/ *adj.* **hug·er, hug·est** Very large: a *huge* box.

hu·man·i·ty /(h)yōō·man′ə·tē/ *n.* **1** The human race. **2** The condition or quality of being human; kindness.

hu·mid /(h)yōō′mid/ *adj.* Containing water vapor; damp: a *humid* day.

hu·mid·i·ty /(h)yōō·mid′ə·tē/ *n.* Moisture or dampness in the air.

hu·mor·ous /(h)yōō′mər·əs/ *adj.* Full of humor; funny; amusing.

hunt·er /hun′tər/ *n.* A person or animal that hunts.

---

act, āte, câre, ärt;　　egg, ēven;　　if, īce;　　on, ōver, ôr;　　bŏŏk, fōōd;　　up, tûrn;
ə = a in *ago*, e in *listen*, i in *giraffe*, o in *pilot*, u in *circus*;　　yōō = u in *music*;　　oil;　　out;
chair; sing; shop; thank; that; zh in *treasure*.

hurl

hurl /hûrl/ *v.* To throw something with force; to fling.

hy·giene /hī'jēn/ *n.* The science of health.

hymn /him/ *n.* A song of praise.

I

ig·nore /ig·nôr'/ *v.* **ig·nored, ig·nor·ing** To pay no attention to.

im- *prefix* Form of *in-* (meaning "not") used before words beginning with *b, m,* and *p: improbable.*

im·age /im'ij/ *n.* **1** A picture or appearance of something, such as produced in the reflection of a mirror or by a lens. **2** A person or thing very similar to another. **3** A mental conception.

im·i·tate /im'ə·tāt/ *v.* **im·i·tat·ed, im·i·tat·ing** To attempt to act or look the same as; to copy; to mimic.

im·i·ta·tion /im'ə·tā'shən/ *n.* **1** The act of imitating or copying. **2** A copy. **3** *adj. use: imitation* leather.

im·ma·ture /im'ə·chŏŏr' or im'ə·t(y)ŏŏr'/ *adj.* Not fully grown; undeveloped. —**im'ma·tur'i·ty** *n.*

im·me·di·ate·ly /i·mē'dē·it·lē/ *adv.* Without delay; at once; instantly.

im·mune /i·myōōn'/ *adj.* **1** Protected from disease, poison, etc., as by inoculation. **2** Not affected by; free from; exempt. —**im·mun'i·ty** *n.*

im·pa·tient /im·pā'shənt/ *adj.* Not willing to accept delay, discomfort, etc.; not patient.

im·per·fect /im·pûr'fikt/ *adj.* Having faults; not perfect.

im·per·son·al /im·pûr'sən·əl/ *adj.* Not in reference to any one person in particular; not personal.

im·po·lite /im'pə·līt'/ *adj.* Rude.

im·port /*v.* im·pôrt', *n.* im'pôrt/ **1** *v.* To bring goods into one country for sale and use from another. **2** *n.* Something that is imported.

im·pos·si·ble /im·pos'ə·bəl/ *adj.* **1** Not able to happen or be done. **2** Not to be tolerated or endured.

im·prove·ment /im·prōōv'mənt/ *n.* **1** The act of making or becoming better. **2** Something done better.

intermission

in- *prefix* Not: *inadequate.*

in·ca·pa·ble /in·kā'pə·bəl/ *adj.* Lacking the ability or skill to do something.

in·com·plete /in'kəm·plēt'/ *adj.* Unfinished; not complete.

in·de·pen·dent /in'di·pen'dənt/ *adj.* **1** Not governed by another country. **2** Not influenced by others. **3** Not dependent on anyone else for support.

in·dus·try /in'dəs·trē/ *n., pl.* **in·dus·tries** **1** Any division of manufacturing or business activity. **2** Manufacturing as a whole.

in·for·ma·tion /in'fər·mā'shən/ *n.* **1** The act or fact of informing. **2** Knowledge or facts about a particular subject.

in·i·tial /in·ish'əl/ *adj., n., v.* **in·i·tialed, in·i·tial·ing** **1** *adj.* Earliest; first. **2** *n.* (*often pl.*) The first letter of a proper name. **3** *v.* To sign one's initials. *Alternate spellings:* **initialled, initialling.**

in·se·cure /in'sə·kyŏŏr'/ *adj.* **1** Not secure, safe, steady, or firm. **2** Not confident; unsure.

in·spect /in·spekt'/ *v.* To look over carefully; to examine.

in·spec·tor /in·spek'tər/ *n.* A person who examines something carefully.

in·stall /in·stôl'/ *v.* To put into place or fix in position for use.

in·stru·ment /in'strə·mənt/ *n.* **1** A mechanical device; tool. **2** A device for measuring, controlling, or recording. **3** *adj. use:* an *instrument* panel. **4** A device for producing musical sounds, as a piano.

in·su·late /in'sə·lāt/ *v.* **in·su·lat·ed, in·su·lat·ing** To cover, surround, or separate with material that prevents or reduces the loss of electricity, heat, sound, etc.

in·ter·est /in'tər·ist or in'trist/ **1** *n.* A desire to learn or experience something. **2** *v.* To hold the attention. **3** *v.* Something that causes attention or curiosity.

in·ter·mis·sion /in'tər·mish'ən/ *n.* A pause or break between periods of activity, especially a break between the acts of a play; recess.

in·tes·tine /in·tes′tin/ *n.* (*often pl.*) A long coiled tube in the abdomen that helps in the digestion of food and the elimination of waste from the body.

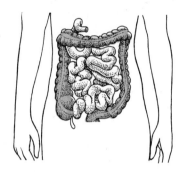

in·tro·duc·tion /in′trə·duk′shən/ *n.* **1** The act of introducing or presenting. **2** The opening part, usually of a book, essay, etc., that is an explanation of what is to follow.

in·ven·tion /in·ven′shən/ *n.* **1** Something designed or developed for the first time. **2** The act of inventing.

in·vis·i·ble /in·viz′ə·bəl/ *adj.* Not visible; not capable of being seen.

in·vi·ta·tion /in′və·tā′shən/ *n.* A spoken or written request asking someone to come to a place or to do something.

-ion *suffix* **1** The act or process of: *rotation.* **2** The result of: *invention.* **3** The condition of being: *relation.*

ir·ri·tate /ir′ə·tāt/ *v.* **ir·ri·tat·ed, ir·ri·tat·ing** **1** To annoy or make angry; to bother. **2** To make sore or raw; to inflame.

-ish *suffix* **1** Like: *childish.* **2** Fond of or inclined to: *bookish.*

-ity *suffix* The condition or quality of being: *reality.*

J

join /join/ *v.* **1** To bring or come together; to connect. **2** To become a member of a group. **3** To meet or be with others: They *joined* us for lunch.

jour·nal /jûr′nəl/ *n.* **1** A daily record of events. **2** A newspaper, magazine, or other periodical.

jour·ney /jûr′nē/ **1** *n.* Travel from one place to another. **2** *n.* The distance traveled. **3** *v.* To travel.

judge /juj/ *n., v.* **judged, judg·ing** **1** *n.* A public official who hears and decides cases in a court of law. **2** *v.* To hear and decide (a case) in a court of law. **3** *n.* A person chosen to settle a problem or decide who wins a contest, race, etc. **4** *v.* To form an opinion or make a judgment.

jum·ble /jum′bəl/ *n., v.* **jum·bled, jum·bling** **1** *n.* A state of confusion; a muddle. **2** *v.* To throw things together in a confused mass; to mix up.

jun·ior /jōōn′yər/ **1** *adj.* Younger or lower in rank. **2** *n.* The younger; usually abbreviated and used to show that a son is named after his father: Carl Bookstone, *Jr.* **3** *adj.* Pertaining to the next-to-last year of high school or college. **4** *n.* A student in this class or year.

junk /jungk/ **1** *n.* Worthless or worn out items; rubbish; trash. **2** *v.* To get rid of or discard as being worthless.

ju·ve·nile /jōō′və·nəl *or* jōō′və·nīl/ **1** *adj.* Young; childlike or immature. **2** *adj.* Something of, like, or for young people. **3** *n.* A young person.

---

act, āte, câre, ärt;   egg, ēven;   if, īce;   on, ōver, ôr;   book, fōōd;   up, tûrn;
ə = a in *ago*, e in *listen*, i in *giraffe*, o in *pilot*, u in *circus*;   yōō = u in *music*;   oil;   out;
chair; sing; shop; thank; that; zh in *treasure.*

K

khak·i /kak′ē/ *n., pl.* **khak·is,** *adj.* **1** *n., adj.* Light-brown in color. **2** *n.* A heavy, light-brown cotton fabric.

knob /nob/ *n.* **1** A round handle to be turned or pulled. **2** A rounded lump on a tree trunk.

knoll /nōl/ *n.* A small round hill; mound.

L

lan·guage /lang′gwîj/ *n.* **1** A body of words and symbols, written or spoken, by which people communicate. **2** Any means used to communicate.

large /lärj/ *adj.* **lar·ger, lar·gest 1** Big, as in size, amount, or extent. **2** Bigger than the average.

las·so /las′ō/ *n., pl.* **lassos** or **las·soes,** *v.* **1** *n.* A long rope having a loop with a slipknot at one end used for catching horses and cattle. **2** *v.* To catch with or as if with a lasso.

late·ly /lāt′lē/ *adj.* Recently.

laun·dry /lôn′drē/ *n., pl.* **laun·dries 1** A room or place where clothes are washed and ironed. **2** Articles that need to be washed or have been washed.

lawn /lôn/ *n.* An area or plot of grassy ground, usually kept short by mowing.

law·yer /lô′yər/ *n.* A person licensed to advise clients about the law and act for them in court; an attorney.

lead·er /lē′dər/ *n.* A person who leads.

learn /lûrn/ *v.* **learned** or **learnt, learn·ing 1** To get or gain knowledge of or skill in. **2** To find out about.

leg·is·la·ture /lej′is·lā′chər/ *n.* A body of people who have the power to make, change, or repeal the laws of a country or state.

lei·sure /lē′zhər or lezh′ər/ **1** *n.* Free time; time away from work, study, or other duties. **2** *adj.* Free from work.

lens /lenz/ *n., pl.* **lens·es** A piece of glass or other clear material that is curved to make light rays passing through it move apart or come together.

li·ar /lī′ər/ *n.* A person who tells lies.

like·ly /līk′lē/ *adj.* **like·li·er, like·li·est,** *adv.* **1** Showing a tendency or possibility to do, be, etc. **2** *adv.* Probably. **3** *adj.* Probably about to happen. **4** *adj.* Probably true.

like·ness /līk′nis/ *n.* Similarity.

limb /lim/ *n.* **1** An arm, leg, or wing. **2** The branch of a tree.

lime·light /līm′līt′/ *n.* **1** A bright light used on the stage as a spotlight. **2** The center of attention or interest.

live·ly /līv′lē/ *adj.* **live·li·er, live·li·est 1** Full of life; spirited. **2** Bright; cheerful: *lively* colors.

lo·ca·tion /lō·kā′shən/ *n.* A place or site.

lodge /loj/ *n., v.* **lodged, lodg·ing 1** *n.* A cabin, inn, etc., where a person can stay. **2** *v.* To get stuck.

lone·ly /lōn′lē/ *adj.* **lone·li·er, lone·li·est 1** Feeling alone and longing for company or friends. **2** Without many people; deserted.

loss /lôs/ *n., pl.* **loss·es 1** Losing or having something lost. **2** A person or thing lost. **3** A defeat.

lum·ber¹ /lum′bər/ *n.* Timber that has been cut down and sawed into boards for use as building materials.

lum·ber² /lum′bər/ *v.* To move along heavily and noisily.

lung /lung/ *n., pl.* **lungs** Either of the two saclike respiratory organs found in the chest of a human being and other vertebrate animals that breathe air.

-ly *suffix* **1** In a certain manner: *logically.* **2** To a certain degree or extent: *highly.* **3** In certain respects or ways: *mentally.* **4** At or in a certain order or time: *recently.*

M

ma·chin·er·y /mə·shēn′(ə·)rē/ *n.* **1** A collection of mechanical devices or machines. **2** The parts of a mechanical device or a machine.

mag·a·zine /mag′ə·zēn′ or mag′ə·zēn/ *n.* A regular publication, usually containing articles, stories, etc., written by various writers.

main·tain /mān·tān′/ *v.* **1** To keep up or carry on; to continue. **2** To keep in

Harcourt Brace School Publishers

good condition: to *maintain* a car.   **3** To support or provide for.

mam·moth /mam′əth/ *adj.* Huge; enormous.

man·i·cure /man′ə·kyŏŏr/ *n., v.* **man·i·cured, man·i·cur·ing**   **1** *n.* The grooming of the hands and fingernails; hand care.   **2** *v.* To groom the hands and fingernails. —**man′i·cur′ist** *n.*

man·u·al /man′yŏŏ·əl/ *adj.*   **1** Of or having to do with the hands.   **2** Done by hand and not by machine.   **3** Requiring or utilizing physical skill and energy.

man·u·script /man′yə·skript/ *n.* A book, article, etc., handwritten or typed.

mar·a·thon /mar′ə·thon/ *n.*   **1** A foot race on a course measuring 26 miles 385 yards, or 42.2 kilometers.   **2** Any long-distance race.

ma·rine /mə·rēn′/   **1** *adj.* Of, having to do with, formed by, or found in the sea.   **2** *adj.* Having to do with shipping or sailing: *marine* law.   **3** *n.* (*sometimes written* **Marine**) A member of the U.S. Marine Corps.

ma·roon[1] /mə·rŏŏn′/ *n., adj.* A dark red color: Mark's shoes are *maroon.*

ma·roon[2] /mə·rŏŏn′/ *v.*   **1** To leave someone on a deserted island or coast.   **2** To leave someone helpless: The tourist felt *marooned* when he missed the bus.

mass /mas/ *n., pl.* **mass·es**   **1** *n.* A quantity of matter having no definite shape or size; lump.   **2** *n.* A great amount or quantity of something.   **3** *adj.* Of or having to do with a great amount of persons or things.   **4** *adj.* On a large scale.

ma·te·ri·al /mə·tir′ē·əl/   **1** *n.* The substance of which something is composed.   **2** *adj.* Having to do with matter; physical.   **3** *n.* Cloth.

ma·ture /mə·t(y)ŏŏr′ *or* mə·chŏŏr′/ *adj., v.* **ma·tured, ma·tur·ing**   **1** *adj.* Fully grown or developed.   **2** *v.* To make or become full-grown or developed.

meas·ure /mezh′ər/ *n., v.* **meas·ured, meas·ur·ing**   **1** *n.* A standard used for comparison, as a pound, meter, etc.   **2** *v.* To find the size, length, weight, etc., of anything.   **3** *v.* To have certain measurements.   **4** *v.* To make or take measurements.

meas·ure·ment /mezh′ər·mənt/ *n.*   **1** The act of measuring.   **2** Extent, size, quantity, etc., found by measuring.   **3** A system of measuring or measures.

me·chan·i·cal /mə·kan′i·kəl/ *adj.*   **1** Having to do with a machine or machinery.   **2** Made or worked by machinery.   **3** Like a machine; automatic. **me·chan′i·cal·ly** *adv.*

med·i·cal /med′i·kəl/ *adj.* Having to do with medicine.

med·i·cine /med′ə·sən/ *n.*   **1** Any substance used in treating an illness.   **2** The science of treating disease and illness and preserving health.

mel·low /mel′ō/ *adj.*   **1** Ripe and sweet, as fruit.   **2** Soft and rich in quality.

mel·on /mel′ən/ *n.* A large, juicy fruit that grows on a vine, as a watermelon.

mem·ber /mem′bər/ *n.*   **1** A person who belongs to a group: Jason is a *member* of a large family.   **2** A part of the body, as an arm or leg.

-ment *suffix*   **1** The act of: *enforcement.*   **2** The result of: *accomplishment.*   **3** A means of or a thing that: *refreshment.*   **4** The condition of being: *excitement.*

act, āte, câre, ärt;   egg, ēven;   if, īce;   on, ōver, ôr;   bŏŏk, fŏŏd;   up, tûrn;
ə = a in *ago*, e in *listen*, i in *giraffe*, o in *pilot*, u in *circus*;   yŏŏ = u in *music*;   oil;   out;
chair;   sing;   shop;   thank;   that;   zh in *treasure*.

men·u /men′yōō/ *n.* **1** A list of the foods to be served at a meal. **2** A list of foods offered at a restaurant.

mer·it /mer′it/ **1** *n.* Worth; excellence; high quality. **2** *v.* To deserve.

mice /mīs/ Plural of *mouse.*

mim·ic /mim′ik/ *v.* **mim·icked, mim·ick·ing,** *n.* **1** *v.* To imitate the speech or actions of. **2** *n.* A person or thing that imitates.

min·er·al /min′ər·əl/ **1** *n.* A natural substance that is not animal or plant, obtained by mining or digging in the earth. **2** *adj.* Like, being, or containing a mineral or minerals.

min·ute¹ /min′it/ *n.* A measure of time; 1/60 of an hour.

min·ute² /mī·n(y)ōōt′/ *adj.* Very tiny.

mir·ror /mir′ər/ **1** *n.* Glass backed by a coating of metal. **2** *v.* To reflect an image of: The lake *mirrored* the trees.

mis·lead /mis·lēd′/ *v.* **mis·led, mis·lead·ing** **1** To lead in the wrong direction. **2** To cause someone to believe something that is not true.

mis·use /*v.* mis·yōōz′, *n.* mis·yōōs′/ *v.* **mis·used, mis·us·ing,** *n.* **1** *v.* To use improperly or in a wrong way. **2** *n.* An incorrect use or usage.

mix·ture /miks′chər/ *n.* A combination of things mixed or blended together.

mod·i·fy /mod′ə·fī/ *v.* **mod·i·fied, mod·i·fy·ing** To change somewhat: The rain forced us to *modify* our plans.

moist /moist/ *adj.* Slightly wet; damp.

mon·i·tor /mon′ə·tər/ **1** *n.* A pupil in school with special duties, as taking attendance, etc. **2** *n.* A device that al-

lows the operation or activity of a thing or person to be observed, checked, or listened to constantly. **3** *v.* To observe, check, or listen to with or as if with such a device.

mon·u·ment /mon′yə·mənt/ *n.* Something built in memory of a person or an event.

mos·qui·to /məs·kē′tō/ *n., pl.* **mos·qui·toes** A small insect with two wings. *Alternate plural:* **mosquitos.**

moss /môs/ *n.* A tiny, flowerless green plant that grows on rocks, trees, etc.

mo·tion /mō′shən/ **1** *n.* Movement. **2** *n.* A signal; gesture. **3** *v.* To signal.

moun·tain /moun′tən/ *n.* A mass of land that rises far above the surrounding area; a very high hill.

mourn /môrn/ *v.* To grieve or show sorrow over a loss, death, etc.

mouse /mous/ *n., pl.* **mice** /mīs/ A small, furry rodent with a long, thin tail and a pointed snout.

mov·a·ble /mōō′və·bəl/ *adj.* Able to be moved: *movable* engine parts.

mul·ti·ple /mul′tə·pəl/ **1** *adj.* Of, like, or having more than one part or element. **2** *n.* In math, a number that contains another number a certain number of times without a remainder: 25 is a *multiple* of 5.

mur·al /myōōr′əl/ *n.* A picture or design painted directly on a wall.

mur·mur /mûr′mər/ **1** *n.* A low, unclear sound. **2** *v.* To make such a sound.

mu·se·um /myōō·zē′əm/ *n.* A place where works of art and other objects of value are kept and exhibited.

mu·sic /myoo′zik/ n.   1 The art of putting together sounds into patterns that are pleasing to hear.   2 A combination of sound patterns.

mu·si·cal /myoo′zi·kəl/ adj.   1 Of, related to, or used to make music: A piano is a *musical* instrument.   2 Skilled or trained in music.   3 Set to, accompanied by, or containing music. —**mu′si·cal·ly** adv.

mu·si·cian /myoo·zish′ən/ n. A person skilled in music or in playing a musical instrument.

mys·te·ri·ous /mis·tir′ē·əs/ adj. Filled with or suggesting something not known or strange; unexplained.

mys·ter·y /mis′tər·ē/ n., pl. **mys·ter·ies**   1 Something that is or seems impossible to know or understand.   2 A story about an event that has this quality.

mys·ti·fy /mis′tə·fī/ v.   **mys·ti·fied, mys·ti·fy·ing** To puzzle or bewilder.

N

nar·row /nar′ō/   1 adj. Not wide.   2 v. To make or become less wide.   3. adj. Limited in scope.   4 adj. Almost unsuccessful or disastrous.

na·tion·al /nash′ən·əl/ adj. Having to do with a nation or country as a whole. —**na′tion·al·ly** adv.

nat·u·ral /nach′ər·əl/ adj.   1 Coming from nature; not artificial.   2 Having to do with the study of nature.   3 Inborn; instinctive.   4 Occurring in the normal course of events.

nat·u·ral·ly /nach′ər·əl·ē/ adv.   1 By a natural way.   2 Certainly.

nav·i·ga·tion /nav′ə·gā′shən/ n.   1 The act or process of sailing, managing, or steering a ship or aircraft.   2 The art of charting a ship's or an aircraft's position and course.

near·ly /nir′lē/ adv. Almost.

nec·es·sar·y /nes′ə·ser′ē/ adj.   1 Needed; essential.   2 Certain to happen.

ne·ces·si·ty /nə·ses′ə·tē/ n., pl. **ne·ces·si·ties**   1 (often pl.) Something that cannot be done without, such as food, water, etc.   2 Extreme need.

neg·a·tive /neg′ə·tiv/   1 adj. Expressing refusal or opposition.   2 n. A word or expression that shows refusal or opposition.   3 adj. Not positive.   4 adj. In math, being less than zero; minus.   5 n. A photographic image in which the lights and shadows are reversed.

neigh·bor /nā′bər/ n. A person who lives near another.

nei·ther /nē′thər or nī′thər/   1 adj., pron. Not one or the other.   2 conj. Not either.

ne·on /nē′on/ n. A colorless, odorless gas that occurs in small amounts in air and does not combine easily with other elements.

-ness suffix   1 The condition or quality of being: *warmness.*   2 An instance of being: *carefulness.*

nice /nīs/ adj. **nic·er, nic·est**   1 Pleasant; kind.   2 Pleasing.

niece /nēs/ n. A daughter of one's brother or sister; a daughter of one's brother-in-law or sister-in-law.

no·bod·y /nō′bod′ē/ pron. No one.

nom·i·na·tion /nom′ə·nā′shən/ n. The act of naming as a candidate or of appointing to an office.

nor·mal /nôr′məl/   1 adj. Agreeing with the usual standard; regular.   2 adj. Not diseased or defective in mind or body.   3 n. The usual state or level.

north·west /nôrth′west′/   1 n. The direction midway between north and west.   2 n. A place in the northwest part.   3 adj. To, in, or from the northwest.

noz·zle /noz′əl/ n. A small opening at the end of a hose or pipe.

nu·cle·ar /n(y)oo′klē·ər/ adj.   1 Having to do with or like a nucleus or nuclei, the central part of a cell or atom: *nuclear* particles.   2 Having to do with atomic energy.

---

act, āte, câre, ärt;   egg, ēven;   if, īce;   on, ōver, ôr;   book, food;   up, tûrn;
ə = a in *ago*, e in *listen*, i in *giraffe*, o in *pilot*, u in *circus*;   yoo = u in *music*;   oil;   out;
chair;   sing;   shop;   thank;   that;   zh in *treasure*.

nu·mer·al /n(y)oo′mər·əl/ *n*. A word, symbol, or group of symbols that represents a number.

nu·mer·a·tor /n(y)oo′mə·rā′tər/ *n*. The number above the line or first in à fraction, as 2 in ⅔ or 2/3. This number is divided by the denominator.

nurs·er·y /nûr′sər·ē/ *n*., *pl*. **nurs·er·ies** 1 A baby's or children's room. 2 A place where trees and plants are raised. 3 A place where children are cared for.

nu·tri·tious /n(y)oo·trish′əs/ *adj*. Providing a living thing with the proper nourishment; nourishing.

o

ob·jec·tion /əb·jek′shən/ *n*. 1 A statement or feeling of disapproval, disagreement, or opposition. 2 A reason or argument against something.

ob·serve /əb·zûrv′/ *v*. **ob·served, ob·serv·ing** 1 To see or notice. 2 To remark or comment. 3 To comply with: to *observe* the speed limit. 4 To celebrate: to *observe* a holiday.

oc·ca·sion·al·ly /ə·kā′zhən·əl·ē/ *adv*. Now and then; sometimes.

oc·cur /ə·kûr′/ *v*. **oc·curred, oc·cur·ring** 1 To take place. 2 To come to mind.

oc·cur·rence /ə·kûr′əns/ *n*. The act or fact of taking place or occurring; something that happens; incident.

o·cean /ō′shən/ *n*. 1 The great body of salt water that covers almost three fourths of the earth's surface. 2 (*often written* **Ocean**) Any one of its four divisions, including the Atlantic, Pacific, Indian, and Arctic.

o·dor /ō′dər/ *n*. A smell or scent.

of·fer /ô′fər/ *n*., *v*. **of·fered, of·fer·ing** 1 *v*. To present for taking if desired; to volunteer. 2 *v*. To give or propose; to suggest. 3 *n*. The act of offering.

of·fi·cer /ôf′ə·sər/ *n*. 1 In the armed forces, a person who has the rank to command others. 2 A person who holds an office or post, as in a corporation, government, or club. 3 A member of the police force. 4 The captain of a merchant or passenger ship or any of the chief assistants.

off·shore /ôf′shôr′/ 1 *adj*. Located or moving away from the shore. 2 *adv*. Away from the shore.

op·er·a·tion /op′ə·rā′shən/ *n*. 1 The act or method of operating or working. 2 The condition of working or being in action. 3 An action done to the body to cure or remedy an illness or injury.

-or *suffix* A person or thing that does something: *actor*.

or·ange /ôr′inj *or* or′inj/ 1 *n*. A round juicy fruit with a thick skin. 2 *n*. The tree this fruit grows on. 3 *n., adj.* Reddish yellow.

or·chard /or′chərd/ *n*. 1 A large group of trees, planted and cultivated for their products. 2 The ground on which these trees grow.

or·deal /ôr·dēl′, ôr·dē′əl, *or* ôr′dēl/ *n*. A very difficult experience.

or·der /ôr′dər/ 1 *n*. A well organized arrangement. 2 *n*. An arrangement of things one after the other. 3 *n*. A command. 4 *v*. To give such an order. 5 *v*. To ask for or request. 6 *n*. A request, usually written, to buy or sell something. 7 *v*. To give an order for.

ore /ôr *or* ōr/ *n*. A mineral or rock that contains a valuable metal or other substance: iron *ore*.

or·gan·ic /ôr·gan′ik/ *adj*. 1 Having to do with the organs of the body. 2 Having to do with or produced by living things: an *organic* diet.

or·gan·ism /ôr′gən·iz′əm/ *n*. A form of life, as an animal or plant, composed of mutually dependent organs or parts that support vital processes.

-ous *suffix* Full of: *humorous*.

out·doors /out·dôrz′/ 1 *adv*. Outside; the opposite of indoors. 2 *n., pl.* (*used with singular verb*) Open spaces.

out·law /out′lô′/ 1 *n*. A criminal. 2 *v*. To make illegal; to prohibit.

out·ra·geous /out·rā′jəs/ *adj*. 1 Shockingly cruel. 2 Insulting; rude.

ov·en /uv′ən/ *n*. An enclosed space, as the inside of a stove, in which food is baked, roasted, or broiled.

overdue

pelican

o·ver·due /ō′vər·d(y)o͞o′/ *adj.* **1** Remaining unpaid when due. **2** Not on time.

ox /oks/ *n., pl.* **ox·en** /ok′sən/ A powerful, four-footed, neutered bull.

P

pain /pān/ **1** *n.* An ache; soreness; mental or physical suffering. **2** *v.* To give pain or cause to suffer.

pale /pāl/ *adj.* **pal·er, pal·est** **1** Without much color; whitish. **2** Not bright; light: *pale* blue.

palm[1] /päm/ *n.* The inside part of the hand between the wrist and the fingers.

palm[2] /päm/ *n.* **1** Any of a group of trees that grow in warm or tropical climates, usually having tall trunks, no branches, and large leaves on the top. **2** A leaf of this tree.

pan·el /pan′əl/ *n., v.* **pan·eled, pan·el·ing** **1** *n.* A section of a wall, ceiling, etc., that is set off from the rest of the surface. **2** *v.* To put up panels. **3** *n.* A group of people chosen to discuss or judge something: a *panel* of experts. *Alternate spellings:* **pan·elled, pan·elling.**

pan·ic /pan′ik/ *n., v.* **pan·icked, pan·ick·ing** **1** *n.* Sudden fear. **2** *v.* To be filled with fear.

par·a·dise /par′ə·dīs/ *n.* **1** Heaven. **2** A place or condition of extreme happiness or beauty.

par·tial /pär′shəl/ *adj.* Not all; part: a *partial* payment.

part·ner /pärt′nər/ *n.* **1** A person who is associated with another or others, especially in a business. **2** One of two or

more people who perform an activity together, as dancing, etc.

pas·sage /pas′ij/ *n.* A way through which a person or thing may pass, as a hall.

patch·work /pach′wûrk′/ *n.* **1** Pieces of cloth of various colors or shapes sewed together. **2** *adj. use:* a *patchwork* quilt.

pat·ent /pat′(ə)nt/ **1** *n.* A government document that gives a person or a company sole rights to make, sell, or use a new invention or process for a certain number of years. **2** *adj.* Given or protected by a patent. **3** *v.* To obtain a patent on.

pa·ti·o /pat′ē·ō *or* pä′tē·ō/ *n., pl.* **pa·ti·os** **1** The courtyard of a Spanish or Spanish-American building. **2** A paved area by the side of a house.

pa·tri·ot·ic /pā′trē·ot′ik/ *adj.* Having or showing love, loyalty, and devotion of one's own country.

pause /pôz/ *v.* **paused, paus·ing,** *n.* **1** *v.* To stop briefly. **2** *n.* A brief stop.

peace·ful /pēs′fəl/ *adj.* Calm; quiet; full of peace. —**peace′ful·ly** *adv.*

peach /pēch/ *n., pl.* **peach·es,** *adj.* **1** *n.* A round fruit with a fuzzy, yellowish-pink skin. **2** *n.* The tree on which this fruit grows. **3** *n., adj.* A yellowish-pink color.

pearl /pûrl/ *n.* **1** A small, round, usually white or tinted gem formed inside an oyster shell. **2** *adj. use: pearl* necklace.

pe·cul·iar /pi·kyo͞ol′yər/ *adj.* Odd or strange. —**pe·cu′li·ar′i·ty** *n.*

pel·i·can /pel′i·kən/ *n.* A large web-footed bird with a pouch below its beak in which it stores food.

---

act, āte, câre, ärt;   egg, ēven;   if, īce;   on, ōver, ôr;   bo͝ok, fo͞od;   up, tûrn;
ə = a in *ago,* e in *listen,* i in *giraffe,* o in *pilot,* u in *circus;*   yo͞o = u in *music;*   oil;   out;
chair; si**ng**; **sh**op; **th**ank; **th**at; **zh** in *treasure.*

pen·ta·gon /pen′tə·gon/ *n.* A closed plane figure having five straight sides and five angles.

per·cent /pər·sent′/ *n.* Parts in each hundred; hundredths: 14 *percent* or 14% = 14/100 or .14. *Alternate spelling:* **per cent.**

perch /pûrch/ **1** *n.* A bar, branch, pole, etc., on which a bird can come to rest. **2** *v.* To sit, rest, or place on or as on a perch.

per·form·ance /pər·fôr′məns/ *n.* **1** The act of performing or doing. **2** A play, concert, or other kind of entertainment. **3** A particular action or deed.

per·fume /*n.* pûr′fyo͞om, *v.* pər·fyo͞om′/ *n.,* *v.* **per·fumed, per·fum·ing** **1** *n.* A liquid that gives off a fragrant or pleasant smell. **2** A fragrant or pleasant smell, as from flowers. **3** *v.* To fill or scent with a fragrant or pleasing smell.

pe·rim·e·ter /pə·rim′ə·tər/ *n.* **1** The circumference or outer boundary of any plane figure, or the length of the circumference, border, or other boundary. **2** The circumference or outer limits of anything.

per·ish /per′ish/ *v.* To be destroyed; to die: The animals *perished* in the fire.

per·ma·nent /pûr′mən·ənt/ *adj.* Intended to go on without change; lasting. —**per′ma·nent·ly** *adv.*

per·se·cute /pûr′sə·kyo͞ot/ *v.* **per·se·cut·ed, per·se·cut·ing** To mistreat or oppress. —**per′se·cu′tor** *n.*

per·son /pûr′sən/ *n.* A human being.

pes·ti·cide /pes′ti·sīd′/ *n.* A chemical used to kill pests, such as mosquitoes, moths, ants, etc.

pe·tro·le·um /pə·trō′lē·əm/ *n.* A crude oil found in the earth, used as a fuel and as the source for gasoline, kerosene, etc.

phar·ma·cy /fär′mə·sē/ *n., pl.* **phar·ma·cies** **1** The science or business of preparing and selling drugs and medicines. **2** A drugstore.

pho·to·cop·y /fō′tō·kop′ē/ *n., pl.* **pho·to·cop·ies,** *v.* **pho·to·cop·ied, pho·to·cop·y·ing** **1** *n.* A photographic copy of printed or written matter. **2** *v.* To make such a copy.

pho·to·gen·ic /fō′tō·jen′ik/ *adj.* Being an attractive subject for photography or having features that photograph well.

phys·i·cal /fiz′i·kəl/ *adj.* **1** Having to do with the body. **2** Having to do with matter or the laws of nature. **3** Having to do with matter and energy, but not chemical composition: a *physical* science. —**phys′i·cal·ly** *adv.*

pic·nic /pik′nik/ *n., v.* **pic·nicked, pic·nick·ing** **1** *n.* A pleasant trip including a meal usually eaten outdoors. **2** *v.* To go on such a trip.

piece /pēs/ *n.* **1** One of the parts into which a thing is separated or broken. **2** A portion or amount of something complete in itself: a *piece* of meat.

pi·geon /pij′ən/ *n.* A bird with a plump body, small head, and short legs.

pi·o·neer /pī′ə·nir′/ *n.* A person who is first to settle a new region of a country.

piv·ot /piv′ət/ **1** *n.* A pin or shaft on which a part turns. **2** *v.* To turn on or as on a pivot or point.

plas·tic /plas′tik/ **1** *n.* Any of a large group of substances chemically made and molded by heat, pressure, etc., into various products. **2** *adj.* Made of plastic. **3** *adj.* Easily molded.

pla·teau /pla·tō′/ *n.* A large stretch of high level land; a high plain.

pleas·ure /plezh′ər/ *n.* **1** A feeling of great satisfaction; delight; enjoyment. **2** Something that pleases.

pledge /plej/ *n., v.* **pledged, pledg·ing** **1** *n.* A serious or formal promise. **2** *v.* To make such a promise.

pli·ers /plī′ərz/ *n., pl.* A pinching tool used for bending, cutting, or holding.

plumb·er /plum′ər/ *n.* A person who installs and repairs pipes and fixtures connected with the water supply in a building.

pneu·mo·nia /n(y)oo·mōn′yə/ *n.* A disease that inflames the lungs.

poach /pōch/ To cook eggs, etc., in gently boiling water, milk, or other liquid.

po·et /pō′it/ *n.* A person who writes poetry.

poise /poiz/ *v.* **poised, pois·ing,** *n.* **1** *v.* To balance. **2** *n.* Balance. **3** *n.* Ease of manner; composure.

poi·son·ous /poi′zən·əs/ *adj.* Being able to make sick or kill; toxic.

pol·i·cy /pol′ə·sē/ *n., pl.* **po·li·cies** A plan or a decision made about how things should be done.

po·lit·i·cal /pə·lit′i·kəl/ *adj.* Having to do with the government or politicians: *political* parties.

pol·i·tics /pol′ə·tiks/ *n., pl.* The way government operates; the art or science of government.

pol·y·gon /pol′i·gon/ *n.* A closed plane figure having three or more straight sides.

pop·u·lar·i·ty /pop′yə·lar′ə·tē/ *n.* The fact or condition of being well liked.

pop·u·la·tion /pop′yə·lā′shən/ *n.* **1** The total number of people living in a country, etc. **2** The total number of people of a specific group, class, etc.

pore /pôr/ *n.* A tiny natural opening in a leaf or in the skin.

por·poise /pôr′pəs/ *n., pl.* **por·pois·es 1** A sea mammal related to the whale, with a blunt, rounded snout. **2** A dolphin. *Alternate plural:* **porpoise.**

port·a·ble /pôr′tə·bəl/ *adj.* Able to be easily carried around or moved.

por·tion /pôr′shən/ **1** *n.* A part or share of something. **2** *v.* To divide into parts or shares.

pos·i·tive /poz′ə·tiv/ *adj.* **1** Admitting no doubt or denial. **2** Certain; affirmative; definite. **3** Very sure of

oneself. **4** Useful. **5** In math, being greater than zero; plus.

po·ta·to /pə·tā′tō/ *n., pl.* **po·ta·toes** The starchy stem or tuber of a cultivated plant, used as a vegetable.

pour /pôr/ *v.* **1** To cause liquid to flow. **2** To rain heavily; to drench.

prac·ti·cal·ly /prak′tik·lē/ *adv.* Almost.

prac·tice /prak′tis/ *v.* **prac·ticed, prac·tic·ing** *n.* **1** *v.* To do something over and over in order to do it better or improve. **2** *n.* An action done over and over in order to do it better or improve. **3** *n.* Skill gained by such an action: to be out of *practice.*

pre- *prefix* Before in time or order: *pre-determined.*

pre·cau·tion /pri·kô′shən/ *n.* **1** Something done beforehand to prevent or avoid danger or injury. **2** Any care or caution taken in advance.

pre·cede /pri·sēd′/ *v.* **pre·ced·ed, pre·ced·ing** To be, go, or come before.

pre·cious /presh′əs/ *adj.* **1** Highly prized; valuable: A diamond is a *precious* gem. **2** Cherished.

pre·ci·sion /pri·sizh′ən/ *n.* Exactness.

pre·dict /pri·dikt′/ *v.* To forecast or foretell. —**pre·dic′tion** *n.*

pre·fer /pri·fûr′/ *v.* **pre·ferred, pre·fer·ring** To like better.

pre·fix /prē′fiks/ *n.* A word part that is added to the beginning of a word to change its meaning.

pre·his·tor·ic /prē′his·tôr′ik/ *adj.* Of or belonging to the era or period before the start of written history: Dinosaurs were *prehistoric* animals.

prej·u·dice /prej′oo·dis or prej′əd·əs/ *n.* An unfair opinion formed without examining facts or evidence.

pre·paid /prē·pād′/ *adj.* Paid for in advance.

prep·a·ra·tion /prep′ə·rā′shən/ *n.* **1** The act of preparing or being prepared. **2** Something done in order to get ready. **3** Something made or prepared.

---

act, āte, câre, ärt;　　egg, ēven;　　if, īce;　　on, ōver, ôr;　　book, food;　　up, tûrn;
ə = a in *ago*, e in *listen*, i in *giraffe*, o in *pilot*, u in *circus*;　　yoo = u in *music*;　　oil;　　out;
chair;　sing;　shop;　thank;　that;　zh in *treasure.*

pre·pare /pri·pâr'/ *v.* **pre·pared, pre·par·ing** To get or make ready.

pre·scrip·tion /pri·skrip'shən/ *n.* **1** A doctor's formula for the preparation and use of a medicine. **2** The medicine itself.

pre·tend /pri·tend'/ *v.* **1** To make believe. **2** To give a false impression.

pre·tense /pri·tens' *or* prē'tens/ *n.* A false act or show of something.

pret·ty /prit'ē/ *adj.* **pret·ti·er, pret·ti·est,** *adv.* **1** *adj.* Attractive; pleasant. **2** *adv.* Somewhat.

pre·vent /pri·vent'/ *v.* **1** To keep something from happening. **2** To stop or hinder. —**pre·ven'tion** *n.*

pre·view /prē'vyoo'/ **1** *n.* An advance showing of all or parts of a motion picture, television show, play, etc. **2** *v.* To show or view in advance.

pre·vi·ous /prē'vē·əs/ *adj.* Being, occurring, or coming before something else in time or order.

print /print/ *n., v.* **print·ed, print·ing** **1** *n.* Letters, words, etc., marked on paper or another material with ink, from type, plates, etc. **2** *n.* A picture or design made from an engraved plate or block. **3** *v.* To stamp or impress letters, words, etc., on or into a surface. **4** *v.* To publish as a newspaper, book, magazine, etc. **5** *v.* To write in letters like those used in print.

pris·on·er /priz'(ə)n·ər/ *n.* A person who is held captive or confined in a prison.

pro·duce /*v.* prə·d(y)oos', *n.* prod'(y)oos *or* prō'd(y)oos/ *v.* **pro·duced, pro·duc·ing,** *n.* **1** *v.* To bring into existence; to yield. **2** *n.* Farm products, especially those grown for market. **3** *v.* To compose or create. **4** *v.* To cause or bring about. **5** *v.* To manufacture. **6** *v.* To bring before the public, as a play, etc.

prod·uct /prod'əkt/ *n.* **1** Something produced, as by growth, labor, study, or skill. **2** A result: Success is often the *product* of hard work. **3** The result obtained by multiplication.

pro·jec·tor /prə·jek'tər/ *n.* A machine that casts or projects images, as slides and movies, onto a screen.

pro·mote /prə·mōt'/ *v.* **pro·mot·ed, pro·mot·ing** **1** To help or work for the progress, development, or growth of. **2** To advance to a higher position, rank, etc. **3** To try to make popular, as by advertising or campaigning.

pro·nun·ci·a·tion /prə·nun'sē·ā'shən/ *n.* The way of saying words or sounds.

proof·read /proof'rēd'/ *v.* **proof·read, proof·read·ing** To read and correct errors in something written.

pro·pel /prə·pel'/ *v.* **pro·pelled, pro·pel·ling** To cause to move forward.

prop·er·ty /prop'ər·tē/ *n., pl.* **prop·er·ties** **1** Anything that a person legally possesses. **2** A piece of land. **3** A particular characteristic.

pro·por·tion /prə·pôr'shən/ *n.* **1** The relative size, number, or degree between things; ratio. **2** In math, the relationship of four numbers when the quotient of one pair equals the quotient of the other pair.

pros·pect /pros'pekt/ **1** *n.* The act of looking ahead; expectation: The *prospect* of a vacation cheered us. **2** *n.* (*often pl.*) The possibility of future success: business *prospects*. **3** *n.* A possible buyer or candidate: a good *prospect* for the job. **4** *n.* A wide view ahead. **5** *v.* To explore or search out.

pro·tec·tion /prə·tek'shən/ *n.* The act or condition of protecting someone or something from harm or injury.

psalm /säm/ *n.* A hymn or poem of praise.

psy·chol·o·gist /sī·kol'ə·jəst/ *n.* A person who studies the mind and behavior.

pub·lic /pub'lik/ **1** *adj.* Of, by, or for the people. **2** *n.* All the people. **3** *adj.* Known by most people.

pub·lish /pub'lish/ *v.* To print and offer for sale or distribution a book, magazine, newspaper, etc.

pueb·lo /pweb'lō/ *n., pl.* **pueb·los** or **pueb·lo** **1** An adobe or stone building or group of buildings of the Indians of the southwestern U.S. **2** (*written* **Pueblo**) A member of one of the Indian tribes that live in such buildings.

pulse /puls/ *n.* **1** The regular beating or throbbing of the arteries caused by contractions of the heart.   **2** Any regular beat, ring, or throbbing.

pure /pyŏŏr/ *adj.* **pur·er, pur·est 1** Not mixed with anything else.   **2** Perfectly clean; free from anything unhealthful.

pu·ri·fy /pyŏŏr′ə·fī/ *v.* **pu·ri·fied, pu·ri·fy·ing** To make or become pure.

pyr·a·mid /pir′ə·mid/ *n.*   **1** A solid geometrical figure having a flat base with three or more triangular sides that meet at the top.   **2** Any of the huge monuments shaped like a pyramid where ancient Egyptian rulers were buried.

Q

quake /kwāk/ *v.* **quaked, quak·ing,** *n.* **1** *v.* To shake or tremble: to *quake* with fear.   **2** *n.* A shaking or trembling. **3** *n.* An earthquake.

qual·i·fy /kwol′ə·fī/ *v.* **qual·i·fied, qual·i·fy·ing** To have the needed ability, as for a job, a school, etc.

qual·i·ty /kwol′ə·tē/ *n., pl.* **qual·i·ties 1** Something special about a person or thing that makes it what it is; characteristic.   **2** The grade or degree of excellence or worth.

quar·rel /kwôr′əl/ *n., v.* **quar·reled, quar·rel·ing   1** *n.* An angry argument; a squabble.   **2** *v.* To argue. *Alternate spellings:* **quarrelled, quarrelling.**

quick·ly /kwik′lē/ *adv.* Fast; swiftly.

qui·et /kwī′ət/ *v., adj.* **qui·et·er, qui·et·est 1** *adj.* Having and making little or no noise.   **2** *adj.* Without stress; calm.   **3** *v.* To make quiet.

quiz /kwiz/ *n., pl.* **quiz·zes,** *v.* **quizzed, quiz·zing 1** *n.* A short test.   **2** *v.* To test by asking questions.

R

ra·di·o /rā′dē·ō/ *n., pl.* **ra·di·os** A device that receives electromagnetic waves and changes them back into sound waves we can hear.

rad·ish /rad′ish/ *n., pl.* **rad·ish·es 1** The small, crisp, red or white bulb-shaped root of a garden plant, usually eaten raw.   **2** The plant itself.

ra·di·us /rā′dē·əs/ *n., pl.* **ra·di·i 1** A straight line extending from the center of a circle to the circumference.   **2** A circular area or boundary measured by the length of the radius: a *radius* of 20 miles. *Alternate plural:* **radiuses.**

rain·fall /rān′fôl′/ *n.*   **1** A shower.   **2** The amount of water that falls as rain, hail, or snow during a certain length of time.

rain·y /rā′nē/ *adj.* **rain·i·er, rain·i·est** Having much rain.

rap·id /rap′id/ *adj.* Quick; fast; swift.

ra·tio /rā′shō *or* rā′shē·ō/ *n., pl.* **ra·tios** The relationship between two quantities; a proportion: If there are 6 dogs and 3 cats, the *ratio* of dogs to cats is 2 to 1 or 2:1.

re- *prefix* **1** Back: *repay.*   **2** Again: *rewrite.*

reach /rēch/ *v.* **reached, reach·ing 1** To touch or get hold of.   **2** To go or extend.   **3** To arrive at.

reb·el *n. or* **re·bel** *v.* /*n.* reb′əl, *v.* ri·bel′/ *n., v.* **re·belled, re·bel·ling 1** *n.* A person who resists authority or fights against it.   **2** *v.* To rise up against a governing power.   **3** *v.* To resist or feel opposition toward.

---

act, āte, câre, ärt;   egg, ēven;   if, īce;   on, ōver, ôr;   bŏŏk, fōōd;   up, tûrn;
ə = a in *ago,* e in *listen,* i in *giraffe,* o in *pilot,* u in *circus;*   yōō = u in *music;*   oil;   out;
chair;   sing;   shop;   thank;   that;   zh in *treasure.*

re·ceipt /ri·sēt′/ *n.* **1** A slip of paper that shows that something has been received or paid for. **2** The receiving of something: the *receipt* of a gift.

re·ceive /ri·sēv′/ *v.* **re·ceived, re·ceiv·ing** **1** To get or accept: to *receive* a package. **2** To suffer: to *receive* an injury. **3** To gain knowledge of; to learn: He *received* the news at noon.

rec·i·pe /res′ə·pē/ *n.* A set of directions for cooking or preparing a certain food or dish.

rec·om·mend /rek′ə·mend′/ *v.* **1** To praise. **2** To advise or suggest.

rec·tan·gle /rek′tang′gəl/ *n.* A parallelogram having four right angles.

re·cy·cle /rē′sī′kəl/ *v.* **re·cy·cled, re·cy·cling** To treat something, as paper, aluminum, etc., in a special way so that it can be used again.

re·duce /ri·d(y)o͞os′/ *v.* **re·duced, re·duc·ing** **1** To make less or smaller. **2** To express in the smallest possible numbers, as a fraction: ⁶⁄₉ can be *reduced* to ⅔.

re·e·val·u·ate /rē′i·val′yo͞o·āt/ *v.* **re·e·val·u·at·ed, re·e·val·u·at·ing** To judge or estimate the worth, importance, or value of something again.

re·fer /ri·fûr′/ *v.* **re·ferred, re·fer·ring** **1** To turn to for help, information, treatment, etc. **2** To send for help, information, treatment, etc.

re·fine /ri·fīn′/ *v.* **re·fined, re·fin·ing** **1** To make or become pure. **2** To make or become polished or cultured: to *refine* one's manners.

re·fined /ri·fīnd′/ *adj.* **1** Free from impurities. **2** Cultured; finished: *refined* manners.

re·flect /ri·flekt′/ *v.* **1** To throw back, as heat, sound, etc. **2** To give back an image of, as a mirror. **3** To think or ponder: Grandpa often *reflects* on the past. **4** To show, exhibit, or express. —**re·flec′tion** *n.*

re·form /ri·fôrm′/ **1** *v.* To make better by correcting wrongs, abuses, faults, etc. **2** *v.* To become better; to improve one's conduct. **3** *n.* A change intended to improve a situation.

re·fuse¹ /ri·fyo͞oz′/ *v.* **re·fused, re·fus·ing** To say that one will not give, take, allow, or agree to something; to decline: to *refuse* help.

ref·use² /ref′yo͞os/ *n.* Trash: Throw out the *refuse*.

reg·u·lar /reg′yə·lər/ *adj.* **1** Usual; habitual; normal. **2** Always happening at the same time.

re·hear·sal /ri·hûr′səl/ *n.* A practice session.

reign /rān/ **1** *v.* To rule or govern. **2** *n.* The period or time during which a sovereign, as a king or queen, rules.

rein·deer /rān′dir′/ *n., pl.* **rein·deer** A kind of deer with large branching antlers found in northern regions.

re·joice /ri·jois′/ *v.* **re·joiced, re·joic·ing** To be filled with joy.

re·la·tion /ri·lā′shən/ *n.* **1** A person related by kinship; a relative. **2** (*pl.*) The connection between people or countries: international *relations*.

re·lease /ri·lēs′/ *v.* **re·leased, re·leas·ing,** *n.* **1** *v.* To set free. **2** *n.* A being set free; freedom. **3** *v.* To let go: *Release* the brake so the car will move.

re·load /rē·lōd′/ *v.* To load again.

re·ly /ri·lī′/ *v.* **re·lied, re·ly·ing** To depend on. —**re·li′a·ble** *adj.*

re·main·der /ri·mān′dər/ *n.* **1** The part left over; the rest. **2** In math, the number left over after subtracting one number from another or dividing one number by another.

rem·e·dy /rem′ə·dē/ *n., pl.* **rem·e·dies,** *v.* **rem·e·died, rem·e·dy·ing** **1** *n.* Something that cures or corrects. **2** *v.* To cure or correct.

re·mem·ber /ri·mem′bər/ v. **1** To call to mind again. **2** To keep in mind.

re·mind /ri·mīnd′/ v. To cause to remember.

re·mote /ri·mōt′/ adj. **re·mo·ter, re·mot·est 1** Far away; distant. **2** From a distance, as by radio waves. **3** Distant in time. **4** Slight.

re·move /ri·mōōv′/ v. **re·moved, re·mov·ing** To take off or move away.

re·pair /ri·pâr′/ **1** v. To fix or mend. **2** n. (often pl.) The act of repairing. —**re·pair′a·ble** adj.

re·peat /ri·pēt′/ v. To say or do again.

re·place /ri·plās′/ v. **re·placed, re·plac·ing 1** To put back in place. **2** To take or fill the place of.

re·play /rē·plā′/ **1** v. To play again. **2** n. The act of replaying. **3** v. To show a TV tape again.

re·port /ri·pôrt′/ **1** v. To tell about something. **2** n. An account of something, often formal or written. **3** v. To state; to announce. **4** n. A statement or announcement. **5** v. To complain about or make known, especially to the authorities.

re·quest /ri·kwest′/ **1** v. To ask for; to demand. **2** n. The act of requesting.

res·cue /res′kyōō/ v. **res·cued, res·cu·ing, n. 1** v. To save or free from danger, confinement, etc.: The fire fighter rescued the man from the burning building. **2** n. The act of saving from danger, confinement, etc.: we were relieved that the rescue was successful. **3** adj. use: rescue attempt.

res·i·dence /rez′ə·dəns/ n. The place where a person lives; home; dwelling.

re·sign /ri·zīn′/ v. **1** To give up or leave, as a job. **2** To give up or yield.

re·source /ri·sôrs′ or rē′sôrs/ n., **re·sourc·es** A supply of something that can be used or drawn on.

re·spect·ful /ri·spekt′fəl/ adj. Showing respect in a manner that exhibits regard, honor, or consideration.

re·store /ri·stôr′/ v. **re·stored, re·stor·ing 1** To bring back to a former condition. **2** To bring back; to establish again: to restore order.

re·tain /ri·tān′/ v. **1** To continue to keep or hold. **2** To remember.

re·turn /ri·tûrn′/ v. **re·turned, re·turn·ing 1** To come or go back. **2** To give or bring back. **3** To repay.

re·u·nite /rē′yōō·nīt′/ v. **re·u·nit·ed, re·u·nit·ing** To get or cause to get together again.

re·veal /ri·vēl′/ v. **1** To make known. **2** To make visible.

re·venge /ri·venj′/ v. **re·venged, re·veng·ing, n. 1** v. To get back at someone by inflicting punishment, injury, etc., in return for a wrong received. **2** n. The act of revenge.

re·verse /ri·vûrs′/ adj., v. **re·versed, re·vers·ing, n. 1** adj. Having the back or rear part facing the observer. **2** v. To turn inside out or upside down. **3** n. The back or rear side of something. **4** v. To turn in the opposite direction.

re·view /ri·vyōō′/ **1** v. To examine or look at again. **2** v. To consider or think about the past. **3** n. A critical article on a book, movie, etc. **4** v. To write such an article.

re·vise /ri·vīz′/ v. **re·vised, re·vis·ing 1** To amend or correct. **2** To change.

rhi·noc·e·ros /rī·nos′ər·əs/ n., pl. **rhi·noc·e·ros·es** A large, heavy, thick-skinned, plant-eating mammal, found in Africa and Asia, having one or two upright horns on its snout. Alternate plural: **rhinoceros.**

ridge /rij/ n. **1** A long, narrow, raised strip. **2** A long, narrow chain of hills or mountains. **3** The line where two sloping surfaces meet.

ri·ot /rī′ət/ **1** n. A violent or wild disturbance involving a large group of people. **2** v. To take part in a riot.

ripe /rīp/ adj. **rip·er, rip·est** Fully grown and ready to eat, as a fruit.

---

act, āte, câre, ärt;   egg, ēven;   if, īce;   on, ōver, ôr;   bŏŏk, fōōd;   up, tûrn;
ə = a in ago, e in listen, i in giraffe, o in pilot, u in circus;   yōō = u in music;   oil;   out;
chair; sing; shop; thank; that; zh in treasure.

rival

ri·val /rī′vəl/ *n., v.* **ri·valed, ri·val·ing** **1** *n.* A competitor; a foe. **2** *adj. use:* a *rival* chess player. **3** *v.* To try to excel or outdo. *Alternate spellings:* **rivalled, rivalling.** ► *Rival* comes from the Latin word *rivalis,* "those who live near the same stream."

roar /rôr/ **1** *v.* To make a loud, deep noise. **2** *n.* A loud, deep noise. **3** *v.* To laugh loudly.

ro·de·o /rō′dē·ō *or* rō·dā′ō/ *n., pl.* **ro·de·os** A public contest and entertainment in which people compete in bronco riding, calf roping, etc.

room·mate /rōōm′māt′/ *n.* A person who shares a room, apartment, house, etc., with another.

roy·al /roi′əl/ *adj.* **1** Having to do with a king or queen, or a member of his or her family. **2** Like or appropriate for a king or queen; splendid.

ru·in /rōō′in/ **1** *n.* (*often pl.*) The remains of something left after destruction, decay, or downfall. **2** *n.* The condition of destruction, decay, or downfall. **3** *v.* To destroy or damage; to spoil.

ru·mor /rōō′mər/ **1** *n.* Information that is not necessarily true, but is spread from one person to another; gossip. **2** *v.* To tell as a rumor.

S

sad /sad/ *adj.* **sad·der, sad·dest** **1** Unhappy. **2** Causing unhappiness.

safe /sāf/ *adj.* **saf·er, saf·est,** *n.* **1** *adj.* Free from danger or harm. **2** *adj.* Not hurt. **3** *adj.* Careful. **4** *n.* A steel or iron box used for keeping money, jewels, etc.

sal·a·ry /sal′ər·ē/ *n., pl.* **sal·a·ries** A fixed amount of money paid at specific times for regular work.

salm·on /sam′ən/ **1** *n.* A large food fish, having a delicate pink color. **2** *n., adj.* A reddish or pinkish orange color.

sa·lute /sə·lōōt′/ *v.* **sa·lut·ed, sa·lut·ing,** *n.* **1** *v.* To recognize or honor in a formal way by raising the hand to the head, firing guns, etc. **2** *n.* The act of saluting.

senator

sau·cer /sô′sər/ *n.* **1** A round, almost flat dish, used to hold a cup. **2** Anything shaped like a saucer.

sau·sage /sô′sij/ *n.* Highly seasoned minced or chopped meat, often packed into a thin tube or skin.

sci·en·tif·ic /sī′ən·tif′ik/ *adj.* Of, having to do with, discovered by, or used in science.

scorch /skôrch/ *v.* To burn slightly on the surface; to singe.

scraw·ny /skrô′nē/ *adj.* **scraw·ni·er, scraw·ni·est** Skinny; very thin; bony.

scrib·ble /skrib′əl/ *v.* **scrib·bled, scrib·bling,** *n.* **1** *v.* To write in a hasty or careless way. **2** *n.* Careless or uncontrolled writing.

sculp·tor /skulp′tər/ *n.* An artist who creates a sculpture from stone, clay, etc.

search /sûrch/ **1** *v.* To examine or look through thoroughly. **2** *v.* To attempt to find by looking; to seek. **3** *n.* The act of searching; examination.

se·cure /si·kyōor′/ *adj., v.* **se·cured, se·cur·ing** **1** *adj.* Safe against loss, danger, etc. **2** *v.* To make safe. **3** *adj.* Firmly fastened. **4** *v.* To firmly fasten.

se·cur·i·ty /si·kyōor′ə·tē/ *n., pl.* **se·cur·i·ties** **1** The feeling or condition of being secure or safe. **2** A person or thing that secures or makes safe. **3** (*pl.*) Stocks or bonds.

seize /sēz/ *v.* **seized, seiz·ing** **1** To take hold of suddenly or with force; to grasp. **2** To capture or arrest.

sel·dom /sel′dəm/ *adv.* Not often; rarely.

self·ish /sel′fish/ *adj.* **1** Caring too much for oneself and not considering others. **2** Exhibiting or caused by too much care or concern for oneself and a disregard of others. —**self′ish·ly** *adv.*

sen·ate /sen′it/ *n.* **1** A governing body, usually possessing law-making powers. **2** (*written* **Senate**) The upper house in the legislative branch of the U.S. government or of a state or other government.

sen·a·tor /sen′ə·tər/ *n.* (*sometimes written* **Senator**) An elected member of a senate; a member of the upper house of the U.S. Congress.

Harcourt Brace School Publishers

sensational

snack

sen·sa·tion·al /sen·sā′shən·əl/ *adj.*
1 Arousing great excitement or interest. **2** Designed to arouse great excitement or interest: a *sensational* news
report.

sep·a·rate /*v.* sep′ə·rāt, *adj.* sep′ər·it *or*
sep′rit/ *v.* **sep·a·rat·ed, sep·a·rat·ing,**
adj. **1** *v.* To move or pull apart; to divide. **2** *adj.* Not connected; detached.
3 *adj.* Not shared; individual. **4** *v.* To
keep apart by being between; to divide.

serve /sûrv/ *v.* **served, serv·ing,** *n.* **1** *v.*
To work for; to help. **2** To wait on or
bring. **3** *v.* In tennis, to put the ball in
play. **4** *n.* In tennis, the act of putting
the ball in play.

sev·er·al /sev′ər·əl *or* sev′rəl/ *adj., pron.*
More than two but less than many.

se·vere /si·vir′/ *adj.* **se·ver·er, se·ver·est**
1 Very harsh; strict. **2** Serious; major.

shad·ow /shad′ō/ **1** *n.* A dark image cast
on a surface by a body or object coming
between the source of light and the surface. **2** *v.* To cast a shadow.

sharp /shärp/ *adv., adj.* **sharp·er, sharp·
est 1** *adj.* Having a fine point or thin
edge; able to cut. **2** *adj.* Turning
suddenly. **3** *adj.* Cutting; piercing.
4 *adj.* Very keen; acute: *sharp* sight.
5 *adj.* Harsh; abrupt. **6** *adv.* Promptly.

sheep /shēp/ *n., pl.* **sheep** An animal
with a thick coat and hoofs, usually
raised for its wool and meat.

sheep·ish /shē′pish/ *adj.* **1** Awkwardly
bashful or embarrassed. **2** Like a
sheep; timid or meek.

shel·lac /shə·lak′/ *n., v.* **shel·lacked,
shel·lack·ing 1** *n.* A liquid that gives
a smooth, shiny appearance to wood,
metal, etc. **2** *v.* To coat with this liquid.

shield /shēld/ **1** *n.* A large board or
broad metal piece with a handle in
back, once carried by warriors to protect themselves in battle. **2** *n.* Something that protects one from harm or
injury. **3** *v.* To protect or guard from
harm or injury.

shore /shôr/ *n.* The coast.

shoul·der /shōl′dər/ *n.* The part of the
body to which a human's arm, an animal's foreleg, or a bird's wing is attached. —**shoulder to the wheel** To
set to work with a hard or strong effort.

shriek /shrēk/ **1** *n.* A loud, sharp, shrill
scream or sound. **2** *v.* To make a loud,
sharp, shrill scream or sound.

siege /sēj/ *n.* An attempt to capture a for-
tified place by surrounding it.

sim·i·lar /sim′ə·lər/ *adj.* Very much alike,
but not completely the same.

sim·ple /sim′pəl/ *adj.* **sim·pler, sim·plest
1** Easy to understand or do. **2** Plain.

sim·pli·fy /sim′plə·fī/ *v.* **sim·pli·fied,
sim·pli·fy·ing** To make easier.

sin·cer·i·ty /sin·ser′ə·tē/ *n.* The quality or
condition of being honest or genuine.

sit·u·a·tion /sich′ōō·ā′shən/ *n.* A state of
affairs caused by particular circum-
stances; condition.

sleep·y /slē′pē/ *adj.* **sleep·i·er, sleep·i·est**
Tired; drowsy.

sleigh /slā/ **1** *n.* A vehicle with runners
for use on snow or ice, usually drawn
by a horse. **2** *v.* To ride in a sleigh.

slim /slim/ *adj.* **slim·mer, slim·mest**
Slender or thin; skinny.

slum·ber /slum′bər/ **1** *v.* To sleep
lightly; to doze. **2** *n.* Sleep. **3** *adj. use:*
slumber party.

snack /snak/ **1** *n.* A light meal. **2** *n.*
Anything eaten between meals. **3** *v.*
To eat a snack.

act, āte, câre, ärt;   egg, ēven;   if, īce;   on, ōver, ôr;   book, food;   up, tûrn;
ə = a in *ago*, e in *listen*, i in *giraffe*, o in *pilot*, u in *circus*;   yoo = u in *music*;   oil;   out;
ch air; si ng; sh op; th ank; th at; zh in *treasure*.

snob·bish /snob'ish/ *adj.* Of or like someone who looks down on others.

so·cial /sō'shəl/ *adj.* **1** Living or liking to live with others. **2** Friendly toward other people. **3** Having to do with friendliness.

so·lar /sō'lər/ *adj.* Having to do with or coming from the sun: *solar* energy.

sol·emn /sol'əm/ *adj.* **1** Serious. **2** Somber; gloomy.

sol·id /sol'id/ **1** *n.* Anything that is not a liquid or a gas. **2** *adj.* Not hollow. **3** *adj.* Strong; without defect.

so·lu·tion /sə·loo'shən/ *n.* **1** The solving of a problem, difficulty, etc. **2** The answer to a problem, difficulty, etc.; explanation. **3** The mixture formed by combining one substance in another so that the molecules of each are evenly distributed.

solve /solv/ *v.* **solved, solv·ing** To find out the answer to something.

some·body /sum'bod'ē *or* sum'bəd·ē/ *pron.* A person unknown or not named.

soothe /sooth/ *v.* **soothed, sooth·ing** To calm or relieve.

source /sôrs/ *n.* A person or place from which anything begins or is obtained.

soy·bean /soi'bēn'/ *n.* **1** The edible seed of an Asian plant. **2** The plant itself.

spe·cies /spē'shēz *or* spē'sēz/ *n., pl.* **spe·cies** A group of animals or plants that have certain characteristics in common and can interbreed.

spend /spend/ *v.* **spent, spend·ing** **1** To use money to buy things. **2** To use or use up. **3** To pass time.

spir·it /spir'it/ *n.* **1** The life-giving or inner force of a human being, as the mind or the soul. **2** A divine or supreme being. **3** A supernatural being: the Holy *Spirit*. **4** Liveliness; vigor;

courage. **5** Vigorous sense of devotion or loyalty: team *spirit*.

splen·did /splen'did/ *adj.* **1** Brilliant; magnificent. **2** Excellent.

sports /spôrts/ **1** *n.* Games, especially outdoor, athletic games. **2** *adj.* Having to do with these games. **3** *adj.* Casual; informal.

squad /skwod/ *n.* A small group or team of persons working together.

squall /skwôl/ **1** *n.* A sudden, fierce wind, which often brings with it rain or snow; a storm. **2** *v.* To cry or scream loudly, as babies do.

square /skwâr/ **1** *n.* A shape having four equal sides and four right angles. **2** *adj.* Having this shape. **3** *n.* An area bordered on four sides by streets.

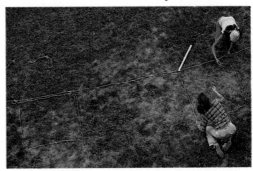

squeak /skwēk/ **1** *n.* A sharp, shrill noise. **2** *v.* To make such a noise. —**squeak'y** *adj.*

squirm /skwûrm/ *v.* To bend and twist the body; to wriggle.

squirt /skwûrt/ *n., v.* **squirt·ed, squirt·ing** **1** *v.* To come out or force to come out in a thin stream; to spurt. **2** *v.* To wet by squirting. **3** *n.* A jet, thin stream, or spurt of liquid.

stalk¹ /stôk/ *n.* The stem of a plant.

stalk² /stôk/ *v.* To approach or pursue without being seen or heard, especially animals and other prey.

starch /stärch/ *n., pl.* **starch·es** **1** *n.* A white vegetable substance having no taste or smell. **2** *n.* A preparation of this substance used to stiffen clothes. **3** *v.* To put starch on clothes.

sta·tion·ar·y /stā'shən·er'ē/ *adj.* Not moving or movable.

Harcourt Brace School Publishers

stead·y /sted′ē/ *adj.* **stead·i·er, stead·i·est,** *v.* **stead·ied, stead·y·ing** **1** *adj.* Not moving; fixed. **2** *adj.* Changing little in movement or actions. **3** *adj.* Reliable. **4** *adj.* Regular: a *steady* customer. **5** *v.* To keep or make steady.

steam /stēm/ *n.* The vapor given off when water is boiled.

steer /stir/ *v.* **steered, steer·ing** To guide or direct the course of, as a car or boat.

step /step/ *n., v.* **stepped, step·ping** **1** *n.* A movement made by lifting one's foot and putting it down in another place. **2** *n.* A stair. **3** *v.* To move by taking steps.

ster·e·o /ster′ē·ō *or* stir′ē·ō/ *n., pl.* **ster·e·os** A shortened form of stereophonic system. A stereophonic system is a way of recording sound with separate microphones and playing it back on separate loudspeakers.

stin·gy /stin′jē/ *adj.* **stin·gi·er, stin·gi·est** **1** Not willing to spend, give, or share; not generous. **2** Very small; scanty or skimpy; meager.

stock·hold·er /stok′hōl′dər/ *n.* A person who owns shares in a corporation.

storm /stôrm/ **1** *n.* A strong wind often accompanied by rain, snow, thunder, etc. **2** *n.* A heavy fall of rain, snow, etc. **3** *n.* A violent outburst. **4** *v.* To be very angry. **5** *v.* To rush or move about violently.

stout /stout/ *adj.* **1** Fat and large; chubby. **2** Firmly built; strong.

stow /stō/ *v.* To pack things away.

straw /strô/ **1** *n.* The dried stalks or stems of grain. **2** *n.* One such stem or stalk. **3** *adj.* Of or like straw. **4** *n.* A thin tube used to suck up a drink.

stream·line /strēm′līn′/ *v.* **stream·lined, stream·lin·ing,** *adj.* **1** *v.* To shape something so that it offers the least resistance to air or water. **2** *adj.* Having a simple, smooth, flowing, or efficient shape: a *streamlined* boat.

stren·u·ous /stren′yoo·əs/ *adj.* Requiring much effort, energy, or work: Running long distances is *strenuous* exercise.

strong /strông/ *adj.* **1** Having a great deal of power or force. **2** Solidly made. **3** Very potent: a *strong* smell. **4** Not easily influenced.

stur·dy /stûr′dē/ *adj.* **stur·di·er, stur·di·est** Very strong: Steel is a very *sturdy* metal.

styl·ish /stī′lish/ *adj.* Having style; fashionable. —**styl′ish·ly** *adv.*

sub·merge /səb·mûrj′/ *v.* **sub·merged, sub·merg·ing** **1** To put or sink below the surface of water or any liquid. **2** To cover with water.

suc·ceed /sək·sēd′/ *v.* **1** To accomplish what is planned or desired. **2** To come after.

suf·fi·cient /sə·fish′ənt/ *adj.* Equal to what is needed; enough; adequate: Donald had a *sufficient* amount of money to buy the basketball. —**suf·fi′ cient·ly** *adv.*

suf·fix /suf′iks/ *n.* A word part that is added to the end of a word to add meaning or change its part of speech.

su·per·vi·sion /soo′pər·vizh′ən/ *n.* Direction; overseeing.

sur·face /sûr′fis/ *n., v.* **sur·faced, sur·fac·ing** **1** *n.* The face of any solid body, or the top of a liquid. **2** *v.* To rise to the surface, as a submarine. **3** *n.* The way a person or situation appears to be: He is always cheerful on the *surface*.

sur·ger·y /sûr′jər·ē/ *n.* **1** The branch of medicine that is concerned with the repair and removal of diseased parts of the body. **2** A surgical operation. **3** A room for surgical operations.

sur·round /sə·round′/ *v.* To enclose completely; to encircle.

sur·viv·al /sər·vī′vəl/ *n.* The act or condition of outlasting or surviving.

sus·pend·ers /sə·spen′dərz/ *n.* A pair of straps worn over the shoulders to hold up a pair of trousers.

---

act, āte, câre, ärt;   egg, ēven;   if, īce;   on, ōver, ôr;   book, food;   up, tûrn;
ə = a in *ago,* e in *listen,* i in *giraffe,* o in *pilot,* u in *circus;*   yoo = u in *music;*   oil;   out;
chair; sing; shop; thank; that; zh in *treasure.*

suspense | **throughout**

sus·pense /sə·spens'/ *n.* A state or condition in which there is a great deal of uncertainty or excitement about what is going to happen.

sus·tain /sə·stān'/ *v.* To maintain the strength or spirits of; to keep up.

swal·low /swol'ō/ *v.* To make food or drink go from your mouth into your stomach.

sweet /swēt/ *adj.* **sweet·er, sweet·est** **1** Having an agreeable or pleasant taste, like that of sugar or honey. **2** Containing sugar in some form. **3** Not salty: *sweet* butter. **4** Gentle; kind; charming.

sys·tem /sis'təm/ *n.* **1** A set or group of parts or things that form a whole. **2** An organized group of facts, principles, beliefs, etc., that are arranged into an orderly plan: a *system* of government. **3** A plan, scheme, or procedure: a *system* for filing papers.

T

tal·ent /tal'ənt/ *n.* A natural ability to do something well: She has a *talent* for ice skating.

taught /tôt/ Past tense and past participle of *teach.*

tax /taks/ **1** *n.* An amount of money paid by individuals, businesses, etc., and used for public purposes. **2** *v.* To put a tax on.

tax·i /tak'sē/ *n., pl.* **tax·is** A car hired to carry passengers; a taxicab.

teach /tēch/ *v.* **taught, teach·ing** **1** To help to learn; to make understand. **2** To give instructions to. **3** To give instruction or lessons, as a teacher.

tel·e·gram /tel'ə·gram/ *n.* A message sent by telegraph: I received a *telegram* telling me when they would arrive.

tel·e·graph /tel'ə·graf/ **1** *n.* A device for sending and receiving messages by means of a series of electrical impulses. **2** *v.* To send or receive a message by this device.

tel·e·scope /tel'ə·skōp/ *n.* An instrument that uses magnifying lenses and sometimes mirrors to make distant objects appear nearer and larger.

tel·e·vise /tel'ə·vīz/ *v.* **tel·e·vised tel·e·vis·ing** To broadcast by means of television.

tel·e·vi·sion /tel'ə·vizh'ən/ *n.* **1** The process of sending and receiving images and sounds over cables or through the air by means of electrical impulses. **2** The apparatus on which these images and sounds can be seen and heard; a television set. **3** *adj. use:* a *television* set.

tem·po·rar·y /tem'pə·rer'ē/ *adj.* Lasting only for a short time; not permanent. **—tem'po·rar'i·ly** *adv.* ► *Temporary* comes from the Latin word *tempus,* "time."

ten·or /ten'ər/ *n.* **1** The highest male voice in music. **2** A person with such a voice. **3** *adj. use: tenor* voice.

ter·mi·nal /tûr'mə·nəl/ **1** *adj.* At, forming, or having to do with a limit or end. **2** *n.* A boundary or end. **3** *n.* A railway or bus station.

ther·mom·e·ter /thər·mom'ə·tər/ *n.* An instrument for measuring temperature.

ther·mos /thûr'məs/ *n.* (*also written* **Thermos**) A bottle or jug that keeps liquids hot or cold: a trademark.

ther·mo·stat /thûr'mə·stat/ *n.* A device that establishes and maintains a certain temperature automatically.

thin /thin/ *adj.* **thin·ner, thin·nest** **1** Narrow. **2** Slim. **3** Watery; not thick or creamy. **4** Flimsy: a *thin* shirt.

thrift·y /thrif'tē/ *adj.* **thrift·i·er, thrift·i·est** Careful about spending money; economical: a *thrifty* consumer.

through·out /thrōō·out'/ *adj., prep.* In or to every part of.

throw

turnpike

throw /thrō/ *v.* **threw, thrown, throw·ing,** *n.* **1** *v.* To toss or fling. **2** *n.* The act of throwing. **3** *v.* To cause to fall. —**throw away** To get rid of something; to discard.

to·ma·to /tə·mā′tō *or* tə·mä′tō/ *n., pl.* **to·ma·toes** A round, red, pulpy fruit, usually used as a vegetable.

tomb /tōōm/ *n.* A place for burying the dead, as a grave or vault.

top·ic /top′ik/ *n.* A subject discussed in speech or in writing.

tor·na·do /tôr·nā′dō/ *n., pl.* **tor·na·does** A violent, destructive whirling wind that forms a funnel-shaped cloud. *Alternate plural:* **tornados.**

tor·toise /tôr′təs/ *n., pl.* **tor·tois·es** A turtle, especially one that lives on land. *Alternate plural:* **tortoise.**

touch /tuch/ *n., v.* **touched, touch·ing** **1** *v.* To place one's hand or another part of one's body on or against something. **2** *v.* To be in contact or in contact with: The table *touches* the wall. **3** *n.* Communication.

touch·down /tuch′doun′/ *n.* In football, a play worth six points made by carrying the ball across an opponent's goal line.

trad·er /trā′dər/ *n.* A person who works in trade or buying and selling.

tra·di·tion·al /trə·dish′ən·əl/ *adj.* Following established social patterns or customs. —**tra·di′tion·al·ly** *adv.*

trag·e·dy /traj′ə·dē/ *n., pl.* **trag·e·dies** **1** A play, movie, etc., that is sad or has an unhappy ending. **2** Any experience that is sad or disastrous.

trait /trāt/ *n., pl.* **traits** A characteristic.

trai·tor /trā′tər/ *n.* A person who turns against or betrays a friend, duty, cause, country, etc.

trans·fer /*v.* trans′fər *or* trans·fûr′, *n.* trans′fər/ *v.* **trans·ferred, trans·fer·ring,** *n.* **1** *v.* To move or send from one person or place to another. **2** *n.* The act of transferring.

trans·fu·sion /trans·fyōō′zhən/ *n.* The process of transferring blood into a person or animal that has lost blood because of bleeding or illness.

trans·por·ta·tion /trans′pər·tā′shən/ *n.* **1** The act or state of being transported. **2** A means or system of transportation: public *transportation.*

treas·ure /trezh′ər/ *n., v.* **treas·ured, treas·ur·ing** **1** *n.* Wealth, riches, or valuables stored up and carefully kept. **2** *n.* Someone or something that is highly valued or loved. **3** *v.* To value or regard highly; to prize.

tri·al /trī′əl *or* trīl/ *n.* **1** The examining and deciding before a court of law whether the charges made in a case are true or false. **2** An attempt to do something; try: three *trials* at swimming the length of a pool.

tri·an·gle /trī′ang′gəl/ *n.* **1** A plane figure that has three sides and three angles. **2** Something having this shape. **3** A metal musical instrument shaped like a triangle.

tri·an·gu·lar /trī·ang′gyə·lər/ *adj.* Having the shape of a triangle.

tri·umph /trī′əmf/ **1** *n.* Victory. **2** *v.* To achieve a victory.

tri·um·phant /trī·um′fənt/ *adj.* Proud or joyful over victory; successful.

trop·i·cal /trop′i·kəl/ *adj.* Of, having to do with, or located in the tropics, the hot, often humid region of the earth near the equator.

trum·pet /trum′pit/ *n.* A brass wind instrument of high range with a long, curved metal tube and a flaring bell at one end.

turn·pike /tûrn′pīk′/ *n.* A highway on which you must pay a toll.

---

act, āte, câre, ärt;   egg, ēven;   if, īce;   on, ōver, ôr;   bŏŏk, fōōd;   up, tûrn;
ə = a in *ago,* e in *listen,* i in *giraffe,* o in *pilot,* u in *circus;*   yōō = u in *music;*   oil;   out;
chair; sing; shop; thank; that; zh in *treasure.*

Harcourt Brace School Publishers

typ·i·cal /tip′i·kəl/ *adj.* Having qualities common or usual to a whole group, class, etc. —**typ′i·cal·ly** *adv.*

U

un·der·wa·ter /un′dər·wô′tər/ **1** *adj.* Found or done under the water. **2** *adv.* Under the water.

un·i·form /yōō′nə·fôrm/ **1** *adj.* Alike; not varying or changing. **2** *n.* A specific outfit worn by members of a group.

u·ni·verse /yōō′nə·vûrs/ *n.* Everything that exists, including the earth, sun, stars, planets, and outer space.

up·set /v., adj. up·set′, n., adj. up′set′/ *v.* **up·set, up·set·ting,** *n., adj.* **1** *v.* To overturn. **2** *v.* To disturb something arranged or ordered. **3** *v.* To disturb or make uneasy. **4** *adj.* Disturbed or worried. **5** *v.* To defeat someone favored to win. **6** *n.* Such a defeat.

up·stairs /up′stârz′/ **1** *n., pl.* (*used with singular verb*) The part of a building above the ground floor. **2** *adj.* Having to do with an upper story. **3** *adv.* Up the stairs.

ur·ban /ûr′bən/ *adj.* Having to do with cities rather than the country.

u·su·al /yōō′zhōō·əl/ *adj.* Common; regular; normal. —**u′su·al·ly** *adv.*

V

va·por /vā′pər/ *n.* Moisture in the air that can be seen, as steam, mist, fog, etc.

va·ri·e·ty /və·rī′ə·tē/ *n.* **1** A lack of sameness; change. **2** An assortment.

veg·e·tar·i·an /vej′ə·târ′ē·ən/ **1** *n.* A person who eats no meat. **2** *adj.* Made up of only fruits and vegetables.

veil /vāl/ *n.* A piece of thin cloth or net worn to protect or hide all or part of the face, or as an ornament.

vein /vān/ *n.* **1** One of the systems of branching vessels that carry blood from parts of the body to the heart. **2** One of the branching ribs forming the structure of a leaf or an insect's wing.

ver·sion /vûr′zhən/ *n.* **1** A particular or personal account of something, possibly inaccurate. **2** A particular variety or form of something.

ver·ti·cal /vûr′ti·kəl/ *adj.* Upright; forming right angles with horizontal lines. —**ver′ti·cal·ly** *adv.*

view /vyōō/ **1** *v.* To look at. **2** *n.* Area of vision. **3** *n.* What is looked at or seen. **4** *n.* An opinion or belief.

vig·or·ous /vig′ər·əs/ *adj.* **1** Full of energy or vigor. **2** Performed with energy or vigor.

vil·lain /vil′ən/ *n.* A wicked person; wrongdoer, as in a play or novel.

vin·e·gar /vin′ə·gər/ *n.* An acid liquid produced by souring cider, wine, etc., used to preserve or flavor foods.

vi·o·let /vī′ə·lit/ **1** *n.* A small plant with flowers that are usually bluish purple. **2** *n.* The flower produced by this plant. **3** *n., adj.* Bluish purple in color.

vi·o·lin /vī′ə·lin′/ *n.* A musical instrument with a wooden body and four strings that is played with a bow.

vi·sion /vizh′ən/ *n.* **1** Sense of sight; ability to see. **2** Something imagined or spiritually revealed, as seen in the mind, in a dream, etc. **3** The ability to see ahead by the imagination or by clear thinking; foresight.

vis·i·tor /viz′ə·tər/ *n.* A person who visits.

vol·ca·no /vol·kā′nō/ *n., pl.* **vol·ca·noes 1** An opening in the earth's surface through which lava, steam, ashes, etc., are released forming a cone-shaped hill or mountain. **2** The hill or mountain itself. *Alternate plural:* **volcanos.**

vow /vou/ **1** *n.* A promise or pledge. **2** *v.* To make a vow.

W

wage /wāj/ *v.* **waged, wag·ing,** *n.* **1** *v.* To be involved or engaged in: to *wage* war. **2** *n.* (*often pl.*) Money paid for work to an employee.

waist /wāst/ *n.* **1** The part of the body below the ribs and above the hips. **2** The part of a garment that covers the body from the neck or shoulders to the waist.

wal·nut /wôl′nut/ **1** *n.* A large nut, with its seed divided in halves, that can be eaten. **2** *n.* The tree this nut grows on. **3** *n.* The wood of this tree. **4** *adj., n.* Dark brown in color.

wa·ter /wô′tər *or* wot′ər/ *n., v.* **wa·tered, wa·ter·ing** **1** *n.* A clear liquid compound of hydrogen and oxygen used for drinking, washing, etc. **2** *v.* To make wet with water. **3** *n.* Any body of water, as an ocean, sea, etc.

wealth·y /wel′thē/ *adj.* **wealth·i·er, wealth·i·est** Having wealth; rich.

weap·on /wep′ən/ *n.* Any object, instrument, or part of the body used in fighting.

wedge /wej/ *n., v.* **wedged, wedg·ing** **1** *n.* Anything shaped like a triangle with two equal sides. **2** *v.* To squeeze or pack into a small space: He *wedged* himself into the crowded car seat.

weigh /wā/ *v.* **1** To have a certain amount of weight or heaviness. **2** To measure the heaviness of something.

what·ev·er /(h)wot′ev′ər *or* (h)wut′ev′ər/ **1** *pron.* Anything or all that. **2** *adj.* Any or all that. **3** *pron.* No matter what.

whim·per /(h)wim′pər/ **1** *v.* To cry with low, mournful, broken sounds. **2** *n.* A cry of this kind.

whole /hōl/ **1** *adj.* All parts of something; complete. **2** *n.* All the parts making up something.

whole·sale /hōl′sāl′/ **1** *n.* The sale of goods in large quantities at a time. **2** *adj.* Having to do with this method of selling goods.

wil·der·ness /wil′dər·nis/ *n.* A wild area or forest where people do not live.

wild·life /wīld′līf′/ *n.* Animals and plants that live in the natural environment.

wind·shield /wind′shēld′/ *n.* A sheet of glass or plastic located in front of the driver and passengers in a car, boat, plane, etc., to block or keep off wind, rain, etc.

wind·y /win′dē/ *adj.* **wind·i·er, wind·i·est** Having much wind.

win·ner /win′ər/ A person who wins.

wit·ty /wit′ē/ *adj.* **wit·ti·er, wit·ti·est** Clever; amusing; very funny.

wom·an /wŏom′ən/ *n., pl.* **wom·en** /wim′in/ An adult human female.

won·der /wun′dər/ *n., v.* **won·dered, won·der·ing** **1** *n.* A feeling of surprise; astonishment; amazement. **2** *n.* An unusual, surprising, or astonishing thing or event. **3** *v.* To be filled with surprise, awe, or astonishment; to marvel. **4** *v.* To be curious about.

won·der·ful /wun′dər·fəl/ *adj.* **1** Causing wonder. **2** Very good; excellent.

wood·cut /wŏod′kut′/ *n.* **1** A block of wood on which a picture or design has been carved. **2** A print made from a carved wood block.

work·shop /wûrk′shop′/ *n.* **1** A shop or building where work is done. **2** A group of people working on or studying a special project together.

wres·tle /res′(ə)l/ *v.* **wres·tled, wres·tling,** *n.* **1** *v.* To throw or force someone into a particular position on the ground. **2** *n.* The act of wrestling. **3** *v.* To struggle.

wrist·watch /rist′woch/ *n., pl.* **wrist·watch·es** A small timepiece, usually worn on the wrist.

Y

yield /yēld/ **1** *v.* To give up or give way; to surrender. **2** *v.* To produce or give in return for work or investment. **3** *n.* The amount yielded or produced.

yolk /yōk/ *n.* The yellow part of an egg.

---

act, āte, câre, ärt;   egg, ēven;   if, īce;   on, ōver, ôr;   bŏok, fōod;   up, tûrn;
ə = **a** in *ago,* **e** in *listen,* **i** in *giraffe,* **o** in *pilot,* **u** in *circus;*   yōo = **u** in *music;*   oil;   out;
chair; si**ng**; **sh**op; **th**ank; **th**at; **zh** in *treasure.*

Harcourt Brace School Publishers

SPELLING THESAURUS

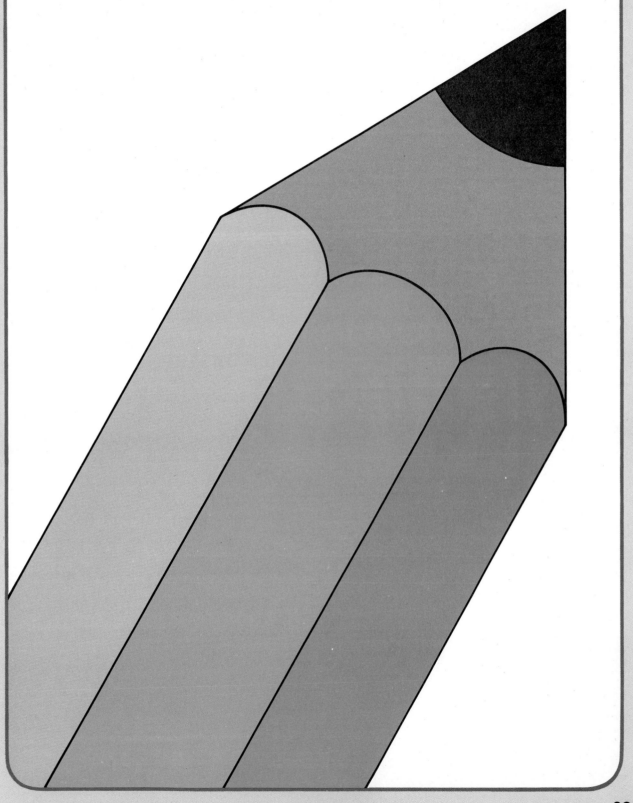

What Is a Thesaurus?

A **thesaurus** lists words and their synonyms. Like a dictionary, a thesaurus lists words in alphabetical order. Each of these words is called an **entry word**. A list of synonyms follows the entry word. Sometimes a thesaurus lists antonyms.

Look at the parts of this thesaurus entry for the word *join*.

The **entry word** is in red letters. It is followed by the part of speech and a definition. An **example sentence** shows how the word can be used.

▶

join *v.* To bring or come together; to connect. The new bridge will join the island with the mainland.

Synonyms for the entry word are in *italic* letters. Each synonym is followed by a definition and an example sentence.

▶

combine To bring or come together; to unite. *Combine* two beaten eggs and a cup of milk in a large bowl.

connect To join together; link. The "chunnel"—a tunnel under the channel—will *connect* England and France.

link To join or connect; unite. The railroad *linked* coal-mining towns to cities where steel was made.

reunite To get or cause to get together again. After being separated during the summer, Jason and his dog were *reunited*.

If an **antonym** is given, it is printed in dark letters.

▶

ANTONYMS: divide, part, separate, split

Harcourt Brace School Publishers

How to Use Your Spelling Thesaurus

Suppose you are writing a news story about performers planning to join together for a benefit concert. You read over your work and see you have used the word *join* too many times. You decide to use the Spelling Thesaurus to find some synonyms. Here are the steps you should follow.

1. Look for the word in the Thesaurus Index. The Index lists every word in the Thesaurus.

2. Find the word in the Index. This is what you will find:

join *v.*

The red print tells you that *join* is an entry word.

3. Turn to the correct page in the Spelling Thesaurus and read the entry carefully. Not every synonym will fit the context of your news story. Choose the synonym or synonyms that will make your writing clearer and stronger.

Remember: Not every synonym will have the precise shade of meaning you want. Look at the sample entry for *join* on page 206. Which synonyms for *join* make the most sense for a news story about a benefit concert?

- Sometimes you may find a word listed in the Index like this:

combine join *v.*

This means you will find the word *combine* listed as a synonym under the entry word *join*. Since *combine* is not printed in red, it is not an entry word. If you look for *combine* in the Spelling Thesaurus as an entry word under the letter *C*, you will not find it!

- You will also see some lines in the Index that look like this:

divide join *v.*

This means that *divide* is listed as an antonym under the entry word *join*.

A

abnormal *adj.*
abnormal normal *adj.*
abnormal usual *adj.*
abruptly quickly *adv.*
accept agree *v.*
accomplish achieve *v.*
accumulate hoard *v.*
accuracy error *n.*
accurate exact *adj.*
achieve *v.*
achieve reach *v.*
acknowledge confess *v.*
active lively *adj.*
actual genuine *adj.*
adequate sufficient *adj.*
adjust alter *v.*
admire appreciate *v.*
admit confess *v.*
advantage loss *n.*
advise recommend *v.*
afraid brave *adj.*
agitate calm *v.*
agree *v.*
agree quarrel *v.*
agreeable friendly *adj.*
agreeable grouchy *adj.*
agreeable nice *adj.*
aide partner *n.*
ailment disease *n.*
alarm panic *n.*
alarming dangerous *adj.*
ally enemy *n.*
alter *v.*
amass hoard *v.*
amazement astonishment *n.*
amiable grouchy *adj.*
amiable nice *adj.*
ample sufficient *adj.*
amusing funny *adj.*
announcement *n.*
annoy irritate *v.*
annoyed grouchy *adj.*

appealing pretty *adj.*
appetizing delicious *adj.*
appreciate *v.*
approach reach *v.*
apt likely *adj.*
arctic hot *adj.*
arid damp *adj.*
arrive reach *v.*
artificial genuine *adj.*
assortment variety *n.*
assured positive *adj.*
astonishment *n.*
astound wonder *v.*
attacker enemy *n.*
attain achieve *v.*
attention *n.*
attractive pretty *adj.*
authentic genuine *adj.*
authority expert *n.*
average usual *adj.*
awareness attention *n.*
awe astonishment *n.*
awful *adj.*
awful excellent *adj.*

B

bad-mannered impolite *adj.*
baffle bewilder *v.*
baffling mysterious *adj.*
baggage freight *n.*
barbaric fierce *adj.*
barren bleak *adj.*
beautiful pretty *adj.*
beg request *v.*
begin cease *v.*
beginner expert *n.*
believe *v.*
beneficial *adj.*
benefit loss *n.*
bewilder *v.*
bind separate *v.*
blaze glow *v.*
bleak *adj.*

blizzard storm *n.*
blunder error *n.*
blurry brilliant *adj.*
border terminal *n.*
bored curious *adj.*
bother irritate *v.*
boundary terminal *n.*
brave *adj.*
brawny fat *adj.*
break repair *v.*
brilliant *adj.*
briskly quickly *adv.*
bristly coarse *adj.*
broad *adj.*
brutal cruel *adj.*
bulletin announcement *n.*

C

calm *v.*
calm irritate *v.*
calm peaceful *adj.*
calm upset *v.*
calmness panic *n.*
carefree happy *adj.*
careful *adj.*
careless careful *adj.*
careless foolish *adj.*
carelessness attention *n.*
cargo freight *n.*
carnival celebration *n.*
catch throw *v.*
cautious careful *adj.*
cease *v.*
celebrate rejoice *v.*
celebration *n.*
certain doubtful *adj.*
certain positive *adj.*
chaos order *n.*
char scorch *v.*
cheerful bleak *adj.*
cheerless bleak *adj.*
chief *n.*
chill scorch *v.*
chubby fat *adj.*

Harcourt Brace School Publishers

chubby thin *adj.*
civil impolite *adj.*
civilized fierce *adj.*
clarify bewilder *v.*
clash agree *v.*
clasp seize *v.*
clear easy *adj.*
clear mysterious *adj.*
clever funny *adj.*
cloth material *n.*
cloudburst rainfall *n.*
coarse *adj.*
collect hoard *v.*
collection variety *n.*
colonist pioneer *n.*
comb search *v.*
combine join *v.*
combine separate *v.*
comical funny *adj.*
command govern *v.*
commander chief *n.*
commence cease *v.*
common usual *adj.*
commonwealth nation *n.*
commotion *n.*
companion partner *n.*
complete incomplete *adj.*
comrade partner *n.*
conceal *v.*
conceal reveal *v.*
concede confess *v.*
concentration attention *n.*
conclude cease *v.*
confess *v.*
confident positive *adj.*
confined broad *adj.*
conflict agree *v.*
conform agree *v.*
confuse bewilder *v.*
confusing easy *adj.*
confusion order *n.*
connect join *v.*
connect separate *v.*
conquer triumph *v.*
consent agree *v.*
consider believe *v.*
continue pause *v.*
coolness panic *n.*

cooperate quarrel *v.*
copy imitate *v.*
cordial grouchy *adj.*
cordial nice *adj.*
correct alter *v.*
correctness error *n.*
costly precious *adj.*
counterfeit genuine *adj.*
courageous brave *adj.*
courteous *adj.*
courteous impolite *adj.*
cover reveal *v.*
cowardly brave *adj.*
cross grouchy *adj.*
crude coarse *adj.*
cruel *adj.*
cruel nice *adj.*
curious *adj.*
curious abnormal *adj.*
curious usual *adj.*
customary usual *adj.*

D

damage *v.*
damage loss *n.*
damp *adj.*
dangerous *adj.*
dangerous beneficial *adj.*
dangerous safe *adj.*
dank damp *adj.*
daring brave *adj.*
dark brilliant *adj.*
dazzling brilliant *adj.*
debatable doubtful *adj.*
debate quarrel *v.*
deceitful disloyal *adj.*
declare confess *v.*
decree announcement *n.*
defeat triumph *v.*
defective imperfect *adj.*
delay pause *n.*
delicate vigorous *adj.*
delicious *adj.*
delight rejoice *v.*
delighted furious *adj.*
delightful awful *adj.*
demand request *v.*
depart reach *v.*

depressed happy *adj.*
depressed sad *adj.*
deserve merit *v.*
despair rejoice *v.*
destroy damage *v.*
destroy repair *v.*
destructive beneficial *adj.*
devoted faithful *adj.*
devour damage *v.*
dewy damp *adj.*
dictate govern *v.*
differ agree *v.*
differ quarrel *v.*
different uniform *adj.*
difficult easy *adj.*
dim brilliant *adj.*
diplomatic courteous *adj.*
director chief *n.*
disagree agree *v.*
disagree quarrel *v.*
disbelieve believe *v.*
disclose conceal *v.*
disclose reveal *v.*
disconnect separate *v.*
discontinue pause *v.*
discourage recommend *v.*
discourteous courteous *adj.*
discover conceal *v.*
discover reveal *v.*
disease *n.*
disguise conceal *v.*
disgusting delicious *adj.*
dislike appreciate *v.*
disloyal *adj.*
dismal funny *adj.*
disorder commotion *n.*
disorder order *n.*
dispensible necessary *adj.*
distract upset *v.*
distribute hoard *v.*
distrust believe *v.*
disturb calm *v.*
disturbance commotion *n.*
divide join *v.*
divide separate *v.*
doubt believe *v.*
doubtful *adj.*
downcast sad *adj.*

downpour rainfall *n.*
dread panic *n.*
dreadful awful *adj.*
dreadful excellent *adj.*
dreary bleak *adj.*
drench water *v.*
drizzle rainfall *n.*
drought rainfall *n.*
drown water *v.*
dry damp *adj.*
dry water *v.*
dull brilliant *adj.*

E

earnest grave *adj.*
earsplitting quiet *adj.*
easy *adj.*
easygoing friendly *adj.*
easygoing furious *adj.*
effortless easy *adj.*
elated happy *adj.*
elated sad *adj.*
elementary easy *adj.*
embrace seize *v.*
empire nation *n.*
enchanted furious *adj.*
enemy *n.*
energetic vigorous *adj.*
enjoy appreciate *v.*
enraged furious *adj.*
entire broad *adj.*
entire incomplete *adj.*
entirety piece *n.*
erroneous exact *adj.*
error *n.*
essential necessary *adj.*
even coarse *adj.*
evident mysterious *adj.*
exact *adj.*
exactness error *n.*
examine quiz *v.*
examine search *v.*
excellent *adj.*
exceptional excellent *adj.*
exclusive broad *adj.*
excursion journey *n.*
expected abnormal *adj.*
expected likely *adj.*

expedition journey *n.*
expensive precious *adj.*
expert *n.*
explain bewilder *v.*
explore search *v.*
extend reach *v.*

F

fabric material *n.*
fail triumph *v.*
faithful *adj.*
faithful disloyal *adj.*
fake genuine *adj.*
false disloyal *adj.*
false faithful *adj.*
false genuine *adj.*
fat *adj.*
fat thin *adj.*
fault error *n.*
faultless imperfect *adj.*
faulty exact *adj.*
faulty imperfect *adj.*
fearful brave *adj.*
feeble strong *adj.*
feeble vigorous *adj.*
ferocious fierce *adj.*
festival celebration *n.*
fierce *adj.*
fiery hot *adj.*
find reveal *v.*
fine coarse *adj.*
finish cease *v.*
finished incomplete *adj.*
fix damage *v.*
flare glow *v.*
flavorful delicious *adj.*
flawed imperfect *adj.*
flawless imperfect *adj.*
fledgling expert *n.*
flimsy strong *adj.*
fling throw *v.*
fluster upset *v.*
foe enemy *n.*
foggy damp *adj.*
foolish *adj.*
fortune treasure *n.*
foul delicious *adj.*
fraction piece *n.*

fragile vigorous *adj.*
fragment piece *n.*
frail vigorous *adj.*
free seize *v.*
freeze scorch *v.*
freezing hot *adj.*
freight *n.*
friend enemy *n.*
friendly *adj.*
fright panic *n.*
frigid hot *adj.*
frisky lively *adj.*
frivolous grave *adj.*
frontier terminal *n.*
frosty hot *adj.*
fulfill achieve *v.*
fuming furious *adj.*
fundamental necessary *adj.*
funny *adj.*
furious *adj.*
fuse separate *v.*

G

gain loss *n.*
gather hoard *v.*
gaunt thin *adj.*
general broad *adj.*
generous cruel *adj.*
genius expert *n.*
gentle cruel *adj.*
gentle fierce *adj.*
genuine *adj.*
gigantic large *adj.*
glacial hot *adj.*
glad sad *adj.*
gleaming brilliant *adj.*
gleeful sad *adj.*
glisten glow *v.*
gloomy bleak *adj.*
gloomy brilliant *adj.*
glory rejoice *v.*
glow *v.*
glue separate *v.*
goods freight *n.*
govern *v.*
grab throw *v.*
graceful pretty *adj.*

gracious friendly *adj.*
gradually quickly *adv.*
grant confess *v.*
grapple wrestle *v.*
grasp seize *v.*
grave *adj.*
grieve rejoice *v.*
grip seize *v.*
grouchy *adj.*
gruff impolite *adj.*
grumble murmur *n.*
grumpy grouchy *adj.*
guarded dangerous *adj.*
guarded safe *adj.*

H

halt cease *v.*
happy *adj.*
happy furious *adj.*
happy sad *adj.*
hardiness disease *n.*
harm loss *n.*
harmful beneficial *adj.*
harmony commotion *n.*
harmony order *n.*
hash jumble *n.*
hastily quickly *adv.*
hateful nice *adj.*
hazardous dangerous *adj.*
hazardous safe *adj.*
head chief *n.*
healthiness disease *n.*
heap jumble *n.*
heartbroken happy *adj.*
heartsick sad *adj.*
hectic peaceful *adj.*
heed attention *n.*
helpful beneficial *adj.*
heroic brave *adj.*
hide reveal *v.*
hideous pretty *adj.*
hoard *v.*
hoard treasure *n.*
hold throw *v.*
holiday celebration *n.*
homely pretty *adj.*
horrible awful *adj.*
horrible excellent *adj.*

horrid awful *adj.*
horror panic *n.*
hostile friendly *adj.*
hot *adj.*
huge large *adj.*
humid damp *adj.*
humorous funny *adj.*
hurl throw *v.*
hurricane storm *n.*
hushed quiet *adj.*

I

ice scorch *v.*
icy hot *adj.*
ideal imperfect *adj.*
identical uniform *adj.*
illness disease *n.*
imitate *v.*
immense large *adj.*
immigrant pioneer *n.*
imperfect *adj.*
impolite *adj.*
impolite courteous *adj.*
improbable likely *adj.*
inaccurate exact *adj.*
inactive lively *adj.*
inadequate sufficient *adj.*
inattentive curious *adj.*
incomplete *adj.*
indifferent curious *adj.*
inexact exact *adj.*
inexact imperfect *adj.*
infection disease *n.*
inferior awful *adj.*
injure damage *v.*
injury loss *n.*
inquisitive curious *adj.*
insecure positive *adj.*
insolent impolite *adj.*
inspect search *v.*
instruct recommend *v.*
insufficient incomplete
 adj.
insufficient sufficient *adj.*
insulting impolite *adj.*
intelligent foolish *adj.*
interrupt pause *v.*
investigate search *v.*

irregular abnormal *adj.*
irritable grouchy *adj.*
irritate *v.*

J

join *v.*
journey *n.*
joyous happy *adj.*
jubilant happy *adj.*
jubilee celebration *n.*
judge believe *v.*
jumble *n.*

K

kind cruel *adj.*
kind fierce *adj.*
kind grouchy *adj.*
kingdom nation *n.*

L

lacking incomplete *adj.*
lacking sufficient *adj.*
large *adj.*
lawful genuine *adj.*
lazily quickly *adv.*
leader chief *n.*
leave reach *v.*
legitimate genuine *adj.*
liable likely *adj.*
lifeless lively *adj.*
likely *adj.*
limit terminal *n.*
link join *v.*
listless lively *adj.*
little large *adj.*
lively *adj.*
lively bleak *adj.*
loose seize *v.*
lose triumph *v.*
loss *n.*
loud quiet *adj.*
loving cruel *adj.*
loyal disloyal *adj.*
loyal faithful *adj.*
luggage freight *n.*
luminous brilliant *adj.*

luscious delicious *adj.*

M

maintain believe *v.*
maintain pause *v.*
malady disease *n.*
mammoth large *adj.*
marvel wonder *v.*
marvelous excellent *adj.*
mask conceal *v.*
master expert *n.*
match agree *v.*
material *n.*
mean friendly *adj.*
mean nice *adj.*
meddlesome curious *adj.*
meek fierce *adj.*
mend repair *v.*
merit *v.*
merrymaking celebration *n.*
message announcement *n.*
mighty strong *adj.*
mimic imitate *v.*
miniature large *adj.*
minute large *adj.*
mirror imitate *v.*
misjudgment error *n.*
mistake error *n.*
misunderstanding error *n.*
mixed uniform *adj.*
mixture variety *n.*
mock imitate *v.*
modify alter *v.*
moist damp *adj.*
mourn rejoice *v.*
mournful funny *adj.*
muddle jumble *n.*
muggy damp *adj.*
mumble murmur *n.*
mumble shriek *n.*
murmur *n.*
murmur shriek *n.*
mutter murmur *n.*
mutter shriek *n.*
mysterious *adj.*
mystify bewilder *v.*

N

narrow broad *adj.*
narrow thin *adj.*
nasty awful *adj.*
nasty nice *adj.*
nation *n.*
nauseating delicious *adj.*
neatness order *adj.*
necessary *adj.*
needless necessary *adj.*
neglect attention *n.*
neighborly friendly *adj.*
nice *adj.*
noiseless quiet *adj.*
noisy quiet *adj.*
normal *adj.*
normal abnormal *adj.*
nosy curious *adj.*
notice announcement *n.*

O

oath vow *n.*
observation attention *n.*
observe search *v.*
occasion celebration *n.*
odd abnormal *adj.*
odd normal *adj.*
odd usual *adj.*
open friendly *adj.*
opponent enemy *n.*
order *n.*
order govern *v.*
orderliness jumble *n.*
ordinary normal *adj.*
organization jumble *n.*
outrageous cruel *adj.*
outstanding excellent *adj.*
overcome triumph *v.*
overjoyed sad *adj.*
oversight attention *n.*
oversight error *n.*
overweight fat *adj.*
overweight thin *adj.*

P

pacify calm *n.*

pacify irritate *v.*
panic *n.*
parch scorch *v.*
parch water *v.*
parched damp *adj.*
parrot imitate *v.*
part join *v.*
partial incomplete *adj.*
partner *n.*
patchwork jumble *n.*
pause *v.*
peace commotion *n.*
peaceful *adj.*
peculiar abnormal *adj.*
peculiar normal *adj.*
peculiar usual *adj.*
perfect exact *adj.*
perfect imperfect *adj.*
perfection error *n.*
perilous dangerous *adj.*
perimeter terminal *n.*
perplex bewilder *v.*
perplexing easy *adj.*
perturb upset *v.*
pester irritate *v.*
phony genuine *adj.*
piece *n.*
pioneer *n.*
plain easy *adj.*
plain mysterious *adj.*
plain pretty *adj.*
playful bleak *adj.*
plead request *v.*
pleasant friendly *adj.*
pledge vow *n.*
plentiful sufficient *adj.*
plump fat *adj.*
poise panic *n.*
polite courteous *adj.*
polite impolite *adj.*
ponder wonder *v.*
portion piece *n.*
positive *adj.*
positive doubtful *adj.*
pour water *v.*
powerful strong *adj.*
precious *adj.*
precise exact *adj.*
pretty *adj.*

probable likely *adj.*
proclamation announcement *n.*
professional expert *n.*
profitable beneficial *adj.*
promise vow *n.*
propel throw *v.*
propose recommend *v.*
protected dangerous *adj.*
protected safe *adj.*
provoke irritate *v.*
pump quiz *v.*
puzzle bewilder *v.*
puzzling easy *adj.*
puzzling mysterious *adj.*

Q

qualify merit *v.*
quarrel *v.*
quest journey *n.*
question believe *v.*
question quiz *v.*
questionable doubtful *adj.*
questioning curious *adj.*
quickly *adv.*
quiet *adj.*
quiet calm *v.*
quiet commotion *n.*
quiet irritate *v.*
quiet upset *v.*
quit cease *v.*
quiz *v.*

R

rainfall *n.*
range variety *n.*
rapidly quickly *adv.*
rash careful *adj.*
rate merit *v.*
reach *v.*
reasonable foolish *adj.*
reckless foolish *adj.*
recommend *v.*
reedy fat *adj.*
refined courteous *adj.*
refined impolite *adj.*

reflect wonder *v.*
regard attention *n.*
regret rejoice *v.*
regular abnormal *adj.*
regular normal *adj.*
regularity variety *n.*
reign govern *v.*
rejoice *v.*
release seize *v.*
release yield *adj.*
reliable disloyal *adj.*
reliable faithful *adj.*
relish appreciate *v.*
remodel repair *v.*
repair *v.*
repair damage *v.*
repetitious uniform *adj.*
republic nation *n.*
request *v.*
required necessary *adj.*
resign yield *v.*
resolve bewilder *v.*
respectful courteous *adj.*
restful peaceful *adj.*
restore damage *v.*
restore repair *v.*
restricted broad *adj.*
resume pause *v.*
reunite join *v.*
reveal *v.*
reveal conceal *v.*
revise alter *v.*
rewarding beneficial *adj.*
riches treasure *n.*
rightness error *n.*
rile calm *v.*
rile irritate *v.*
risky dangerous *adj.*
risky safe *adj.*
rival enemy *n.*
robust vigorous *adj.*
rookie expert *n.*
rough coarse *adj.*
routine normal *adj.*
rude courteous *adj.*
rude impolite *adj.*
ruffle upset *v.*
ruin damage *v.*
rule govern *v.*

ruler chief *n.*
ruthless cruel *adj.*

S

sad *adj.*
sad funny *adj.*
sad happy *adj.*
safe *adj.*
safe dangerous *adj.*
sameness variety *n.*
satisfactory sufficient *adj.*
savage fierce *adj.*
scald scorch *v.*
scarce precious *adj.*
scarce sufficient *adj.*
scatter hoard *v.*
scorch *v.*
scorn appreciate *v.*
scratchy coarse *adj.*
scrawny thin *adj.*
scream murmur *n.*
scream shriek *n.*
screech shriek *n.*
screen conceal *v.*
scuffle wrestle *v.*
search *v.*
secrete reveal *v.*
section piece *n.*
secure dangerous *adj.*
secure positive *adj.*
seek search *v.*
seize *v.*
seize throw *v.*
self-control panic *n.*
selfish nice *adj.*
senseless foolish *adj.*
sensible foolish *adj.*
separate *v.*
separate join *v.*
serene peaceful *adj.*
serious grave *adj.*
service repair *v.*
settle upset *v.*
settler pioneer *n.*
shabby precious *adj.*
shatter repair *v.*
sheltered safe *adj.*

undecided positive *adj.*
uneven coarse *adj.*
unexpected normal *adj.*
unfaithful disloyal *adj.*
unfaithful faithful *adj.*
unfeeling cruel *adj.*
unfinished incomplete
   adj.
unfriendly friendly *adj.*
unhappy happy *adj.*
unhealthy beneficial *adj.*
unhurriedly quickly *adv.*
uniform *adj.*
uniformity variety *n.*
unit piece *n.*
unite separate *v.*
unlike uniform *adj.*
unlikely likely *adj.*
unnecessary necessary
   adj.
unreal genuine *adj.*
unrest commotion *n.*
unrest order *n.*
unruly peaceful *adj.*
unsafe safe *adj.*
unsettle upset *v.*
unsure positive *adj.*
unusual normal *adj.*

uproar commotion *n.*
upset *v.*
upset furious *adj.*
urge recommend *v.*
usual *adj.*
usual abnormal *adj.*
utter broad *adj.*

V

vague doubtful *adj.*
valiant brave *adj.*
valuable precious *adj.*
value appreciate *v.*
valueless precious *adj.*
vandalize damage *v.*
varied uniform *adj.*
variety *n.*
vicious cruel *adj.*
vigorous *adj.*
vital necessary *adj.*
vivid lively *adj.*
vow *n.*

W

warlike friendly *adj.*
wary careful *adj.*

waste hoard *v.*
water *v.*
weak strong *adj.*
weak vigorous *adj.*
weird mysterious *adj.*
whisper murmur *n.*
whisper shriek *n.*
whole piece *n.*
wholesome beneficial *adj.*
whoop shriek *n.*
widespread normal *adj.*
wild fierce *adj.*
wild peaceful *adj.*
wilt water *v.*
wise foolish *adj.*
witty funny *adj.*
wonder *v.*
wonderful awful *adj.*
wonderful excellent *adj.*
worthless precious *adj.*
wrestle *v.*

Y

yell murmur *n.*
yield *v.*
yield triumph *v.*

A

abnormal *adj.* Not normal, unusual. In Death Valley, daytime temperatures above 110 degrees are not abnormal.

curious Unusual; odd; strange. She had a collection of *curious* dolls made of corn cobs.

irregular Not in accord with customary standards. A pacemaker is used to correct an *irregular* heartbeat.

odd Strange or unusual; peculiar. Felix is an *odd* cat; he enjoys swimming.

peculiar Odd or strange. The trapdoor spider has a *peculiar* habit of pitching pebbles into the air as it digs its burrow.

ANTONYMS: expected, normal, regular, typical, usual

achieve *v.* To accomplish. The school achieved its goal of raising fifty thousand dollars to build a gym.

accomplish To carry out; effect. Through teamwork, the students *accomplished* their task of cleaning the classroom.

attain To gain or arrive at by hard work; achieve, as a desired end. The student *attained* success in school by studying frequently and completing assignments carefully.

fulfill To carry out, as a promise or prediction. Sarah *fulfilled* her promise to her mother by walking her brother to school.

agree *v.* To have the same ideas or opinions. Three-fourths of the states must agree before the Constitution can be amended.

accept To agree or approve. Not all historians *accept* that Betsy Ross designed the first American flag.

conform To be or act in accord with customs, rules, or accepted ideas. To enter the restaurant, diners must *conform* to the dress code.

consent To give approval; agree. In a republic, the people *consent* to be governed by those they elect.

match To be alike or go with. *Match* the lucky number and win a fabulous prize!

ANTONYMS: clash, conflict, differ, disagree

alter *v.* To change. Over the years, hurricanes altered the shape of the coastline by washing away the land.

adjust To change something so that it fits or matches. On a sunny day, *adjust* the camera to let less light through the lens.

correct To adjust, alter, or set right. The bridge builders must *correct* their plans to account for the curve of the earth's surface.

modify To change somewhat. They asked the architect to *modify* the house plan so that Jamie could have his own bedroom.

revise To amend or correct. In 1907, a committee *revised* the rules of baseball, which, before that time, didn't allow many plays legal today.

transform To change the form or appearance of. During the pupal stage, the sleeping caterpillar is *transformed* into a butterfly.

announcement *n.* A public or formal declaration or notice. The announcement of the end of World War II came on September 2, 1945.

bulletin A short account of the latest news. Frequent news *bulletins* kept the public informed about the latest election results.

decree A formal order or decision, as by a government or court. The Magna Carta was a *decree* signed by King John of England that guaranteed the right of a jury trial.

message Information that is told or sent

to another person. Before the invention of the telegraph, the Pony Express was the fastest way to send a *message* in the Old West.

notice A written or printed announcement. The electric power company posted a *notice* that work would begin on Clay Street tomorrow.

proclamation An official, public announcement. The mayor issued a *proclamation* honoring the heroic firefighters.

appreciate *v.* To recognize the value or quality of something. Few people appreciated Van Gogh's paintings while he lived, but all that changed a few years after his death.

admire To regard or look upon with wonder, pleasure, and approval. Many people *admire* the beauty of birds and their freedom in flight.

enjoy To receive pleasure or delight from. I couldn't *enjoy* the concert because the man behind me kept coughing.

relish To have an appetite for; like or enjoy. The woodpecker eats ants and especially *relishes* cocoons.

value To regard highly; prize. The ancient Romans *valued* salt so highly that it was sometimes used as money.

ANTONYMS: **dislike, scorn**

astonishment *n.* Great surprise; amazement. The Everglades tourists stared in astonishment as the tree frog hung upside down from leaves.

amazement Bewilderment resulting from surprise; astonishment. The world watched in *amazement* as the weak American colonies threw off the yoke of the mighty British.

awe A feeling of fear and wonder, as at the size, power, or majesty of something. Having never seen horses, American Indians looked at the mounted Spaniards with *awe*.

shock A sudden and severe upset of the mind or feelings, as in fright or great sorrow. The *shock* of failing the test made Mike gloomy all day.

attention *n.* Careful looking or listening. Pay attention to the directions or else you won't know what to do.

awareness Consciousness. The people went about their business calmly, with no *awareness* of the disaster about to strike.

concentration Complete attention. The difficult experiment required all my *concentration*.

heed Careful attention. The French king paid no *heed* to the demands of the people.

observation The act, ability, or habit of observing. After close *observation* of the sun and the stars, sailors were able to navigate accurately without modern instruments.

regard A look, especially an attentive look. No movement escaped the *regard* of the watchful falcon.

ANTONYMS: **carelessness, neglect, oversight**

awful *adj.* Very bad; unpleasant; terrible. The entire potato harvest failed, and many Irish people came to America to escape the awful famine.

dreadful Very bad; shocking; awful. The *dreadful* sound could mean only one thing: Dad had backed the car into the trash cans again.

horrible Causing horror; frightful. Losing my keys and wallet made the day *horrible* for me.

horrid Frightful; horrible. The *horrid* smell chased everyone from the chemistry lab.

inferior Not so good, as in quality, worth, or usefulness. You can't expect to do good work with *inferior* tools.

nasty Bad, ugly, or painful. Be careful with that rusty fishhook, or you'll get a *nasty* cut!
ANTONYMS: **delightful, wonderful**

B

believe *v.* To think or accept something as being real or true. We had believed that Joan was from Texas, but later we discovered that she was born in New York.

consider To believe to be. Many people *considered* the problem mystifying until the detective solved the case.

judge To form an opinion or make a judgment. The art expert *judged* the painting to be from the fifteenth century.

maintain To state or declare; insist. The man *maintained* his innocence throughout the long trial, but the jury found him guilty.
ANTONYMS: **disbelieve, distrust, doubt, question**

beneficial *adj.* Useful; helpful; worthwhile. The Finns believe that a brisk dip in ice water is beneficial to one's health.

helpful Useful or beneficial. Here's a *helpful* hint: Put flea powder in your vacuum cleaner bag to control fleas.

profitable Bringing a benefit or gain. The dance club held a *profitable* car wash that raised $250.

rewarding Giving pleasure or satisfaction. Baking your own bread is a time-consuming but *rewarding* experience.

wholesome Beneficial to health; healthful. A *wholesome* diet helped him recover quickly.
ANTONYMS: **dangerous, destructive, harmful, unhealthy**

bewilder *v.* To baffle or confuse; to puzzle. Her unpredictable moves in the chess match bewildered her opponent.

baffle To confuse; bewilder; perplex. The new chemistry book, with all its strange formulas and symbols, *baffled* Denise.

confuse To perplex; mix up. Driving in a strange city always *confuses* me.

mystify To puzzle or bewilder. How ancient people moved the enormous stones to Stonehenge *mystifies* everyone.

perplex To cause to hesitate or doubt; confuse; bewilder; puzzle. The poorly written directions for my new watch *perplexed* me when I tried to change the time.

puzzle To confuse or perplex; mystify. The unexplained giant statues on Easter Island still *puzzle* scientists.

stump To baffle or confuse. The last question on the test *stumped* everyone, and the teacher agreed not to count it.
ANTONYMS: **clarify, explain, resolve**

bleak *adj.* Gloomy; dismal. William predicted a bleak season for the team now that the star player was benched for the year.

barren Empty; lacking. The *barren* landscape of the Gobi desert covers large sections of China and Mongolia.

cheerless Sad and gloomy. The rain did nothing to improve our *cheerless* afternoon.

dreary Full of or causing sadness or gloom. After his *dreary* day, Father was looking forward to the comfort of a hot meal and a good night's sleep.

gloomy Dark; dismal. The *gloomy* old house was surely abandoned, thought the boys.
ANTONYMS: **cheerful, lively, playful, sunny**

brave *adj.* Courageous; not afraid. Davy Crockett and a band of brave Texans

Harcourt Brace School Publishers

died defending the Alamo in 1836.

courageous Having or showing courage. The *courageous* lifeguard braved the high waves to save the drowning boy.

daring Brave and adventurous; fearless. We read of the *daring* adventures of Daniel Boone, a frontier hero who was captured by Indians but escaped.

heroic Of, like, or proper for a hero. One hundred *heroic* men defended the desert town against an army of 2000.

valiant Having or showing courage. It was a time of legendary kings and *valiant* knights who rode off to defend their land.

ANTONYMS: **afraid, cowardly, fearful, timid**

brilliant *adj.* Shining brightly; glowing; sparkling. Dust particles in the air are the reason for brilliant tropical sunsets.

dazzling Blinding or dimming the vision with too much light. The deer stood frozen in the *dazzling* headlights.

gleaming Shining, as light reflected on a surface. The *gleaming* tea set had obviously been polished just before our arrival.

luminous Full of light; glowing. Saint Elmo's fire, long reported by sailors, is caused by a *luminous* electrical discharge surrounding an object.

shiny Bright; gleaming. I hoped that the *shiny* new car parked in the garage was my birthday present.

ANTONYMS: **blurry, dark, dim, dull, gloomy**

broad *adj.* Having a wide range; extensive. An encyclopedia covers a broad range of subjects, but only briefly.

entire Complete; full; total. By naming Adele director, they gave her control over the *entire* program.

general Not limited or specialized.

Several breeds, including German shepherds, belong to the *general* class of herding dogs.

total Complete; absolute. Although I did poorly on some parts of the test, the *total* test score was good.

utter Complete; total. The meal, from the watery soup to the burnt chicken, was an *utter* failure.

ANTONYMS: **confined, exclusive, narrow, restricted**

C

calm *v.* To make quiet. To calm an overly frisky dog, pat its chest, not its head.

pacify To bring peace to. You may not be able to *pacify* the crying baby.

quiet To make quiet. Linda read a story to *quiet* the children before their nap.

soften To make or become soft or softer. Iris lowered the shades to *soften* the harsh light.

soothe To calm or relieve. Perhaps relaxing in a tub of warm water will *soothe* you.

ANTONYMS: **agitate, disturb, rile**

careful *adj.* Cautious; done with care or effort. Careful planning was the secret of her success.

cautious Using care; careful not to take chances or make mistakes; watchful. A *cautious* driver, Mark inched out of the driveway.

suspicious Inclined to suspect; distrustful. Being a *suspicious* person, Helen did not trust anyone else to make the bank deposits.

timid Fearful or shy. Susanne is too *timid* to speak before an audience.

wary Watchful or suspicious; cautious. The *wary* mail carrier checked for dogs before opening the gate to the yard.

ANTONYMS: **careless, rash, trusting**

cease *v.* To come to an end or put an end to. As soon as I give the signal that time is up, cease writing and pass your papers to the front.

conclude To end; finish. This *concludes* our concert for today, but tune in next week for a new program of songs.

finish To end or bring to an end. Dr. Hook *finished* his experiments in 1958 and sent his findings to a journal.

halt To stop. The guards *halted* all cars crossing the border.

quit To cease from; stop. Julia *quit* working in the garden early today because it began to rain.

ANTONYMS: **begin, commence, start**

celebration *n.* Special activities held to express joy, honor, or respect for a particular person, event, time, or day. A celebration is held at this time each year to honor the founder of the town.

carnival A fair or festival with rides and games. During the New Orleans *carnival*, many people dress in costumes to march in the parade.

festival A particular feast, holiday or celebration, especially an annual one. At the Garlic *Festival*, held yearly in Gilroy, California, you can sample hundreds of dishes made with garlic.

holiday A day on which most business is stopped in remembrance of an important event. Before Presidents' Day was decided on, we celebrated two separate *holidays* on the birthdays of Washington and Lincoln.

jubilee A time of festivity or rejoicing. Queen Victoria celebrated her diamond *jubilee* in 1897, 50 years after first taking her throne.

merrymaking Fun and gaiety; laughter and joking. The *merrymaking* went on long after the party was supposed to end.

occasion An important event. Emily tried to make Michael's twelfth birthday a special *occasion*.

chief *n.* A person highest in command or authority. Sitting Bull was a great chief of the Sioux Indians.

commander A person who is in command, as of a ship or military force. The *commander* of the fleet ordered the ships into the middle of the Pacific Ocean.

director A person who directs or is in charge, as one in charge of a play, movie, etc. The *director* made sure that each member of the cast understood his or her part in the play.

head A leader; boss. As *head* of the building crew, Mr. Forrest distributed paychecks and gave out work assignments.

leader A person who leads. Sir Francis Drake was *leader* of several expeditions against the Spanish.

ruler A person who rules or governs, as a king or queen. The *ruler* of the ancient Egyptians was called the pharaoh.

supervisor A person who oversees and directs others. Our *supervisor* is a good organizer and gives each person the job he or she does best.

coarse *adj.* Rough; not fine or smooth. To smooth a rough surface, first use coarse sandpaper.

bristly Of, like, or covered with bristles. The hedgehog protects itself by rolling up into a *bristly* ball of spines.

crude Roughly made; not well finished. The logs of the *crude* cabin were not stripped of their bark.

rough Not smooth or even; bumpy; irregular. The car bounced and lurched over the *rough* cobblestone street.

scratchy That scratches or irritates. I find wool too *scratchy* to wear next to the skin.

uneven Not even, smooth, level, or equal.

The *uneven* brick surface was not good for roller skating.

ANTONYMS: **even, fine, silky, smooth**

commotion *n.* Great confusion or excitement; disturbance. The commotion caused by the appearance of the blimp distracted some people from their work.

disorder A condition of untidiness or confusion. After just five minutes, the mischievous twins created complete *disorder* in Felicia's tidy kitchen.

disturbance Confusion; tumult; commotion. The loud alley cats caused such a *disturbance* that no one in the neighborhood could sleep.

turmoil A condition of great confusion or agitation; disturbance; tumult. After the *turmoil* of the war years, Europe was eager for peace.

unrest Angry discontent or turmoil sometimes not far from rebellion. Labor *unrest* finally led to the riots and strikes of the 1930's.

uproar A condition of violent agitation, disturbance, or noisy confusion. The whole company was in an *uproar* when the cafeteria closed.

ANTONYMS: **harmony, peace, quiet**

conceal *v.* To hide; to keep secret. Mark concealed the flowers behind his back.

disguise To conceal or give a false idea of. Tony tried to *disguise* her black eye with make-up.

mask To hide or conceal; disguise. By whistling, Tim *masked* his fear of being in the crowded elevator.

screen To hide, shield, or shelter with or as if with a screen. The new barn *screened* our house from the road.

ANTONYMS: **disclose, discover, reveal, uncover**

confess *v.* To admit, concede, or acknowledge. Kevin confessed to

having eaten the pickle from my lunch tray.

acknowledge To admit the truth or reality of. Stubborn as ever, Jack never *acknowledged* the possibility that he could be wrong.

admit To confess; to acknowledge. Russell finally *admitted* that he disliked the shirt Sarah had given him.

concede To admit as true; acknowledge. Patty *conceded* that she couldn't have finished without Kit's help.

declare To make known to be; announce formally; proclaim. When did Fred *declare* that he was running for class president?

grant To accept as true; concede. "I'll *grant* that the Wolves are a fine team," Bob said, "but they don't stand a chance against the Gophers."

courteous *adj.* Considerate; respectful; polite. Leticia was always courteous on the phone, even when speaking to people who had called to complain.

diplomatic Tactful. Amy desperately tried to think of a *diplomatic* way to tell Lorrie that no one liked her singing.

polite Showing consideration for others; mannerly. Don't interrupt; it's not *polite*!

refined Free from vulgarities or coarseness; cultured. In the *refined* court of Louis XVI, the French claim, even the horses had good manners.

respectful Showing respect in a manner that exhibits regard, honor, or consideration. His *respectful* answer softened his teacher's anger.

ANTONYMS: **discourteous, impolite, rude**

cruel *adj.* Causing or resulting in pain and suffering. They struggled to make headway against the cruel, biting wind.

brutal Of or like a brute; cruel; savage. The *brutal* force of the earthquake

Harcourt Brace School Publishers

brought down entire city blocks.

outrageous Shockingly cruel. In the 1790's the French rebelled against the *outrageous* treatment of the peasants.

ruthless Without pity, mercy, or compassion; cruel. The kind volunteers were anything but *ruthless.*

unfeeling Not sympathetic; hardhearted. Only an *unfeeling* person would not be moved by the pictures of the homeless people.

vicious Spiteful or mean. Long pictured as *vicious,* the gorilla is really a gentle beast.

ANTONYMS: **generous, gentle, kind, loving, tender**

curious *adj.* Eager to learn. From the earliest times, humans have been curious about the stars.

inquisitive Full of questions; eager for knowledge; curious. An *inquisitive* child wants to know the reason for everything.

meddlesome Tending to interfere or tamper carelessly. A *meddlesome* neighbor likes to know everything that is going on.

nosy Prying and snooping into other people's affairs. Celia called him *nosy* for peeking in the oven.

questioning Expressing inquiry, curiosity, or doubt. Not knowing what to do, the child gave his father a *questioning* look.

snooping Looking or prying into things that are none of one's business. A *snooping* raccoon has gone through the garbage pail.

ANTONYMS: **bored, inattentive, indifferent**

D

damage *v.* To cause injury to. Looking into the sun will damage your eyes.

destroy To ruin completely; wreck; smash. The incoming waves *destroyed* the sand castle.

devour To destroy. The uncontrolled fire *devoured* the entire block of buildings.

injure To hurt, harm, or damage. Gymnasts observe safety rules carefully so they don't *injure* themselves.

ruin To destroy or damage; to spoil. The heavy rains *ruined* our picnic in the park.

vandalize To damage property maliciously. The principal asked us to take pride in our school by not *vandalizing* school property.

See also loss.

ANTONYMS: **fix, repair, restore**

damp *adj.* Slightly wet; moist. Plant the seeds in the soil and keep the ground damp until they sprout.

dank Unpleasantly cold and wet. Shivering with cold, we sloshed through the *dank* forest.

dewy Moist with or as if with dew. My dog loves to roll in the *dewy* grass and then dry off by the fire.

foggy Full of fog or mist. You can barely see the bridge on a *foggy* day.

humid Containing water vapor; damp. The *humid* air from the sea drops its moisture on the slopes of the coastal mountains.

moist Slightly wet or damp. My turkey always turns out dry. How do you keep yours so *moist?*

muggy Warm, humid, and close. It was too *muggy* in the steam room for me to stay long.

steamy Misty; consisting of, like, or full of steam. To get the wrinkles out of a wool suit, hang it in a *steamy* bathroom.

ANTONYMS: **arid, dry, parched**

dangerous	doubtful

dangerous *adj.* Not safe. Hiking was forbidden on the dangerous cliffs.

alarming Frightening. The citizens were upset at the *alarming* news of the earthquake.

hazardous Full of danger or risk. Wilma was cautious driving on the *hazardous* mountain road.

perilous Full of peril; risky; dangerous. Bands of robbers made the desert journey *perilous*.

risky Full of risk; dangerous; hazardous. Jane and Mario realized that the boat ride through the sharp reefs would be *risky*.

threatening Dangerous; menacing. The *threatening* clouds promised a thunderstorm.

ANTONYMS: **guarded, protected, safe, secure**

delicious *adj.* Tasty; very good. The president arranged a delicious feast to welcome the visitors.

appetizing Pleasing or stimulating to the appetite. Arrange the food on the plate so that it looks *appetizing*.

flavorful Full of good flavor; tasty. Dried apricots are more *flavorful* than fresh ones, I think.

luscious Very good to taste and smell. Martin hungrily eyed the *luscious* peaches on Mr. Neff's tree.

tasty Having a good flavor; savory. My cat's idea of a *tasty* treat is a sardine.

ANTONYMS: **disgusting, foul, nauseating, sickening**

disease *n.* An illness. Hiccups can be a serious disease

ailment An illness of the mind or body. Ruth suddenly came down with a mysterious *ailment* on the morning of the test.

illness An ailment; disease. Her *illness* forced her to stay in bed for a week.

infection A disease or other harmful condition caused by an invasion of germs. It was just a little scratch, but it turned into an *infection*.

malady A disease, sickness, or illness. Henry VIII suffered from gout, a painful *malady* common among the wealthy.

sickness A particular disease or disorder; illness. Sailors used to suffer from scurvy, a *sickness* caused by lack of Vitamin C.

ANTONYMS: **hardiness, healthiness, soundness**

disloyal *adj.* Not loyal, faithful or trustworthy. A disloyal employee sold the company's secrets to an overseas firm.

deceitful Tending to deceive; lying or treacherous. Not wishing to appear *deceitful*, Martha told us the story.

false Not faithful; disloyal. Jeremy proved himself a *false* friend by not helping Gus when he really needed it.

treacherous Likely to betray; disloyal; unreliable. A group of *treacherous* knights plotted to overthrow the king.

unfaithful Breaking promises or ignoring duty. My *unfaithful* dog prefers the neighbor's company to mine.

ANTONYMS: **faithful, loyal, reliable, steadfast, true**

doubtful *adj.* Unsure. The outcome was doubtful until the very end, when our team scored a field goal to win.

debatable Open to doubt or disagreement. The benefit of the road project is *debatable* because, though it will ease traffic, it will cost millions.

questionable Likely to be questioned or doubted. It was unlikely that Mrs. Simmons would believe Jake's *questionable* story.

uncertain Not certain; unsure; doubtful. Our travel plans are still *uncertain* because my vacation may be delayed.

undecided Not yet settled or decided. The question will remain *undecided* until Alice casts her vote to break the tie.

vague Not definite, clear, precise, or distinct. Your *vague* statements leave us with many questions.

ANTONYMS: **certain, positive, sure**

E

easy adj. Not difficult. Henry's house is an easy downhill walk from here.

clear Plain and understandable. Merle's directions were *clear*, and we found the house in no time.

effortless Requiring or showing little or no physical or mental power. Although dancing is extremely difficult, the trick is to make it look *effortless*.

elementary Simple and undeveloped. Sam mastered the *elementary* parts of the job quickly.

plain Easy to understand; clear; obvious. The police officer's directions were *plain* and easy to follow.

simple Easy to understand or do. After reading the *simple* instructions, Ed put the table together with ease.

ANTONYMS: **confusing, difficult, perplexing, puzzling**

enemy n. A person or country who tries to harm or fight another. Heather does not have enemies because she tries to get along with everyone.

attacker One who sets upon another with violence. The *attackers* scaled the high walls silently, hoping to catch the guards sleeping.

foe An enemy or rival; opponent. Fear is the only *foe* that can defeat you.

opponent A person who opposes another, as in sports, war, or debating. Chess is more challenging if your *opponent* plays as well as you do.

rival A competitor; a foe. Although they were *rivals* on the golf course, Nat and Terry were the best of friends.

ANTONYMS: **ally, friend**

error n. The condition of being incorrect. Since you made two errors, your test score is ninety-eight.

blunder A stupid mistake. David's *blunder*, mistaking the salt for the pepper, almost ruined the meal.

fault A mistake or blunder. I had to concede that there was no *fault* in his reasoning.

misjudgment A wrong or unfair judgment. The captain's *misjudgment* caused the ship to stray off course.

mistake An error or blunder. I found my *mistake*, and now the totals match.

misunderstanding A failure to understand someone or something correctly. Teresa misread the invitation, and the *misunderstanding* caused her to be late.

oversight An unintentional failure to do, notice, or remember something. Rudy claimed that my not being invited was an *oversight*.

ANTONYMS: **accuracy, correctness, exactness, perfection, rightness**

exact adj. Accurate, correct, precise. An exact speaker, Stevenson always chose his words carefully.

accurate Having or making no error; exact; true. As ship's reporter, Chuck had to be an *accurate* typist.

perfect Accurate; exact. To avoid misunderstandings, they asked for a *perfect* translation of the contract into French.

precise Strictly accurate; exact. People who direct air traffic in busy airports must pay *precise* attention to many details.

strict Exact; precise. To determine road use, they kept a *strict* count of the

number of cars that passed over the bridge.
ANTONYMS: **erroneous, faulty, inaccurate, inexact**

excellent *adj.* Very good. Stan did an excellent job painting the house, much better than I could.

exceptional Not ordinary; unusual; extraordinary. A salesperson needs an *exceptional* memory for faces and names.

marvelous Causing astonishment and wonder; amazing. News of the *marvelous* invention spread quickly.

outstanding More excellent or important than others of its kind. The museum gladly accepted a gift of several *outstanding* examples of Chinese clay pots.

splendid Brilliant; magnificent. What *splendid*, sunny weather for the beach!

superior Much better than the usual; extremely good. Morgan praised the *superior* workmanship of the handmade chairs.

wonderful Very good; excellent. Your short story made me laugh and shows a *wonderful* sense of humor.
ANTONYMS: **awful, dreadful, horrible, terrible**

expert *n.* A person who is very knowledgeable or skilled in some special area. Two things make a person an expert: study and experience.

authority A person with special knowledge. An *authority* on early movies, Gail has a library of over 100 silent films.

genius A person with an extremely high degree of mental ability or creative talent. Some *geniuses* excel only in one field, such as mathematics, science, or music.

master A person who is especially gifted or skilled. After studying for fifteen years, he became a *master* at his craft.

professional A person highly skilled in some art or craft. Proud of being a *professional*, the actress performed even though she was hoarse.

specialist A person who concentrates on one particular activity or subject. The doctor called in a *specialist* to perform the delicate operation.
ANTONYMS: **beginner, fledgling, rookie, tenderfoot**

F

faithful *adj.* Loyal; true. The faithful dog wouldn't leave its master's side.

devoted Feeling or showing love or devotion; true. A *devoted* friend, Lou was always ready to help.

loyal Constant and faithful to one's family, friends, or obligations. Six *loyal* knights defended the king.

reliable Dependable; trustworthy. We're looking for a *reliable* worker who will always be on time.

sincere Honest; faithful. When you have a problem, a *sincere* friend will not desert you.

steadfast Not moving or changing; constant. Tim's *steadfast* loyalty to the company helped him advance quickly.

trustworthy Worthy of confidence; reliable. A *trustworthy* employee was chosen to handle the money.
ANTONYMS: **false, treacherous, unfaithful**

fat *adj.* Having too much weight on the body; plump. Fat after eating all summer, bears can hibernate all winter.

brawny Muscular, strong. The *brawny* young man decided to try out for the high school wrestling team.

chubby Plump; rounded. Some children begin to lose their *chubby* appearance at about age five.

overweight Weighing too much. According to the chart, you're not *overweight* for your height.

plump Slightly fat or rounded. After soaking in hot water for ten minutes, the raisins should be soft and *plump*.

stout Fat or thickset in body. The *stout* legs of the table made it perfect for displaying the heavy statue.

ANTONYMS: **reedy, skinny, slight, slim, thin**

fierce *adj.* Cruel, violent, savage, or angry. The lion's fierce roar would scare most people.

barbaric Of or like barbarians; uncivilized. The Huns and Goths were called *barbaric* because they were uncivilized and warlike tribes.

ferocious Extremely fierce or savage. The Great Wall of China was meant to hold back the Tartars, a *ferocious* tribe from central Asia.

savage Wild, untamed, and often fierce. *Savage* winds tossed the ship about like a toy.

wild Savage or primitive; uncivilized. Farmyard pigs set loose in California have become *wild* and should be avoided.

ANTONYMS: **civilized, gentle, kind, meek, tame**

foolish *adj.* Silly or unwise; showing a lack of good sense. Tying someone's shoelaces together is a very foolish prank.

careless Reckless; done without care or effort. The *careless* remark hurt his feelings.

reckless Taking foolish risks; rash; careless. Driving class taught us how not to be *reckless* drivers.

senseless Stupid; foolish. Going out in the rain without an umbrella was *senseless*.

silly Lacking good sense; foolish; stupid. I like the *silly* suggestion that we hold the Winter Festival Dance in July.

ANTONYMS: **intelligent, reasonable, sensible, shrewd, wise**

freight *n.* Goods transported by train, truck, ship, or plane. The first trains carried freight, not people.

baggage The trunks, suitcases, and packages of a person traveling; luggage. We went to claim our *baggage*, but our suitcases were missing.

cargo The freight carried by a ship, train, etc. Without its heavy *cargo*, the ship rode higher in the water.

goods Anything made to be sold. The *goods* were sold to the highest bidder at public auction.

luggage Suitcases, bags, and trunks used in traveling. I got off the plane in New Orleans only to discover that my *luggage* had gone on to Miami.

shipment Anything that is shipped. The bookstore owner eagerly awaited the *shipment* of new books.

friendly *adj.* Like a friend; pleasant; helpful; neighborly; kindly. Copperville was a friendly town, and newcomers were always welcome.

agreeable Giving pleasure; pleasing. Josh was an *agreeable* boy ready to help anyone.

easygoing Not hurried, strained, or upset about things; relaxed. An *easygoing* person, Josephine made friends quickly.

gracious Kind and polite. Being away from home, we gladly accepted his *gracious* invitation to Thanksgiving dinner.

neighborly Being like a good or pleasant

Harcourt Brace School Publishers

neighbor; friendly; considerate. The Beachams made a *neighborly* gesture by helping us to move in.

open Generous; willing to consider other views and opinions. An *open* child, Claire was ready to like her new babysitter.

pleasant Agreeable or friendly, as in manner or appearance. If you expect to be a successful salesperson, you must develop a *pleasant* manner.

ANTONYMS: **hostile, mean, unfriendly, warlike**

funny *adj.* Able to cause laughter; amusing. Apparently, everyone found the joke very funny, but I missed the point.

amusing Causing amusement, fun, laughter, or merriment. Everyone predicted that the *amusing* new comedy would be a hit.

clever Exhibiting skill, wit, or sharp thinking. A *clever* mimic, Richard could imitate almost anyone's voice and gestures.

comical Causing laughter; funny. The long droopy ears and black spot over one eye gave the dog a *comical* appearance.

humorous Full of humor; funny; amusing. To make a *humorous* story even funnier, practice not smiling or laughing as you tell it.

witty Clever; amusing; very funny. The book is a collection of funny stories, jokes, and *witty* sayings.

ANTONYMS: **dismal, mournful, sad, sorrowful, tragic**

furious *adj.* Very angry. Holding the broken flowerpot, she had every right to be furious.

enraged Filled with rage; angry or furious. The *enraged* hen pecked at our fingers as we took her eggs.

fuming Angry; in a rage. Brooke promised to be home by seven. By eight Mother was annoyed, and by nine she was *fuming*.

upset Disturbed or worried. My mother gets *upset* if I don't hang up my clothes.

ANTONYMS: **delighted, easygoing, enchanted, happy**

G

genuine *adj.* Real; authentic. Mr. Reiner insisted the painting was genuine even though the art expert said it was an imitation.

actual Existing in fact; real. This is a copy of the Declaration of Independence; the *actual* document is in Washington, D.C.

authentic Genuine; real. No one believed the old paper was an *authentic* treasure map.

lawful Permitted or not forbidden by the law. *The Prince and the Pauper*, a novel by Mark Twain, is about the *lawful* heir to the throne of England and his look-alike.

legitimate Genuine; real; authentic. Mrs. Thornton thinks heavy traffic is a *legitimate* excuse for lateness.

ANTONYMS: **artificial, counterfeit, fake, false, phony, unreal**

glow *v.* To shine because of intense heat, especially without a flame. The barbecue fire is ready when the coals glow softly.

blaze To shine; glow. The skyscraper's windows *blazed* in the golden afternoon sun.

flare To blaze up suddenly with a glaring, unsteady light. Astronomers study the burning gases that *flare* out from the sun's surface.

glisten To shine or sparkle, as with reflected light. Hung with dewdrops, the spider's web *glistened* like a jeweled necklace.

shimmer To shine with an unsteady, glimmering light. The walls *shimmered* in the reflected light of the oil lamp.

shine To give off or reflect light. The sparkling diamonds *shine* in the sunlight.

govern *v.* To rule or guide. A viceroy, a representative of the king, was sent to govern a colony.

command To be in control of or authority over. The President of the United States *commands* all the armed forces of the country.

dictate To give orders. Paris, the fashion capital of the world, *dictates* the clothing styles for the coming year.

order To give a command. The conductor *ordered* the musicians to begin to play.

reign To rule or govern. In Marco Polo's time, the Mongol emperor Kublai Khan *reigned* over much of China.

rule To have authority or control over; govern. The captain *ruled* his ship in a friendly way.

grave *adj.* Very important; serious. The situation is grave, and we must take immediate action to prevent a flood.

earnest Very serious, determined, or sincere. An *earnest* young woman made a moving speech about our duty to help the homeless.

serious Grave; solemn; thoughtful. This important problem deserves our *serious* attention.

solemn Serious. The *solemn* mourners stood silently by the side of the grave.

thoughtful Full of or occupied with thought. After reading the same book, they had a *thoughtful* discussion about the challenges of growing up.

ANTONYMS: **frivolous, silly, trifling, trivial**

grouchy *adj.* Bad-tempered; sulky. The baby was grouchy because he needed a nap.

annoyed Bothered; irritated. The cat was *annoyed* at being awakened from its nap.

cross Bad-tempered; irritable. Mrs. Padula warned the boys in a *cross* voice not to chase her cat again.

grumpy Cranky or grouchy. Mr. Fields woke up with a headache and was in a *grumpy* mood for the rest of the day.

irritable Easily annoyed or angered; snappish. The baby gets *irritable* if he doesn't have his afternoon nap.

ANTONYMS: **agreeable, amiable, cordial, kind, sweet**

H

happy *adj.* Showing joy or pleasure. Some people are happiest when they are fishing.

carefree Without worries; happy. The family spent three *carefree* weeks on the beach.

elated Filled with joy or pride, as over success or good fortune. The people of Colorado were *elated* when theirs became the thirty-eighth state to enter the Union.

joyous Joyful. The *joyous* colors of spring are everywhere.

jubilant Expressing great joy; joyful; exultant. Upon finding gold, the *jubilant* miners went into town to celebrate.

thrilled Feeling great emotion or excitement. *Thrilled* by the news, the excited crowd danced in the street.

ANTONYMS: **depressed, heartbroken, sad, unhappy**

hoard *v.* To save and store away for preservation or future use, often in a greedy way. Grandma used to hoard pennies in an old roasting pan.

accumulate To heap or pile up; gather together; collect. Gladys *accumulated* many beautiful rugs during her travels.

amass To heap up; accumulate, especially as wealth or possessions for oneself. Mother has *amassed* an amazingly large collection of recipes.

collect To accumulate. A person who *collects* stamps is called a philatelist.

gather To collect over a period of time; accumulate. The library *gathered* books from all over the world. See also treasure.

ANTONYMS: **distribute, scatter, spend, waste**

hot *adj.* Very warm; having a high temperature. On such a hot day, we should be at the beach.

fiery Hot as fire; burning. The burning meteor fell to the ground in a *fiery* streak.

sizzling Giving off a hissing sound when very hot. To keep the steaks hot, they serve them on *sizzling* metal platters.

torrid Very hot; scorching; burning. This summer's *torrid* weather destroyed many crops.

ANTONYMS: **arctic, freezing, frigid, frosty, glacial, icy**

imitate *v.* To attempt to act or look the same as; to copy; to mimic. When she answered the phone, Jan tried to imitate her sister's voice, but I knew who it was.

copy To make a copy or copies of. Please *copy* this and return the original to me.

mimic To imitate the speech or actions of. Arlene's parrot can *mimic* the voice of everyone in her family.

mirror To reflect an image of. Although the book is supposed to be fiction, the plot *mirrors* true events closely.

mock To mimic or imitate. The mockingbird is so named because it can *mock* the calls of many other birds.

parrot To imitate or repeat without understanding. In this class, I expect you to think for yourselves, not just to *parrot* the ideas and words of others.

imperfect *adj.* Having faults; not perfect. Even though the diamond was imperfect, Ann chose the ring because she liked the setting.

defective Having a defect; not perfect. The *defective* radio is a good buy for someone who knows how to fix it.

faulty Having faults; imperfect. The cause of the accident was *faulty* tires, not bad driving.

flawed Having a crack, blemish, or other defect. The movie is very funny but *flawed* by a chase scene that lasts too long.

inexact Not completely accurate or true. The *inexact* directions caused us to get lost.

ANTONYMS: **faultless, flawless, ideal, perfect**

impolite *adj.* Rude. In some farm communities, guests who refuse food are considered impolite.

bad-mannered Having an offensive way of behaving. The *bad-mannered* parrot always seemed to interrupt our conversations.

gruff Rude or surly; unfriendly. Don't be misled by his *gruff* manner; he's really a kind person.

insolent Deliberately rude; insulting; sneering. Roger has great respect for his boss and is never *insolent*.

insulting Scornful or full of contempt. The *insulting* review attacked the singer's appearance and didn't even mention her voice.

rude Having no courtesy; impolite. It is very unpleasant to speak with someone *rude* on the telephone.
ANTONYMS: **civil, courteous, polite, refined, sociable**

incomplete *adj.* Unfinished; not complete. We are returning your application because the forms are incomplete.
insufficient Not enough; not adequate. We have an *insufficient* number of players for our baseball team.
lacking Not having; absent; insufficient. *Lacking* the price of admission to the movie, the girls went for a walk instead.
partial Not all; part. The weather report has called for *partial* sunshine.
short Not having a sufficient amount of. I am only two baseball cards *short* of having a complete collection.
unfinished Not completed. Though *unfinished*, the Second Piano Concerto is quite beautiful.
ANTONYMS: **complete, entire, finished, total**

irritate *v.* To annoy or make angry; to bother. The chatter in the hall irritated Paul as he tried to work.
annoy To bother; to make slightly angry. Jamie *annoyed* the babysitter with his endless questions.
bother To annoy or trouble. Don't let his silly jokes *bother* you.
pester To annoy or bother. A cloud of mosquitoes *pestered* the picnickers all afternoon.
ANTONYMS: **calm, pacify, quiet, soften, soothe**

J

join *v.* To bring or come together; to connect. The new bridge will join the island with the mainland.
combine To bring or come together; to unite. *Combine* two beaten eggs and a cup of milk in a large bowl.
connect To join together; link. The "chunnel"—a tunnel under the channel—will *connect* England and France.
link To join or connect; unite. The railroad *linked* coal-mining towns to cities where steel was made.
reunite To get or cause to get together again. After being separated during the summer, Jason and his dog were *reunited*.
ANTONYMS: **divide, part, separate, split**

journey *n.* Travel from one place to another. The journey from Paris to New York takes eight hours by plane.
excursion A short pleasure trip or outing. We took the Skunk Railroad on an *excursion* through the redwoods.
expedition An organized journey made for a specific purpose. The Lewis and Clark *expedition* explored the unknown territory from the Mississippi River to the West Coast.
quest A seeking or looking for something; search. The scouts were on a *quest* for the hidden map.
tour A trip during which one visits a number of places for pleasure or to perform. The theater company is on a *tour* of Canada.
trek A journey, especially a slow or difficult one. The knee-high mud made it a difficult *trek* through the swamp.

jumble *n.* A state of confusion; a muddle. How can I make sense of this crazy jumble?
hash A jumble; mess. The cat jumped on my desk and made a *hash* of my papers.
heap A collection of things piled up; pile; mound. The jigsaw puzzle fell to the floor in a *heap*.
muddle A condition of confusion; mix-up.

Your drawing is a *muddle* of colors and lines.

patchwork Anything made up of different materials. When seen from the sky, the newly plowed and planted fields made a *patchwork* of green and brown.

ANTONYMS: **orderliness, organization, tidiness**

L

large *adj.* Big in size, amount, extent, etc. The large dog befriending the tiny hamster was quite a sight.

gigantic Huge; giant. Even the *gigantic* pyramids are dwarfed by modern skyscrapers.

huge Very large. The *huge* red spot on Jupiter, seven times as large as Earth, is really a magnetic storm.

immense Very large; huge. Because of its *immense* size and strength, the elephant has no natural enemies.

mammoth Huge; enormous. Building the Golden Gate Bridge was a *mammoth* task that took many workers four years to complete.

ANTONYMS: **little, miniature, minute, small, tiny**

likely *adj.* Probably true. Studying regularly is the likeliest way to improve grades.

apt Having a natural tendency; likely. My parents are *apt* to make a splendid meal when my grandparents visit.

expected Certain or almost certain. The *expected* high temperature for tomorrow is 83 degrees.

liable Likely; apt. Not *liable* to tire easily, Malcolm is the right person for the job.

probable Likely to be true or to happen. The *probable* cause of the forest fire was lightning.

ANTONYMS: **improbable, unlikely**

lively *adj.* Full of life; spirited. The band struck up a lively tune, and all the merrymakers began to dance.

active Showing action; busy. My grandmother leads an *active* lifestyle, traveling and entertaining often.

frisky Lively or playful. The *frisky* otters kept sliding down the bank into the pond.

spry Quick and agile. Uncle Jerome was *spry* well into his nineties and kept up the vegetable garden by himself.

vivid Full of life or seeming very much alive. The author's *vivid* character seemed to be someone I would like to have for a friend.

ANTONYMS: **inactive, lifeless, listless, sluggish**

loss *n.* Losing or having something lost. Loud music can cause hearing loss

damage Harm or injury. The *damage* from the hailstorm was very severe.

harm Injury; damage. The tornado did great *harm*.

injury Hurt, harm, or damage done to someone or something. Seat belts save lives and prevent *injury*.

ANTONYMS: **advantage, benefit, gain**

M

material *n.* Cloth. Canvas is a sturdy and relatively inexpensive material

cloth A fabric made of fibers, as wool, cotton, or rayon. Bolts of *cloth* lined the shelves at the sewing center.

fabric A material made of woven, knitted, or matted fibers. The Chinese were the first to discover that *fabric* could be made from the cocoon of the silkworm.

textile A woven fabric. Although cotton grew in the South, many *textile* mills were in the North.

tissue Any gauzelike fabric. The bride's veil was made of the finest silk *tissue.*

merit *v.* To deserve. His fine artwork merits recognition.

deserve To be worthy of; to merit. That unimportant event doesn't *deserve* all the attention the newspapers have given it.

qualify To have the needed ability, as for a job, school, etc. To *qualify* for a raise, Daniel had to work for the company for three months.

rate To have a certain worth or rank. Prima Donna, a terrier, *rated* first prize in the show.

murmur *n.* A low, unclear sound. Sitting on the porch, we could hear the faint murmur of the slow stream.

grumble A low, muttered complaint. The crowd answered the referee's decision with a *grumble* of disapproval.

mumble A soft, unclear voice. It was difficult for the actor to learn to speak with a *mumble.*

mutter A low, unclear utterance or tone. She answered in a low *mutter*, and I couldn't tell whether she wanted to dance with me or not.

whisper A low, rustling sound; murmur. A *whisper* of wind fluttered through the leaves.

ANTONYMS: **scream, shout, shriek, yell**

mysterious *adj.* Filled with or suggesting something not known or strange; unexplained. No one could explain the source of the mysterious noise.

baffling Confusing; bewildering; perplexing. These *baffling* directions don't give a clue about how to assemble the model plane.

puzzling Confusing; perplexing; mystifying. The *puzzling* disappearance of the watch was finally explained when we came across

the nest of the pack rat hidden on a rocky ledge.

weird Strange; eerie. The *weird* landscape reminded Laura of the surface of the moon.

ANTONYMS: **clear, evident, plain**

N

nation *n.* A country. Though the home of many cultures, Italy did not become a nation until 1861.

commonwealth A group of states or nations linked by common ties and interests. Though an independent country, Canada is part of the *Commonwealth* of Nations.

empire A group of different, often widespread states, nations, or territories under a single ruler or government. France was once part of the Roman *empire* and had a Roman governor.

kingdom A country ruled by a king or queen. The king and queen were searching for the bravest knight in the *kingdom.*

republic A government in which the power is given to officials elected by and representing the people. The French people overthrew the king and set up a *republic.*

necessary *adj.* Needed; essential. We used to think that light was necessary for plant growth until scientists discovered plants growing in total darkness in the deep oceans.

essential Extremely important or necessary; vital. A balanced diet is *essential* to good health.

fundamental Essential; basic. I can't play the piano, but I have a *fundamental* knowledge of how to read music.

required Needed. There are many classics on the *required* reading list.

vital Having great or essential importance. The compass was *vital* to our survival; without it, we'd be lost at sea.
ANTONYMS: **dispensible, needless, unnecessary**

nice *adj.* Pleasant; kind. Trying to be nice, Joanne invited the new neighbors to dinner.
agreeable Giving pleasure; pleasing. The nurse had an *agreeable* manner that soothed her patients.
amiable Pleasing in disposition; agreeable; friendly. The *amiable* dog wagged its tail when it saw the child.
cordial Warm and hearty; sincere. The boss gave all the workers a *cordial* welcome at the party.
sweet Gentle; kind; charming. Isn't that the *sweetest* kitten you've ever seen?
ANTONYMS: **cruel, hateful, mean, nasty, selfish**

normal *adj.* Agreeing with the usual standard; regular. The normal body temperature of adults can range from 96.8 to 99.2 degrees.
ordinary Average in quality or ability; not special. His teachers said that Einstein, the great genius of this century, was an *ordinary*, even a slow, student.
regular Usual; habitual; normal. Even if nothing hurts, you should have *regular* dental checkups every six months.
routine Habitual; customary. Don't be upset; that's just a *routine* letter the bank sends to all its customers.
widespread Spreading over, happening in, or affecting a large area. Sending greeting cards did not become a *widespread* custom until this century.
ANTONYMS: **abnormal, odd, peculiar, unexpected, unusual**

O

order *n.* An arrangement of things one after the other. The dog trainer sadly noted the usual order of events: Joe would throw the ball, Rex would grab it, and then Joe would chase Rex to get the ball back.
harmony An orderly and pleasing arrangement, as of colors or parts. Carefully study how the artist has balanced his colors and shapes to create *harmony* in the painting.
neatness Precision. The crowd admired the *neatness* and skill of the figure skater's movements.
system An organized group of facts, principles, beliefs, etc., that are arranged into an orderly plan. Mabel arranged her music tapes according to this *system*: female singers on the top shelf, male singers on the middle shelf, and groups on the bottom shelf.
tidiness Neatness; orderliness. Charley's room seemed a model of *tidiness* until Mother opened the closet door and a jumble of clothes fell at her feet.
See also govern.
ANTONYMS: **chaos, confusion, disorder, unrest**

P

panic *n.* Sudden fear. Calm action and avoiding panic can save lives in a fire.
alarm A sudden feeling of fear. The *alarm* and restlessness of the chickens meant that a fox was nearby.
dread Great fear or uneasiness, especially over something in the future. Some people have a *dread* of the unknown, but I welcome new experiences.
fright Sudden, violent alarm or fear. The loud noise gave me such a *fright*!
horror A feeling of extreme fear, dread, or loathing. The people fled in *horror* as

they heard the roar of water from the broken dam.

ANTONYMS: **calmness, coolness, poise, self-control**

partner *n.* One of two or more people who perform an activity together, as dancing, etc. The dance partners practice every afternoon.

aide An assistant, as an aide-de-camp or an executive who helps run a business. The general sent his *aide* ahead to set up headquarters and find suitable lodging.

companion A person who goes with or accompanies someone else; one who shares in what another is doing. Scientists found that dogs named Fido were faithful *companions*, while dogs named Rover tended to roam.

comrade A close companion or friend. Jason agreed to meet his *comrades* on the soccer field at noon.

sidekick A steady friend or companion. In western movies, the dashing hero usually shared his adventures with a comical *sidekick*.

pause *v.* To stop briefly. Sally paused to collect her thoughts before answering the question.

delay To make late by stopping or slowing up. The ad read, "Don't *delay*—send us your order today!"

discontinue To stop having, using, or making; break off or end. The factory *discontinued* the pattern, so I won't be able to replace the broken plate.

interrupt To cause (something or someone) to stop by breaking in. The audience frequently *interrupted* the show by clapping and cheering.

ANTONYMS: **continue, maintain, resume**

peaceful *adj.* Calm; quiet; full of peace. A loud bang shattered the peaceful afternoon and the checkers game.

calm Quiet; peaceful; still. Scarcely a ripple disturbed the *calm* surface of the pond.

restful Quiet; serene. You'll feel better after a *restful* night's sleep.

serene Peaceful; tranquil; unruffled; calm. Teresa's *serene* face gave no clue that she had just had an angry argument.

ANTONYMS: **hectic, stormy, unruly, wild**

piece *n.* One of the parts into which a thing is separated or broken. The cup broke into three pieces, but I glued it back together.

fraction Part of a whole. Only a small *fraction*—about one-ninth—of an iceberg floats above water.

fragment A part broken off or incomplete. Until recently, some tourists carried off *fragments* of Greek ruins as souvenirs.

portion A part or share of something. I'm not very hungry, so please give me just a small *portion*.

section A separate part or division; portion. A *section* in the front of the telephone book tells you what to do in emergencies.

ANTONYMS: **entirety, unit, whole**

pioneer *n.* A person who is first to settle a new region of a country. Daniel Boone was a pioneer who found a way across the Appalachian Mountains into Kentucky.

colonist A person who begins, settles, or lives in a colony. The first *colonists* to settle in New York were Dutch.

immigrant A person who comes into a country or region where he or she was not born, in order to live there. Between 1900 and 1914 some nine million *immigrants* came from Europe to the United States.

settler A person who settles or makes a home in a new country or colony. The first thing a *settler* had to do, even before building a house, was to clear the land for crops.

positive *adj.* Certain; affirmative; definite. Molly was positive she had returned the library book.

assured Guaranteed; sure. Her fine speaking skills won Katherine an *assured* place on the debate team.

certain Completely sure, confident, or convinced. I'm not *certain* that's the phone number; perhaps you should look it up.

confident Having confidence; assured. *Confident* that help would arrive soon, Sylvia managed to calm the others.

secure Safe against loss, danger, and so on. Since her neighbors were home, Bonnie felt *secure* in the apartment.

ANTONYMS: **insecure, uncertain, undecided, unsure**

precious *adj.* Highly prized; valuable. The locket was precious to Lynn, not because it was gold, but because Perry had given it to her.

costly Costing very much; expensive. The carved moldings of the old house would be too *costly* to replace today.

expensive Costing a great deal. Keith feared flying and so took the train, even though it was slower and more *expensive*.

scarce Hard to find or get; not common; not plentiful. Once found everywhere, Indian arrowheads are now *scarce* and difficult to obtain.

valuable Being worth money or effort. This rare stamp is the most *valuable* in the collection.

ANTONYMS: **valueless, worthless**

pretty *adj.* Attractive; pleasant. Linda is pretty because she always smiles.

appealing Attractive or interesting. People often did favors for Bill because of his *appealing* personality.

attractive Pleasing. The flower bed was flanked by an *attractive* border of daisies.

beautiful Lovely; pretty. The ugly duckling grew into a *beautiful* swan.

graceful Having or showing beauty or delicacy of form or movement. Though clumsy on land, penguins are *graceful* swimmers.

ANTONYMS: **hideous, homely, plain, ugly, unattractive**

Q

quarrel *v.* To argue. The two drivers quarreled over which one had the right to the parking place.

debate To discuss or argue for or against. Even as we *debate* what to do, time is running out.

differ To have a difference of opinion; disagree. The two witnesses to the accident *differed* about what happened.

disagree To have a different opinion; differ. The second cook *disagreed*, saying that chili should never be made with beans.

squabble To have a petty quarrel; wrangle. My sisters are always *squabbling* about whose turn it is to use the telephone.

ANTONYMS: **agree, cooperate**

quickly *adv.* Fast; swiftly. Leave the building calmly and quickly by the nearest exit.

abruptly Suddenly; hastily. He stopped speaking *abruptly*, as if struck with a new thought.

briskly Acting or moving quickly; lively. Hold the thermometer by the end opposite the bulb and shake it downward sharply and *briskly*.

hastily Quickly; speedily. I write this *hastily* because I'm at the station and my train has been called.

rapidly Very quickly; swiftly. As a meteor falls *rapidly* through the atmosphere, friction causes it to burn and glow.

ANTONYMS: **gradually, lazily, slowly, sluggishly, unhurriedly**

quiet *adj.* Having or making little or no noise. The children were enjoying a quiet hour of reading by the fire.

hushed Quiet; still; silent. To my horror, everyone in the *hushed* room heard my remark.

noiseless Causing or making little or no noise; quiet; silent. With *noiseless* steps, the lion stalked the zebra.

silent Not having or making any sound or noise; noiseless. The courtroom was *silent* when the judge spoke.

speechless Temporarily unable to speak, especially because of strong emotion. Almost *speechless* with surprise, I could only sputter "Thanks!"

See also calm.

ANTONYMS: **earsplitting, loud, noisy**

quiz *v.* To test by asking questions. The excited boys quizzed Marvin about his ride in the hot-air balloon.

examine To look closely and carefully; to investigate. To "candle" an egg means to *examine* it by holding it up to a light.

pump To get information by asking many questions. The police officer *pumped* the witness about what had happened.

question To ask a question. The judge, too, can *question* a witness on the stand in court.

test To subject to a series of questions to measure something, as knowledge or skills. This program *tests* the user's quickness in responding to sudden hazards on the road.

R

rainfall *n.* The amount of water that falls as rain, hail, or snow during a certain length of time. The highest average annual rainfall is on Mount Waialeale, Hawaii, the wettest spot on Earth.

cloudburst A sudden, heavy downpour of rain. Everything looks fresh and bright after a summer *cloudburst* washes the land clean.

downpour A heavy fall of rain. Caught in the *downpour* without an umbrella, we were sopping wet in just seconds.

drizzle A mistlike rain. We were hoping for a good dousing to end the drought, but all we got was a brief *drizzle*.

shower A brief fall of rain, hail, or sleet. People in the tropics know to expect a *shower* at four o'clock nearly every afternoon.

ANTONYM: **drought**

reach *v.* To arrive at. The captain says we'll reach land in two days.

achieve To accomplish. You'll never *achieve* your goal if you don't practice.

approach To come nearer in space or time. Everyone was excited as the blast-off *approached*.

arrive To reach a place after a journey. The opera singer Enrico Caruso *arrived* in San Francisco shortly before the great earthquake of 1906.

extend To stretch, reach, or last. The Sahara covers much of North Africa and *extends* westward toward the Atlantic.

ANTONYMS: **depart, leave**

recommend *v.* To advise or suggest. Janice asked the waiter to recommend a favorite dish.

advise To give advice to. He *advised* me to pull up the baited string slowly and have the crab net ready.

instruct To order, direct, or command.

The duke *instructed* his cooks to prepare a great feast for the king.

propose To put forward for acceptance or consideration. I *propose* that we visit our grandparents this afternoon.

suggest To put forward as a proposal; propose. The teacher *suggested* an easy way to remember the names of the planets and their order from the sun.

urge To recommend or advocate strongly. My family *urged* me to take lessons if I was really serious about scuba diving.

ANTONYM: **discourage**

rejoice *v.* To be filled with joy. After his long solo flight across the Atlantic, Charles Lindbergh *rejoiced* when he saw the shores of France.

celebrate To observe or honor in a special manner. We *celebrated* Mom's birthday by taking her on a rafting trip.

delight To take great pleasure. The twin girls *delighted* in the way the kitten played.

glory To rejoice proudly; take pride. The family *gloried* in their son's first steps.

ANTONYMS: **despair, grieve, mourn, regret, suffer**

repair *v.* To fix or mend. I'm especially glad that Dad didn't *repair* the broken mower since it's my turn to mow the lawn.

mend To repair. How long does it take for a broken bone to *mend*?

remodel To make over, with changes of design or purpose. They *remodeled* the theater so that it would hold more people.

restore To bring back to a former condition. The boy didn't realize how much work it would take to *restore* a 1932 automobile to prime condition.

service To maintain or repair. Liz signed a

contract to have her new car *serviced* if it breaks down.

ANTONYMS: **break, destroy, shatter, smash**

request *v.* To ask for; to demand. Mrs. Collins requested a meeting with the president of the company.

beg To ask earnestly. The hysterical mother *begged* the firefighters to save her child.

demand To ask for forcefully. Professor Kantor *demanded* an explanation for my lateness.

plead To ask earnestly; to beg. The president sent an ambassador to *plead* for a meeting.

reveal *v.* To make known. If you know how to read its secrets, this rock reveals much about the history of the earth.

disclose To expose to sight; uncover. We cannot *disclose* that private information without Mr. Squire's consent.

discover To find out, get knowledge of, or come upon before anyone else. No one has been able to *discover* the reason for the disappearance of the Mayan people.

find To learn; discover. John *found* that the new neighbors had a son his age.

uncover To make known; believe. The reporter *uncovered* a plot by the dealer to sell stolen artworks.

ANTONYMS: **conceal, cover, hide, secrete**

S

sad *adj.* Unhappy. With their droopy faces, basset hounds always look sad.

depressed Gloomy or sad. Scientists now believe that *depressed* people feel better after being in a room with bright light.

downcast Low in spirits; sad. *Downcast* by the news of the accident, the

Harcourt Brace School Publishers

worried families waited for word of the fate of the miners.

heartsick Very disappointed. Joan was *heartsick* about losing the ring her grandmother had given her.

ANTONYMS: **elated, glad, gleeful, happy, overjoyed**

safe *adj.* Free from danger or harm. Keep these important papers in a safe place.

guarded Carefully protected or defended; closely watched. Well *guarded* against invasion, the castle withstood many attackers.

protected Shielded or defended from attack, harm, or injury. *Protected* by its envelope of air, the earth is shielded from most of the sun's damaging rays.

sheltered Covered or protected. Plant these seedlings in a *sheltered* spot, away from wind and cold.

undamaged Not damaged or hurt. The fragile vase arrived *undamaged* because it had been carefully packed in straw.

ANTONYMS: **dangerous, hazardous, risky, unsafe**

scorch *v.* To burn slightly on the surface; to singe. I scorched my new shirt with a hot iron.

char To burn or scorch slightly. Hal *charred* the toast because he forgot to take it out of the oven.

parch To make or become dry with heat; shrivel. The hot sun *parched* the fields of newly planted corn.

scald To burn with hot liquid or steam. Mother *scalds* tomatoes in boiling water for ten seconds so that they will be easy to peel.

ANTONYMS: **chill, freeze, ice**

search *v.* To examine or look through thoroughly. Howard searched the library shelves for books on ships.

comb To search carefully. Alice *combed* her room for her missing homework and found it under her bed.

examine To look at closely and carefully; to investigate. The dentist *examined* Phil's teeth but found only one cavity.

explore To travel in or through in order to learn or discover something. People who *explore* caves are called spelunkers.

inspect To look over carefully; to examine. Sherlock Holmes *inspected* the room for clues to solve the mystery.

investigate To look into thoroughly in order to find out the facts or details. The insurance company *investigated* the fire and found that faulty wiring started the blaze.

observe To see or notice. Guides take tourists to a place where they can *observe* the elephant seals safely.

seek To go in search of. According to the myth, Jason left to *seek* the fabulous golden fleece, owned by the king of Colchis.

seize *v.* To take hold of suddenly or with force; grasp. The Southern forces fired on and later seized Fort Sumter, held by Union troops.

clasp To grasp or embrace. She *clasped* the kitten to her chest and said, "Mommy, can I keep it?"

embrace To take or accept willingly. The class eagerly *embraced* the offer to go to the museum.

grasp To take hold of firmly, as with the hand. The mountain climber *grasped* the rope as she moved up the mountain.

grip To grasp or hold on firmly. *Grip* the bat firmly near the base.

ANTONYMS: **free, loose, release**

separate *v.* To move or pull apart; to divide. We learned how to separate the yolk from the white of a raw egg.

disconnect To break or undo the connection of or between. First, *disconnect* the plug marked *A* from the socket marked *B.*

divide To split or separate into parts or groups. Imaginary lines *divide* the earth into twenty-four time zones.

split To divide into shares. Since there are three partners, we'll *split* the profits three ways.

ANTONYMS: **bind, combine, connect, fuse, glue, unite**

shriek *n.* A loud, sharp, shrill scream or sound. Startled by the spider, Miriam gave a shriek of surprise.

scream A loud, piercing cry or sound. The old friends *screamed* with excitement when they were reunited.

screech A shrill, harsh cry or sound. This kind of owl is named for its piercing, shrill *screech.*

whoop A loud cry, as of excitement or surprise. Shirley's silly costume drew *whoops* of delighted laughter.

ANTONYMS: **mumble, murmur, mutter, whisper**

step *v.* To move by taking steps. Please step closer to the microphone and tell us your name.

tramp To step or walk heavily. The weary soldiers *tramped* through the deserted streets.

trample To walk or stamp on heavily. "You've *trampled* my beautiful rug with your muddy boots," he said.

trot To move at a rapid but not too fast run. The dog *trotted* onto the field during the game, angering some players but delighting the fans.

trudge To walk wearily or with great effort. The exhausted firefighters *trudged* to camp to get some sleep.

storm *n.* A strong wind often accompanied by rain, snow, thunder, and so on. A sudden storm drove the sailboats back to harbor.

blizzard A heavy snowstorm accompanied by strong, freezing wind. Caught in a two-day *blizzard*, the mountain climbers were forced to make camp and delay their climb.

hurricane A storm of heavy rains and whirling winds of 75 miles per hour or more, usually beginning in the tropics, often the West Indies. The *hurricane* toppled 100-year-old oaks along the Gulf Coast.

squall A sudden, fierce wind, which often brings with it rain or snow; a storm. The Coast Guard sent ships to search for the two fishing boats missing in the *squall.*

tornado A violent, destructive whirling wind that forms a funnel-shaped cloud. The survivors said that the *tornado* was louder than a train and blew out all the windows in the house.

strong *adj.* Solidly made. Bruce feared that the delicate chair wasn't strong enough to support his weight.

mighty Extremely strong; powerful. Darius believed that Alexander the Great could not possibly defeat his *mighty* army.

powerful Having great physical strength or force. A parrot can snap a thick twig with its *powerful* jaws.

solid Strong; without defect. A *solid* stone foundation supports the statue.

sturdy Very strong. It's foolish to go hiking unless you're wearing *sturdy* shoes with nonslip soles.

ANTONYMS: **feeble, flimsy, slight, weak**

sufficient *adj.* Equal to what is needed; enough; adequate. Never try to read unless there is sufficient light.

adequate Enough; sufficient. Our present power plant is *adequate* to supply our electricity needs until the year 2010.

ample Sufficient; adequate. The nearby coal mine guaranteed an *ample* supply of fuel for the mill.

plentiful Existing in great quantity; more than enough. The coastal Indians established communities near *plentiful* quantities of shellfish.

satisfactory Giving satisfaction; good enough to meet needs or expectations. This year's wheat harvest was *satisfactory*, but it didn't match last year's record crop.

ANTONYMS: **inadequate, insufficient, lacking, scarce**

T

terminal *n.* A boundary or end. The western terminal of the railroad line was San Francisco.

border A margin or edge. Thousands of cars cross the *border* into Canada each day.

boundary Something that indicates an outer limit or edge. The river forms the *boundary* between the two states.

frontier The part of a country lying along another country's border. The Spanish refugees made their way to the French *frontier*.

limit The farthest or utmost point beyond which something does not or cannot go. A white line indicated the *limit* beyond which only passengers could cross.

perimeter The circumference or outer limits of anything. A fence enclosed the *perimeter* of the lot.

thin *adj.* Slim. Less water is lost from the surface of long, thin pine needles than from the broad, flat surface of oak leaves and elm leaves.

gaunt Very thin and bony, as from illness or hunger; worn. Roland looked *gaunt* when he was sick, but now he looks healthy.

narrow Not wide. This road is too narrow for two trucks to pass.

scrawny Skinny; very thin; bony. You don't expect that *scrawny* chicken to feed four people, do you?

slim Slender or skinny. The typical two-year-old has a rounded face and stomach; by age six, children are *slimmer* and begin to resemble small adults.

ANTONYMS: **chubby, fat, overweight, stout**

throw *v.* To toss or fling. Melinda asked the guests to throw birdseed, not rice, at her wedding because raw rice harms the birds who eat it.

fling To throw, especially with force; hurl. See if you can *fling* the stone into the pond so that it skips across the water.

hurl To throw something with force; to fling. The giant wave picked up the boat as if it were a toy and *hurled* it onto the beach.

propel To cause to move forward. A great jet of flame *propels* the rocket into space.

sling To fling or hurl as from a sling. Safely beyond the range of the enemy archers, soldiers used catapults to *sling* immense stones at the castle walls.

ANTONYMS: **catch, grab, hold, seize**

treasure *n.* Wealth, riches, or valuables stored up and carefully kept. The sailors found a treasure of gold and jewels.

fortune A great sum of money; wealth. The company is so huge that it spends a *fortune* on paper clips alone.

hoard A pile or stock of something hoarded. One squirrel stayed behind to guard the *hoard* of nuts against the birds.

riches Much money or many valuable possessions; great wealth. Thinking only of gold, the explorers were blind to the natural *riches* of the world they had discovered.

store Something that is laid up or put away for future need. They stockpiled vast *stores* of grain inside the city walls in case of attack.

triumph *v.* To achieve a victory. Thomas Alva Edison *triumphed* over his reading handicap and became a great inventor.

conquer To overcome by effort. In 1952, a Swiss expedition *conquered* Mount Everest and set the world's climbing record.

defeat To gain victory over; conquer; beat. The great period of Greek history began after the Greeks *defeated* the Persians in a series of wars lasting fifty years.

overcome To get the better of; triumph over; conquer. Practice your speech to gain confidence, and you'll *overcome* your nervousness.

subdue To gain power over, as by force; conquer. The army *subdued* the enemy with a surprise attack.

ANTONYMS: **fail, lose, yield**

U

uniform *adj.* Alike; not varying or changing. To build the fence, we'll need sixty boards of uniform height and width.

identical Exactly alike. No two zebras have *identical* stripes, just as no two people have identical fingerprints.

repetitious Full of repetition, especially in a useless or tiresome way. He soon grew tired of his *repetitious* job: stacking box after box as they came off the assembly line.

similar Very much alike, but not completely the same. Both buildings have *similar* pointed arches, but otherwise they are very different.

ANTONYMS: **different, mixed, unlike, varied**

upset *v.* To disturb or make uneasy. Celia promised herself that she wouldn't let Fran's teasing upset her.

distract To confuse or bother, as by dividing the attention. The noise of the jackhammers *distracted* the students taking the exam.

fluster To make confused or upset. Dick *flustered* the other golfers by asking them questions as they drew their clubs back to swing.

perturb To disturb greatly; alarm; agitate. Mother was already anxious because Andy was late, and the news of an accident on Mare Road *perturbed* her.

ruffle To disturb or irritate; upset. Just as we decided that nothing could *ruffle* the cool-headed Rita, Bev walked in wearing a dress identical to Rita's.

unsettle To make or become confused, disturbed, or upset. The plane's sudden dip *unsettled* the passengers, but the pilot calmed them by saying that flying over the Rockies is always a little bumpy.

See also furious.

ANTONYMS: **calm, quiet, settle, smooth, soothe**

usual *adj.* Common, regular, normal. The day trip made a nice change in our usual schoolday routine.

average Typical or common. The *average* heart pumps five quarts of blood per minute through its chambers.

variety

wonder

common Widespread; general. Raccoons are *common* in almost every part of the country, even in many cities.

customary Based on custom; usual. Flowers are a *customary* gift given on Mother's Day.

typical Having qualities common or usual for a whole group, class, etc. I run six miles on a *typical* day.

ANTONYMS: **abnormal, curious, odd, peculiar, strange**

V

variety *n.* An assortment. The nearer the equator you go, the greater the number and variety of plants and animals you'll find.

assortment A collection or group of various things; variety. The same shoe is available in an *assortment* of colors.

collection Things gathered or assembled. Mattie has a *collection* of small spoons from all over the world.

mixture A combination of things mixed or blended together. You can make paste from a *mixture* of flour and water.

range A set, selection, or variation within limits. A department store carries a wide *range* of clothing styles.

ANTONYMS: **regularity, sameness, similarity, uniformity**

vigorous *adj.* Full of energy or vigor. Louis was exhausted after his vigorous workout.

energetic Full of energy; lively; vigorous. Diana was thrilled by the quick, *energetic* style of the dancers.

robust Strong; sturdy; vigorous. The young child seemed *robust* and healthy.

ANTONYMS: **delicate, feeble, fragile, frail, weak**

vow *n.* A promise or pledge. John kept his vow to his grandfather and stayed in school.

oath A formal appeal to God or other authority to witness to the truth of a promise or statement. The knights made an *oath* to defend the king forever.

pledge A serious or formal promise. Kenneth made a *pledge* to pay his brother's debts.

promise A positive statement made by one person to another about performing (or not performing) a certain act. I *promised* to drive Jean to the dentist.

W

water *v.* To make wet with water. Water the petunias as soon as they begin to droop.

drench To wet completely; to soak. The cloudburst *drenched* the fans in the stands, but many stayed on to see the end of the game.

drown To cover or wet with a liquid. The heavy rains *drowned* my tomato seedlings.

pour To cause liquid to flow. Just to be sure, *pour* water on the campfire before you leave.

soak To make completely wet by placing or keeping in a liquid. In science class, we *soaked* a chicken bone in vinegar until the bone was rubbery.

squirt To come out or force to come out in a thin stream; to spurt. Lulu *squirted* Bubba with her new water pistol.

ANTONYMS: **dry, parch, wilt**

wonder *v.* To be curious about; to wish to know. The scouts wondered about the tribe that had lived in the place where they were now camping.

wrestle	yield

astound To stun with amazement. The sinking of the Armada *astounded* the Spanish and the English.

marvel To be astonished or awestruck; wonder. Crowds gathered to *marvel* at the treasures from the pharaoh's tomb.

ponder To consider carefully; puzzle over. Sue *pondered* the meaning of the mysterious, unsigned message she received in the mail.

reflect To think or ponder. Take a moment to *reflect* on what happened.

wrestle *v.* To struggle. According to legend, the lion could not be harmed by weapons, so Hercules wrestled him to the ground and strangled him.

grapple To struggle closely; contend. The twins *grappled* over the toy fire engine; neither wanted the puzzle.

scuffle To fight roughly or in a confused way. The two boys *scuffled* briefly before the babysitter separated them.

tackle v. To seize and stop, especially by forcing to the ground. Brian lunged to *tackle* the runner on the five-yard line.

tussle To fight or struggle roughly. Stop *tussling* over the doll, or you'll break it.

Y

yield *v.* To give up or give away; to surrender. If there are no road signs at an intersection, the driver on the left yields the right of way.

release To set free. Mildred *released* the firefly from the jar.

resign To give up or yield. Since my family and I are moving, I must *resign* my position of class president.

surrender To give up, as to an enemy; yield. Realizing that they were outnumbered, they *surrendered* the field to the enemy.

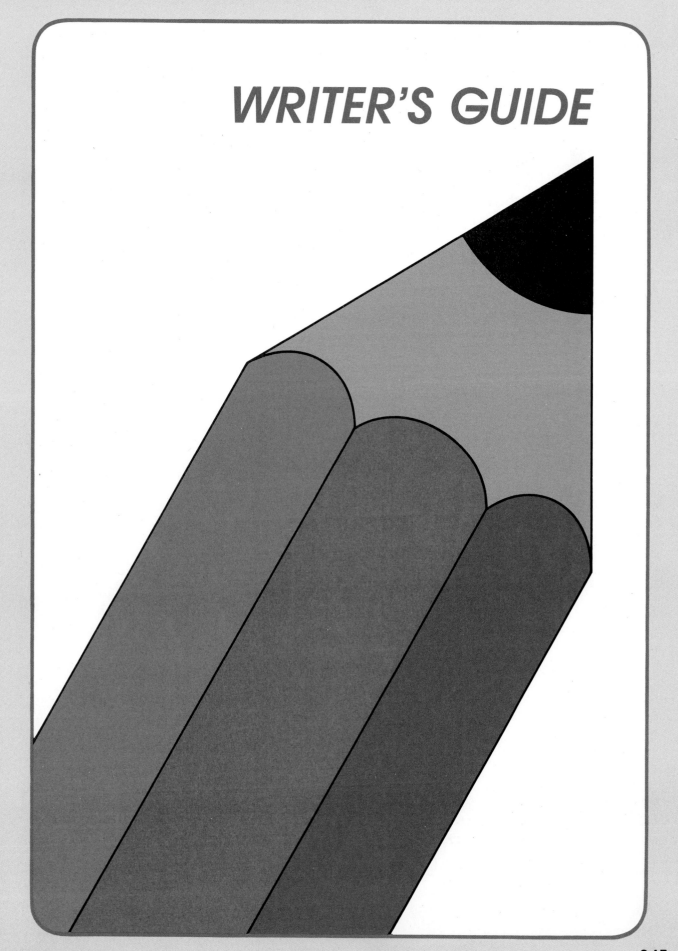

WRITER'S GUIDE

SPELLING RULES

Unit 1: Short Vowel Sounds

The short vowel sounds are usually spelled with one vowel letter.

- /a/ is spelled with **a**, as in *snack*.

- /e/ is spelled with **e**, as in *depth*.

- /i/ is spelled with **i**, as in *glimpse*.

- /o/ is spelled with **o**, as in *bronze*.

- /u/ is spelled with **u**, as in *pulse*.

Unit 2: Long Vowel Sounds

Some long vowel sounds are spelled with two letters. Here are five ways to spell long vowel sounds.

- /ā/ is spelled with **ai**, as in *complain*.

- /ē/ is spelled with **ea**, as in *cease*.

- /ō/ is spelled with **oa**, as in *coach*.

- /ō/ is spelled with **ow**, as in *blown*.

- /ō/ is spelled with **ou**, as in *shoulder*.

☐ In *aisle* the letters **ai** do not spell /ā/, but another long vowel sound: /ī/.

Unit 3: More Long Vowel Spellings

The two vowel letters *e* and *i* combine in different ways to spell long vowel sounds.

- Most of the time, the spelling for /ē/ is *i* before *e*, as in *niece*.

- If the word has a sound /ā/, *e* comes before *i*, as in *vein*.

- If the word has the sound /ē/ after the sound /s/, the spelling is also *ei*, as in *receive*.

Unit 4: **Plurals**

- To form the plural of words ending with s, ss, x, sh, ch, tch, and zz, add es.

  starch—starches radish—radishes

- To form the plural of words that end with a consonant and o, add es.
  domino—dominoes

- To form the plural of words that end with a vowel and o, add s.
  stereo—stereos

☐ *Autos* is an exception to the rules for plurals; add just s to form the plural.

Unit 5: **The Sounds /kw/, /ks/, /gz/**

Three consonant letters do not have regular sounds: c, q, and x.

- The letter **c** represents two different sounds: /k/, as in *picnic*, and /s/, as in *excellent*.

- The letter **q** always combines with the vowel letter **u** and usually spells the sounds /kw/, as in *quiz*.

- The letter **x** usually represents two different sounds: /ks/, as in *suffix*, and /gz/, as in *exact*.

Unit 7: **The Sound /j/**

Here are two ways to spell /j/ at the beginnings of words.

- with **g** before e or i, as in *genuine*

- with **j** before a, o, or u as in *junior*

☐ *Objection* is an exception you will need to remember.

Here are two ways to spell /j/ at the ends of words.

- with **ge**, as in *image*

- with **dge** after short vowel sounds, as in *pledge*

☐ In *pigeon*, **ge** spells /j/ in the middle of the word.

Unit 8: **The Sounds /sh/ and /zh/**

Here are two ways to spell /sh/.

- with **ti**, as in *friction*

- with **ci**, as in *gracious*

Here are three ways to spell /zh/.

- with **s**, as in *treasure*

- with **si**, as in *division*

- ☐ In *equation*, /zh/ is spelled with *ti*.

Unit 9: **The Sounds /ou/ and /oi/**

Here are two ways to spell /ou/.

- with **ou**, as in *flounder*

- with **ow**, as in *chowder*

Here are two ways to spell /oi/.

- with **oi**, as in *rejoice*

- with **oy**, as in *employer*

- ☐ In *porpoise* and *tortoise*, the letters *oi* are in the unstressed syllable and have the sound /ə/.

Unit 10: **The Sounds /yo͞o/ and /yo͝o/**

Here are three ways to spell /yo͞o/.

- with **u**, as in *musician*

- with **u**-consonant-**e**, as in *fuse*

- with **iew**, as in *view*

Here are two ways to spell /yo͝o/.

- with **u**, as in *mural*

- with **u**-consonant-**e**, as in *cure*

Unit 11: Compound Words

- A **compound word** is made up of two or more words. The words are usually written together as one word. Usually the spellings of the separate words remain the same when they are combined.
    earth + quake = earthquake
    rain + fall = rainfall

- Sometimes, when two words become a compound word, a letter is dropped.
    all + ready = already

Unit 13: Words with *ed* and *ing*

The endings *ed* and *ing* can be added to action verbs.

- If a word ends with *ic*, add *k* before adding the ending.
    frolic—frolicked—frolicking

- If a word ends with *er* or *ur*, double the *r* before adding the ending if the accent is on the last syllable.
    oc cur′—occurred—occurring

- If a words ends with *er* or *ur*, just add the ending if the accent is on the first syllable.
    fil′ter—filtered—filtering

- If a word ends with two consonants or two vowels and a consonant, just add the endings.
    steer—steering   coast—coasting

Unit 14: The Sound /ô/

Here are four ways to spell /ô/.

- with **a** before **l**, as in *stalk*

- with **au**, as in *pause*

- with **aw**, as in *dawn*

- with **o**, as in *broth*

Harcourt Brace School Publishers

☐ The word *broad* is an exception. In *broad*, /ô/ is spelled *oa*.

Unit 15: The Sounds /ûr/

Here are four ways to spell /ûr/.

- with **ur**, as in *hurl*
- with **our**, as in *courage*
- with **ear**, as in *search*
- with **er**, as in *terminal*

Unit 16: The Sounds /ôr/

Here are four ways to spell /ôr/.

- with **or**, as in *cord*
- with **our**, as in *mourn*
- with **ore**, as in *restore*
- with **oar**, as in *hoarse*

Unit 17: Science Words

- Many science words are used to describe how we live.
  ecology   environment

Unit 19: "Silent" Letters

Some words contain letters that are not pronounced. These letters are called "silent" letters. Here are some common "silent" letters.

- the letter *b* after *m*, as in *crumb*
- the letter *n* after *m*, as in *hymn*
- the letter *g* before *n*, as in *foreign*
- the letter *l* before *m* and *k*, as in *calm* and *chalk*

☐ In the words *palm* and *calm*, the letter *l* is usually not pronounced.

Unit 20: **Words with *er* and *est***

Here are some rules for adding *er* and *est* to form a comparative adjective or a superlative adjective.

- When a word ends with one vowel letter and one consonant letter, double the consonant letter before adding *er* or *est*.
  fat—fatter   sad—saddest

- When a word ends with *e*, drop the *e* before adding *er* or *est*.
  pale—paler   simple—simplest

- When a word ends with *y*, change *y* to *i* before adding *er* or *est*.
  creamy—creamier   lonely—loneliest

Unit 21: **The Sounds /ər/**

Here are three ways to spell /ər/ at the end of words.

- with **er**, as in *computer*

- with **or**, as in *director*

- with **ar**, as in *beggar*

Unit 22: **Prefixes**

- A **prefix** is a word part that can be added to the beginning of a word to change the word's meaning.

Here is a chart of some prefixes and their meanings.

PREFIX	MEANING	EXAMPLE
re-	"back" or "again"	*reunite*
com- or **con-**	"with"	*companion*
pre-	"before"	*predict*
in- or **im-**	"not"	*impatient*

Unit 23: **Suffixes**

A **suffix** is a word part that is added to the end of a word. A suffix often changes the part of speech of a word.

- The suffixes *-ish* and *-al* change nouns into adjectives.
  fool, *n.*—foolish, *adj.*
  nation, *n.*—national, *adj.*

- The suffix *-ly* usually changes adjectives into adverbs.
  practical, *adj.*—practically, *adv.*

When you add a suffix, follow the usual rules for adding an ending.

- If a word ends with *y*, change *y* to *i* before adding *-ly*.
  easy—easily

- If a word has a short vowel sound, double the final consonant before adding an ending.
  snob—snobbish

Unit 25: **Noun Suffixes**

The suffixes *-ment*, *-ion*, and *-ity* are added to words to form nouns.

- You add *-ment* and *-ion* to verbs to make nouns.
  arrange—arrangement   decorate—decoration

- You add *-ity* to some adjectives to make nouns.
  equal—equality

Sometimes spelling changes are made when suffixes are added to base words.

- Always drop *e* before adding a suffix that begins with a vowel.
  locate—location   secure—security

- Notice how these words change.
  curious—curiosity
  solve—solution

Unit 26: **Word Families**

- Words with a common word part belong to the same **word family.**

WORD PARTS	EXAMPLES
form	in*form*ation, re*form*
duce	re*duce*, pro*duce*
fine	re*fine*d, con*fine*d
mote	re*mote*, e*mot*ional
spect	in*spect*, pro*spect*
tain	con*tain*, main*tain*

Unit 27: Mathematics Words

Here are two ways to spell /əl/.

- with **al**, as in *numeral*

- with **le**, as in *multiple*

Here are three ways to spell /ər/.

- with **er**, as in *diameter*

- with **ure**, as in *measurement*

- with **or**, as in *numerator*

Unit 28: The Sound /ə/

Here are four ways to spell /ə/.

- with **a**, as in *salary* /sal′ər·ē/

- with **e**, as in *comedy* /kom′ə·dē/

- with **i**, as in *delicate* /del′ə·kit/

- with **o**, as in *gasoline* /gas′ə·lēn/

Unit 29: Syllable Patterns

A **syllable** is a word or part of a word. Each syllable in a word has one vowel sound. Here are some rules for dividing words into syllables.

- When a word has two vowel sounds between two consonants, divide the word between the two vowels.
  poet—po et   diet—di et

- When a word has two consonant letters between two vowels, divide the word between the two consonants.

  funnel—fun nel   cabbage—cab bage

Unit 31: More Syllable Patterns

Some words have two syllables. Listen for the accented syllable. The middle consonant in each word is part of the accented syllable. Divide the words so that the consonant letter is with the accented syllable.

    bal′ ance   pre tend′   ma roon′

Unit 32: Words from Latin and Greek

Here is a chart that shows four Greek or Latin roots.

ROOTS	EXAMPLES
tele, "at a distance"	*telegraph*, "writing sent over a distance"
port, "carry"	*import*, "carry into a country"
auto, "self"	*autograph*, "signature by oneself"
part, "divide"	*apart*, "divide in pieces"

Unit 33: Synonyms and Antonyms

- A **synonym** is a word that has almost the same meaning as another word.

  rival—foe

- An **antonym** has the opposite meaning of another word.

  backward—forward

Unit 34: Three-Syllable Words

- Some words have three syllables. Each syllable in a word has one vowel sound.

  prop′ er ty   mys′ ter y   cir′ cu lar

- ☐ The word *interest* can be said with three syllables or with two syllables.

  in′ ter est   in′ terest

Harcourt Brace School Publishers

Unit 35: **Four-Syllable Words**

Some words have four syllables. A syllable has just one vowel sound.
Pronounce each syllable to spell each word correctly.

     e vap' o rate   pa tri ot' ic   a' vi a tor

TROUBLESOME WORDS TO SPELL

already	have	quite	today
am	haven't	receive	together
and	hello	remember	tomorrow
are	her	right	tonight
awhile	here	school	too
because	I'll	some	two
before	I'm	sometimes	until
can't	isn't	stationery	very
close	it's	suppose	want
couldn't	know	teacher	we
cousin	letter	Thanksgiving	went
didn't	maybe	that's	we're
don't	Mr.	their	won't
down	Mrs.	there	would
everybody	name	there's	write
football	now	they're	writing
for	off	think	you
friend	our	thought	your
from	outside	time	you're
grammar	pretty	to	yours

LANGUAGE: A Glossary of Terms and Examples

Grammar

Sentences

- A **sentence** is a group of words that expresses a complete thought. It always begins with a capital letter. It always ends with a punctuation mark.

- A **declarative sentence** makes a statement. It ends with a period (.).
  This is the best show on TV.

- An **interrogative sentence** asks a question. It ends with a question mark (?).
  Where is the soccer ball?

- An **exclamatory sentence** shows strong feeling or surprise. It ends with an exclamation point (!).
  What a beautiful day!

- An **imperative sentence** makes a request or gives a command. It ends with a period.
  Be careful riding on that street.

- The **subject** of a sentence tells whom or what the sentence is about. It may be one word or a group of words.
  My aunt and uncle from Connecticut visited us.

- The **predicate** of a sentence tells something about the subject. It includes an action verb or linking verb and other words that go with it.
  They live in a small town near New Haven.

Nouns

- A **noun** is a word that names a person, place, or thing.

- A **common noun** names any person, place, or thing. It is a general word that begins with a small letter.
  niece   foam   rainfall   avenue

- A **proper noun** names a *particular* person, place, or thing. A proper noun begins with a capital letter.

    Abigail Adams   Santa Fe

- A **singular noun** names *one* person, place, or thing.

    field   veil   author   psalm

- A **plural noun** names *more than one* person, place, or thing.

    autos   pizzas   tornadoes   losses

- To form the plural of most nouns, add *s*. Add *es* to nouns that end in *z, s, x, sh,* or *ch.*

    liar—liars   starch—starches

- To form the plural of a noun that ends in *y* with a vowel before it, add *s*. If the noun ends in *y* with a consonant before it, change *y* to *i* and add *es.*

    bay—bays   ceremony—ceremonies

- To form the plural of nouns that end in a vowel and *o*, add only *s*. For some nouns that end in a consonant and *o*, add *es.*

    radio—radios   echo—echoes

- To form the plural of most nouns ending in *f* or *fe*, change the *f* to *v* and add *es*. For others, add an *s.*

    life—lives   wolf—wolves   chief—chiefs

- The plurals of some nouns are formed by a vowel change within the singular form. Others are the same in both the singular and plural.

    goose—geese   sheep—sheep   politics—politics

- A **possessive noun** shows ownership or possession.

- To form the possessive of a singular noun, add an apostrophe and an *s.*

    kitten—kitten's   Bob—Bob's   pony—pony's

- To form the possessive of a plural noun that ends in *s*, add an apostrophe.

    classes—classes'   boys—boys'   hats—hats'

- To form the possessive of a plural noun that does not end in *s*, add an apostrophe and an *s.*

    women—women's   children—children's   geese—geese's

Verbs

- A **verb** expresses action or being.

- An **action verb** expresses physical or mental action. It is often the key word in the predicate of a sentence. It tells what the subject does.

  Angela <u>adopted</u> a gray kitten.

- A **linking verb** links, or joins, the subject of a sentence with a word or words in the **predicate**. It tells what the subject is or is like. The most common linking verbs are forms of *be*.

  The kitten <u>is</u> beautiful. It <u>will be</u> her only pet.

- The **main verb** is the verb in a sentence that expresses the action or being.

  does <u>contain</u> is <u>reminding</u> will <u>prevent</u>

- A **helping verb** helps the main verb express an action or make a statement. These words are often used as helping verbs: *am, has, have, had, was, were, do, does, did, will*.

  <u>has</u> reduced <u>were</u> inspecting <u>did</u> reign

Verb Tenses

- The time expressed by a verb is called its **tense**.

- **Present tense** expresses action that happens now or regularly.

  Mayor Johnson <u>governs</u> this city. She <u>promotes</u> it as a vacation spot.

- Most present tense verbs that follow singular subjects end in *s* or *es*.

  She <u>appoints</u> good workers to help her.

- Present tense verbs that follow plural subjects do not take an *s* or *es* ending.

  The mayor's guests <u>inspect</u> City Hall.

- **Past tense** expresses action that happened in the past. Many verbs use *ed* to show past tense.

  They all <u>appeared</u> at our last charity drive.

- Regular verbs are verbs that form the past and past participle by adding *d* or *ed* to the singular form.

Present	Past	Past Participle
furnish(es)	furnished	(have, has, had) furnished
flourish(es)	flourished	(have, has, had) flourished

- **Irregular verbs** are verbs that do not add *d* or *ed* to form the past or past participle.

Present	Past	Past Participle
write(s)	wrote	(have, has, had) written

Adjectives

- An **adjective** is a word that modifies a noun or pronoun. It answers the questions *what kind*, *which one*, *whose*, or *how many*.

    The <u>two sleepy</u> children fell asleep near the <u>murmuring</u> stream.

- Adjectives can describe by comparing.

- The **comparative degree** of an adjective is used when two things are compared. One-syllable adjectives add *er* to make comparisons. Adjectives of two or more syllables usually use *more* or *less*.

    Chicago is <u>larger</u> than Miami.
    This area is <u>less remote</u> than that one.

- The **superlative degree** of an adjective is used when *three or more* things are compared. One-syllable adjectives add *est*. Adjectives of two or more syllables usually use *most* or *least*.

    Jan was the <u>calmest</u> swimmer at the meet.
    She was the <u>most patient</u> when the meet was delayed.

Adverbs

- An **adverb** is a word that modifies a verb, an adjective, or another adverb. It answers the questions *how*, *when*, *where*, and *to what extent*.

    They danced <u>beautifully</u>.   (modifies verb *danced*)
    The sun is <u>very</u> bright.   (modifies adjective *bright*)
    The snail moved <u>quite</u> fast.   (modifies adverb *fast*)

- Some adverbs can be formed by adding *ly* to adjectives.

  typical—typically   generous—generously

- Adverbs can be used to compare actions.

- The **comparative degree** of an adverb is used when *two* things are compared. One-syllable adverbs add *er* to make comparisons. Adverbs of two or more syllables usually use *more* or *less*.

  Steve seemed steadier today than he did yesterday.
  Alan writes more carefully than Sam does.

- The **superlative degree** of an adverb is used when *three or more* things are compared. One-syllable adverbs add *est* to make comparisons. Adverbs of two or more syllables usually use *most* or *least*.

  Of all the players, Margaret left the earliest.
  She plays the most carefully of all.

Vocabulary

Antonyms

- Words that have contrary, or opposite, meanings are called **antonyms.**

  permanent—temporary   typical—exceptional

Synonyms

- Words that have the same or similar meanings are called **synonyms.**

  admitted—confessed   adequate—sufficient

Homophones

- **Homophones** are words that sound alike but have different spellings and meanings.

  Can you play this chord on the guitar?
  Tie the cord to the tree.

Homographs

- **Homographs** are words that are spelled alike but have different meanings and sometimes different pronunciations.

Harcourt Brace School Publishers

I will <u>forward</u> my phone calls to you while I am gone.
Will she step <u>forward</u>?

Prefixes

- A **prefix** is a word part that can be added to the beginning of a word to change its meaning.

     visible—invisible   satisfy—dissatisfy

Suffixes

- A **suffix** is a word part that is added to the end of a word. A suffix changes the word's *part of speech*.

     sheep—sheepish   vigor—vigorous

Word Family

- A **word family** is a group of words that have the same base word.

     elevate—elevator, elevation

Idioms

- An **idiom** is an expression that has a specialized meaning. Often the meaning of an idiom is different from the meaning of the separate words.

     <u>in fine feather</u> = in very good humor or health

Analogies

- An **analogy** shows the relationship between two pairs of words.

     <u>Salmon</u> is to <u>river</u> as <u>elephant</u> is to <u>jungle</u>.

WRITER'S GUIDE

DICTIONARY: A Glossary of Terms and Examples

Alphabetical Order

- The order of letters from A to Z is called **alphabetical** order. Words in a dictionary are listed in alphabetical order. These words are in alphabetical order.

  preview
  produce
  pulse
  quake
  question
  radius

Guide Words

- There are two **guide words** at the top of each dictionary page. The word on the left is the first word on the page. The word on the right is the last word. All the other words on the page are in alphabetical order between those words.

mammoth	-ment
mam·moth /mam′əth/ *adj.* Huge; enormous. **man·i·cure** /man′ə·kyŏŏr/ *n., v.* **man·i·cured, man·i·cur·ing** **1** *n.* The grooming of the hands and finger-	**ma·ture** /mə·t(y)ŏŏr′ *or* mə·chŏŏr′/ *adj., v.* **ma·tured, ma·tur·ing** **1** *adj.* Fully grown or developed. **2** *v.* To make or become full-grown or developed.

Entry Word

- On a dictionary page, an **entry word** is a word in dark print that is followed by its meaning. Entry words appear in alphabetical order and are divided into syllables.

  meas·ure /mezh′ər/ *n., v.* **meas·ured, meas·ur·ing** **1** *n.* A standard used for comparison, as a pound, meter, etc. **2** *v.* To find the size, length, weight, etc., of anything. **3** *v.* To have certain measurements. **4** *v.* To make or take measurements.

meas·ure·ment /mezh′ər·mənt/ *n.* **1** The act of measuring. **2** Extent, size, quantity, etc., found by measuring. **3** A system of measuring or measures.

med·i·cal /med′i·kəl/ *adj.* Having to do with medicine.

- Words that have the same spelling but are different in meaning and origin are listed as separate entries in the dictionary.

re·fuse[1] /ri·fyōoz′/ *v.* **re·fused, re·fus·ing** To say that one will not give, take, allow, or agree to something; to decline: to *refuse* to help; to *refuse* candy.

ref·use[2] /ref′yōos/ *n.* Trash: Throw out the *refuse*.

Entry

- An **entry** is all the information about an entry word.

Pronunciation

- A **pronunciation** follows each entry word. Letters and symbols show how the word is pronounced.

mel·on /mel′ən/ *n.* A large, juicy fruit that grows on a vine, as a watermelon.

Part of Speech

- A **part of speech** tells whether the word is a noun, a verb, or some other part of speech. The names are abbreviated.

Definition

- A **definition** tells what a word means in the dictionary. Many words have more than one definition.

me·di·um /mē′dē·əm/ *n., pl.* **me·di·a** or **me·di·ums,** *adj.* **1** *n.* A condition or degree between two extremes. **2** *adj.* Between two conditions or degrees in quantity, quality, etc.; middle. **3** *n.* A means by which something is made or done; the news *media.* **4** *n.* (*often written* **the media**) Radio, television, newspapers, magazines, and other such means of mass communication.

Word History

- A **word history** explains the origin or history of a word. It is marked by the symbol ▶ and sometimes follows the definition of a word.

Pronunciation Key

- A pronunciation key explaining the pronunciation marks appears at the beginning of a dictionary. A brief key is often found at the bottom of dictionary pages as well.

act, āte, câre, ärt;		egg, ēven;	if, īce;	on, ōver, ôr;	bŏŏk, fōōd;	up, tûrn;

ə = **a** in *ago*, **e** in *listen*, **i** in *giraffe*, **o** in *pilot*, **u** in *circus*;   yoo = **u** in *music*;   oil;   out;

ch**air**;   si**ng**;   **sh**op;   **th**ank;   **th**at;   **zh** in *treasure*.

Syllables

- A word is made up of several parts called **syllables.** Each syllable has a vowel sound.

- A word can be divided between **syllables** with a hyphen when the word will not fit at the end of a line.

- In a word with two or more syllables, the accent mark (′) in the pronunciation shows which syllable is said with the most force.

- The syllable with the accent mark is called the **accented syllable**.

- A **secondary accent** shows a syllable said with less force.

COMPOSITION

Guides for the Writing Process

Prewriting

Use this checklist to plan your writing.

- Choose a topic.
- Choose a purpose for writing.
- Ask yourself questions about your topic.
- Choose a prewriting plan that works best for the form of writing you have chosen.
- Add more ideas as you think of them.
- Read over your plan.
- Begin to put your ideas in order.

Here are some prewriting plans.

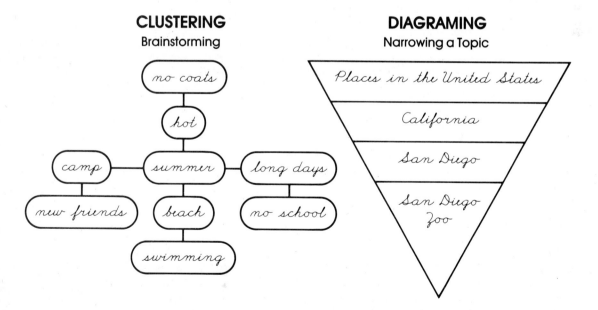

CLUSTERING
Brainstorming

DIAGRAMING
Narrowing a Topic

▶ WRITER'S GUIDE

CHARTING
Organizing Facts

Who	What	When	Where	Why
Anne	mows lawn	week-ends	local homes	to earn money
José	feeds horses	every day	the ranch	to help family
Ray	waters plants	once a week	in house	likes growing things

OUTLINING
Organizing Research

Dinosaurs

Kinds of
A. Lizard-hipped
  1. Brontosaurus
  2. Tyrannosaurus
B. Bird-hipped
  1. Stegosaurus
  2. Triceratops

Living Habits
A. Lived in swamps
B. Got food from plants

MAPPING
Drawing a Plan

Beginning

Val wants to be on the U.S. Olympic Swim Team.
She wants to practice every day for hours at a time.

Middle

Val wins many local and state races.
Val signs up for a national race to qualify for the Olympic team.
One week before the race Val gets the flu.

Ending

Val must stay in bed. She cannot practice.
On race day Val does swim. She finishes third. She makes team.

Harcourt Brace School Publishers

Composing

Use this checklist as you write.

- Read over your plan.

- Think about your purpose and audience.

- Use your plan to put your ideas on paper quickly.

- Do not worry about spelling, punctuation, or grammar at this time.

- Remember that you may get more ideas as you write.

- Add more new ideas as you think of them.

Revising

Use this checklist when you edit and proofread your work.

Editing

- Read over your work.

- Be sure your audience has enough information.

- Be sure the order of your sentences makes sense.

- Check that each sentence is a complete thought.

- Be sure each paragraph has a clear topic sentence.

- Check that all the detail sentences support the main idea.

- Be sure the words are lively and interesting.

Proofreading

- Be sure you used capital letters correctly.

- Be sure you used punctuation marks correctly.

- Check the spelling of each word.

- Be sure you used each word correctly.

- Be sure the grammar is correct.

WRITER'S GUIDE

- Be sure the first line of each paragraph is indented.

- Be sure your handwriting is neat and readable.

Editing and Proofreading Marks

- Use **Editing and Proofreading Marks** when you revise your writing. These marks help you see the changes you want to make.

- Remember that you can go back and change words or sentences as often as you want to or need to.

	Editing and Proofreading Marks
	capitalize
	make a period
	add something
	add a comma
	add quotation marks
	take something away
	spell correctly
⊓	indent the paragraph
/	make a lowercase letter
	transpose

The school fair will be held next tuesday afternoon. All students are going to attend. There will be a *writing* contest and a crafts show. Science projects will also be displayed. Teachers, families, and friends will be invited. The school band will play "The Star-Spangled Banner." Then the principal and the coach will give a speech. *Prizes* (Prises) will be given for the best compositions and drawings. The fair has always been a highlight of the school year. Plans are already being made for the fair next year. It will place take in April instead of in May.

Harcourt Brace School Publishers

A Glossary of Terms and Examples

Kinds of Sentences

- A **sentence** is a group of words that expresses a complete thought. It begins with a capital letter and ends with a punctuation mark.

     Saturn is the second largest planet.

- A **declarative sentence** makes a statement. It ends with a period (.).

     Margaret is an excellent dancer.

- An **interrogative sentence** asks a question. It ends with a question mark (?).

     Where is Sylvia?

- An **exclamatory sentence** shows strong feeling or surprise. It ends with an exclamation point (!).

     What a difficult test that was!

- An **imperative sentence** makes a request or gives a command. It ends with a period (.).

     Please bring me the paper.

Paragraph

- A **paragraph** is a group of sentences that develops a single topic or main idea.

- The **topic sentence** expresses the main idea of the paragraph.

- **Detail sentences** in the paragraph help develop the main idea.

- The first line of every paragraph is indented.

Descriptive Paragraph

- Paragraphs that **describe** should appeal to the senses of the reader. As much as possible, they should allow the reader to *see, feel, hear, taste,* and *smell* the object or scene described.

- The descriptive paragraph begins with a **topic sentence** that tells what the subject is.

- **Detail sentences** in the paragraph support the topic and reinforce the feelings of the writer. Vivid words help the scene or topic come alive for the reader.

Here is an example of a descriptive paragraph.

> *Margy flopped down on a prickly cushion of pine needles under a tall evergreen. The ridges of the tree's bark cut into her back as she tried to catch her breath. The air was cold and clean, full of the tree's sharp scent. Wondering how it would taste, Margy bit into a pine needle. A bitter, piney tang filled her mouth.*

How-to Paragraph

- A **how-to paragraph** begins with a **topic sentence** that tells what process is being explained.

- The **detail sentences** of the paragraph name the materials that are needed and give the steps of the process in the order in which they should be done.

- The steps are linked together with transitional expressions, such as *first, then, next,* and *finally.*

Here is an example of a how-to paragraph.

> *A photo collage is a wonderful gift that is inexpensive and easy to make. Choose five or six pictures that are the same size. You'll also need a large piece of sturdy cardboard for backing, a large sheet of colored paper, scissors, a pencil, and tape. First, arrange the pictures on the colored paper. Then, with the pencil, trace around the edges of each picture. Cut along the lines you drew to make a "window" for each photo. Next, tape the pictures to the back of the colored paper so that they show through the windows. Make sure the pictures are straight before you tape the colored paper and pictures to the cardboard backing.*

Harcourt Brace School Publishers

Opinion Paragraph

- A **paragraph of opinion** gives reasons for one's beliefs on a specific topic, often with the hope of persuading others to share that opinion.

- The **topic sentence** tells the writer's opinion.

- **Detail sentences** give reasons to support the opinion.

- The last sentence might summarize what has been said.

Here is an example of a paragraph of opinion.

> I enjoy roller-skating for three reasons. First, it is healthful exercise, which I badly need. Secondly, it helps my sense of balance. I feel more graceful and sure-footed in my daily life after I have skated. Finally, I enjoy it for social reasons. My friends and I always meet on Wednesdays to skate for an hour or two. Roller-skating has certainly helped me in many ways!

Comparison Paragraph/Contrast Paragraph

- A **comparison paragraph** tells how two things are *alike*.

- A **contrast paragraph** tells how two things are *different*.

- The **topic sentence** expresses the main idea and states whether the paragraph will compare or contrast. The qualities to be discussed are named in this sentence.

- **Detail sentences** explain each quality mentioned in the topic sentence in the order in which they are named in the topic sentence.

Harcourt Brace School Publishers

Here is an example of a comparison paragraph.

> The alligator and the crocodile are alike in several important ways: appearance, living environment, and the way they reproduce. Alligators and crocodiles both have long, flat bodies covered with thick, horny skin. They have short legs, long snouts, and powerful jaws. They both live in warm, wet areas. Alligators and crocodiles are both reptiles, which means they are cold-blooded and reproduce by laying eggs.

Here is an example of a contrast paragraph.

> Buses and trains are different in three important ways: the surface on which they ride, their outward appearance, and their services. First, buses run on ordinary roads and highways, and trains require a system of tracks. Secondly, a bus is a single vehicle, whereas a train is a series of cars linked together. Finally, buses provide standard comfort but no added services. Trains, on the other hand, have conductors and porters, and quite often offer dining services on board.

Friendly Letter

- The friendly letter has five parts.

- The **heading** contains the letter writer's address and the date. A comma is written between the name of the city and state and between the day and the year in the date.

- The **greeting** welcomes the person who receives the letter. It begins with a capital letter and is followed by a comma.

- The **body** of the letter contains the message. Each paragraph in the body is indented.

- The **closing** is the end of the letter. The first word of the closing is capitalized. A comma follows the closing.

- The **signature** is the name of the letter writer.

Here is an example of a friendly letter.

3108 South Street
Milwaukee, Wisconsin 53233
June 27. 20——   **Heading**

Dear Andy.   **Greeting**

  I have some really exciting news! My calf won first prize at the County Fair. There were over 200 calves in the contest, so I feel really lucky that Elsie won.
  Elsie received a beautiful blue ribbon. I got a big trophy. I've already found a place for it in my room. I hope you can come visit soon so you can see it.   **Body**
  Please write and tell me what is new with you.

      Your friend.   **Closing**
      Tom   **Signature**

Business Letter

- A **business letter** is written to accomplish a specific business purpose. A business letter may make a request, place an order, or register a complaint.

- A business letter has six parts.

- The **heading,** which includes the writer's address and date, is in the upper right corner.

- The **inside address** starts at the left margin. It gives the name and address of the person who is receiving the letter.

- The **greeting** begins at the left margin. It begins with a capital letter and is followed by a colon.

- The **body** tells why the letter is being written.

- The **closing** is at the end of the letter, in line with the heading. The first word of the closing is capitalized. A comma follows the closing.

- The **signature** of the writer is in line with the closing. It includes the writer's full name.

Here is an example of a business letter.

96 Oakton Plaza
Richmond, Virginia 23227
September 12, 20—

Heading

Famous Hat Company
4729 North Howard Street
Tucson, Arizona 85716

Inside Address

Dear Sir or Madam:

Greeting

   Please send me nine baseball caps, catalog number 662F, in red. Four of the caps should be size small, two should be size medium, and three should be size large. All caps should have a white felt letter "A" on the crown. I have enclosed a money order for $21.50 to cover the cost of the caps at $2.00 each plus $3.50 for postage and handling.
   Thank you for your prompt attention to this order.

Body

Sincerely yours,

Maria Bustillo

Maria Bustillo, Coach

Closing

Signature

Journal

- A **journal** is a daily record of events. What someone writes in a journal in a day is called an **entry**.

- Each **journal entry** gives the day and date and tells *who, what, when, where,* and *why* about events.

Here is an example of a journal entry.

> *February 18. 20--*
>
> *Mom and I spent the afternoon together. We went skating at Bittersweet Lake. Boy. was it cold! The skating was great. and so was the hot soup we had when we went back to the apartment to defrost our toes. Mom sure is a good sport!*

Story

- A **story** has a beginning, a middle, and an ending.

- The **beginning** of the story introduces the characters, the setting, and the problem.

- The **middle** of the story shows how the characters try to solve the problem. It usually tells how the main character grows and changes.

- The **ending** shows how the problem is solved.

- A story usually has a title that suggests its subject and catches the reader's attention. The first word and each important word in the title begin with a capital letter.

Here is the beginning of a story.

> *Jeremy's Secret*
>
> *As Jeremy stood at the foot of the hill and looked up, the climb seemed clearly impossible. He had already traveled twenty miles on foot since dawn of that day. His tired muscles and bruised feet begged for rest. The young boy sighed wearily, knowing he couldn't stop now. Freedom from the dangerous secret that threatened him lay in a little town just beyond this hilly range. Doggedly, putting all thoughts of rest and comfort out of his head, Jeremy placed one aching foot in front of the other and began to climb.*

Conversation

- A **conversation** is a dialogue between two or more people.

- The exact words of a speaker are enclosed in quotation marks.

- Each quotation begins with a capital letter.

- Quotations are separated from the rest of the sentence by a comma, a question mark, or an exclamation point. Here are two examples.
    "Please give me a loaf of bread," said Andy.
    "Is this kind all you have?" he questioned the baker.

- A new paragraph begins each time the speaker changes.

- Conversation is used in a story to reveal character, develop the plot, and help set the tone for the story.

Here is an example of conversation.

> *"Come back here, Paulie," ordered Mrs. Jefferson. "You shouldn't go to school wearing those sneakers. Come back and put on your brown oxfords."*
>
> *"Oh, Mom," Paulie protested. "These are my favorite shoes. Besides, my oxfords are at the shoemaker's being fixed. I think my sneakers look just fine."*

Harcourt Brace School Publishers

Biography

- A **biography** is the story of a person's life written by another person. It follows the events of the person's life in time order.

- The facts in a biography usually begin with birth and continue through old age or death in the order that they happened.

- Short, interesting stories, called **anecdotes**, are often included in a biography.

Here is an example of the beginning of a biography.

> When Mark Twain wrote about life in America in the 1800's, he was writing about a country he knew from his own experience. He was born in Florida, Missouri, on November 30, 1835, and was named Samuel Langhorne Clemens. His most famous books, <u>Tom Sawyer</u> and <u>The Adventures of Huckleberry Finn</u>, were inspired by memories of boyhood adventures he had while growing up in Hannibal, Missouri, then a small town on the Mississippi River.

Book Report

- A **book report** gives the title and author of a book.

- The title of the book is underlined.

- A book report gives a brief summary of the book. It tells about the main characters and one or two important events in the story.

- A book report does not tell the ending of the story.

- A book report includes a reader's opinion of the book.

Here is an example of a book report.

Title	*The Yearling*
Author	*Marjorie Kinnan Rawlings*
Summary	*This book tells the story of a boy named Jody. He lives in the woods of Florida in the early part of this century. Jody finds a young deer and it becomes his pet. Then one day Jody's father tells him that he cannot keep the deer any longer. You will be surprised at what happens next.*
Opinion	*I enjoyed this book. I learned about the relationships among a boy, his family, and his pet.*

News Story

- A **news story** reports facts.

- Most news stories consist of a **headline**, a **lead paragraph**, and the **body** of the story.

- The **headline** sums up the main idea. The first word and each important word begin with a capital letter.

- News stories open with a **lead paragraph** that answers the six basic questions: *who, what, when, where, why,* and *how.*

- The **body** of a news story gives additional details that support the lead.

Here is an example of a lead paragraph for a news story.

City, State Elections Draw Record Crowds of Voters

Poll-watchers, citizens, and candidates were pleased by a record-high voter turnout on Election Day. More citizens than ever before voted yesterday, November 4, in this Wyoming mountain village. A total of 68% of the voting population of 13,642 cast ballots for mayoral candidates, state representatives, and county officials. "The weather was cool but the issues were certainly not," said mayor-elect Janet Birdshaw. "Citizens of Alpine exercised their right to show their opinions by voting. That's something we can all be proud of."

Research Report

- A **research report** has several paragraphs that give facts about one subject.

- To begin research for a report, first take notes on the subject from two or more books. List the books you use in a bibliography.

- Make an outline using your notes.

- Follow your outline to write the paragraphs of the report.

Here is an example of the first paragraph of a research report.

> Imagine a million tons of snow hurtling down a mountainside at 200 miles an hour, churning up a cloud of snow dust hundreds of feet high. Does that send chills down your spine? It should. An avalanche is one of nature's most dangerous and unpredictable forces. In this report, I will explain how avalanches begin. I will also tell how scientists and snow rangers are trying to find ways to control the savage power of the avalanche.

Lyric Poem

- A **lyric poem** expresses a poet's feelings, usually in a brief, song-like manner.

- The subject matter usually includes nature, love, or sadness. It *describes* people and things.

- Often, but not always, a lyric poem has a definite rhythm and rhyme.

Here is an example of a lyric poem.

> Dark.
> Rain-slick streets.
> Windy, whispery.
> Like shadowed alleys
> Dead-end in mystery.

MECHANICS: A Glossary of Rules

Capital Letters

Names and Titles of People

- Capitalize names, initials, and titles of people.
  Ms. Janet Dunne   President Franklin D. Roosevelt

- Capitalize the pronoun *I*.

Names of Places and Times

- Capitalize geographical names and the names of holidays and historical periods.
  Switzerland   Labor Day   Middle Ages

- Capitalize each important word in abbreviations and addresses.
  Blvd. (Boulevard)   12 Oak Dr. (Drive)   Ave. (Avenue)

- Capitalize days of the week and months of the year and their abbreviations.
  Tuesday   Thurs.   Nov.   May   Feb.

Sentences and Their Parts, and Titles of Written Works

- Capitalize proper adjectives.
  Italian city   Greek mountain

- Capitalize the first word of a sentence.
  Did you hear the explosion? No, I didn't.

- Capitalize the first word in a direct quotation.

- Capitalize the first word, the last word, and all other important words in the title of a written work. These include titles of books, reports, stories, poems, songs, magazines, newspapers, articles, record albums, and television shows.
  Car and Driver (magazine)   "Fog" (poem)
  Moby Dick (book)

Harcourt Brace School Publishers

Punctuation

Period

- Place a period at the end of a declarative or an imperative sentence.
  Oranges contain vitamin C.   Please eat your okra.

- Place a period after an abbreviation.
  Mr. (Mister)   yd. (yard)   Gen. (general)

- Place a period after an initial.
  Ulysses S. Grant   Rutherford B. Hayes

- Place a period after a number in the main topic and after a letter in the subtopic of an outline.
  I. Antique cars
      A. Cars through 1912
      B. Cars 1913-1927

Question Mark and Exclamation Point

- Place a question mark at the end of an interrogative sentence.
  Who made this error?

- Place an exclamation point at the end of an exclamatory sentence.
  The baby has crawled outdoors!

- Place an exclamation point after a strong interjection.
  Help! I'm going to drop these dishes.

Comma

- Place a comma between the day and the year in a date. If the year is followed by more words in the sentence, place a comma after the year.
  The fiftieth star was added to the flag on July 4, 1960.
  On July 8, 1835, the Liberty Bell cracked.

- Place a comma between the city and the state in an address.
  Tacoma, Washington   Wichita, Kansas

- Place a comma after the greeting in a friendly letter and after the closing of any letter.

    Dear Jennifer,   Sincerely yours,   Love,

- Use commas to separate three or more items in a list, or series, in a sentence.

    I boiled the cabbage, the carrots, and the potatoes.

- Place a comma before the conjunction *and*, *or*, or *but* in a compound sentence.

    Our team made another touchdown, but it still lost the game.

- Use commas to set off a noun in direct address.

    Turn off the light in the hallway, Frank, when you leave.

- Place a comma after the words *yes* and *no*, after mild interjections, and after two or more prepositional phrases when these items introduce a sentence.

    Yes, I bought the album.
    My, you have a lot of energy!
    Under the table in the kitchen, you will probably find Rover, asleep.

- Place a comma between the closing marks of a direct quotation and the rest of the sentence unless a question mark or exclamation point is needed.

    "I like that mural," she said.

- Use commas to set off most appositives.

    Harriet Quimby, a magazine writer, was the first licensed U.S. woman pilot.

Quotation Marks and Underlining

- Place quotation marks around minor titles (titles of songs, articles, short stories, chapters in books, and minor poems).

    "The Mysterious Cat" (poem)

- Underline titles of books, plays, newspapers, magazines, movies, record albums, television shows, and musical compositions.

<u>The New York Times</u> (newspaper)
<u>Cats</u> (musical)
<u>Anne of Green Gables</u> (book)

- Place quotation marks directly before and after each direct quotation. If the quotation is divided into two parts by other words, place quotation marks only around the quoted words.

  "What movie shall we see?" I asked.
  "I saw the movie at the Rialto," said Jan. "Let's go to the Strand."

- If a direct quotation consists of several sentences, do not close the quotation until the speaker is finished.

  Mark announced, "Tryouts for the hockey team will be held tomorrow. Sign up now if you wish."

- Always place commas and periods *inside* the closing quotation marks. Place question marks and exclamation points inside the closing quotation marks only if the quotation itself is a question or an exclamation.

  "My mind always seems fresher and clearer after I exercise," said Alice. "I really enjoy a good workout."
  Who said, "A sound mind in a sound body"?

Apostrophe

- Add an apostrophe and an *s* to singular nouns to show possession. Such nouns are singular possessive nouns.

  <u>Angela's</u> cat   <u>kite's</u> tail   <u>Steve's</u> books

- Add an apostrophe and an *s* to plural nouns that do not end in *s*. These will be plural possessives.

  <u>women's</u> hats   <u>oxen's</u> stalls

- Add an apostrophe to plural nouns that end in an *s* to show possession. These are also plural possessives.

  <u>elephants'</u> trunks   <u>pets'</u> leashes   <u>girls'</u> sweaters

- Use an apostrophe for possessive nouns but not for possessive pronouns.

  Uncle <u>Bill's</u>   lawyers'   Kim's
  hers   its   ours

- Use an apostrophe to form contractions of verbs and the adverb *not*.
  we're   she's   wouldn't   can't

Colon

- Use a colon after the greeting in a business letter.
  Dear Senator Stanley:

Hyphen

- Use a hyphen to syllabicate at the end of a line. Do not syllabicate before a single final letter.
  car-pen-try   ra-di-us   pyr-a-mid

HANDWRITING: Letter Forms

Uppercase and Lowercase Manuscript Letters

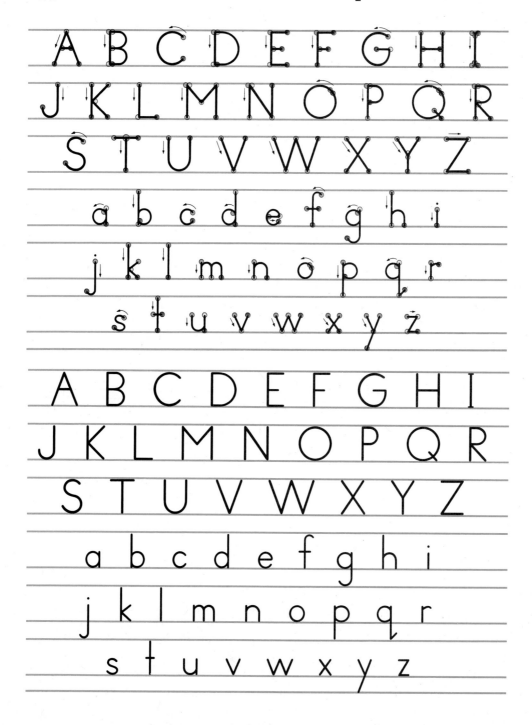

Uppercase and Lowercase Cursive Letters

A B C D E F G H I
J K L M N O P Q R
S T U V W X Y Z
a b c d e f g h i
j k l m n o p q r
s t u v w x y z

A B C D E F G H I
J K L M N O P Q R
S T U V W X Y Z
a b c d e f g h i
j k l m n o p q r
s t u v w x y z

Harcourt Brace School Publishers